WORKING DIFFERENCE

A book in the series

Comparative and International

Working-Class History

General editors:

Andrew Gordon, Harvard University

Daniel James, Duke University

Alexander Keyssar, Duke University

WORKING DIFFERENCE

Women's Working Lives in Hungary and Austria, 1945–1995

ÉVA FODOR

DUKE UNIVERSITY PRESS   Durham and London 2003

© 2003 Duke University Press
All rights reserved
Printed in the United States of America on acid-free paper
Typeset in Trump Mediaeval by Keystone Typesetting, Inc.
Library of Congress Cataloging-in-Publication Data
appear on the last printed page of this book.

Szüleimnek

Contents

Acknowledgments

This book has long been in the making and has benefited from advice and encouragement from a number of people in various stages and arenas of my life. The project started out as a Ph.D. dissertation, inspired by the frustration I experienced when I arrived in Los Angeles from Budapest in 1990 and was confronted with my inability to describe gender relations in state socialist Hungary to my American friends. I had never heard the term "homemaker" before. They had never met anyone who took for granted three-year paid maternity leaves.

My professors and friends and my readings and discussions in the Department of Sociology at the University of California at Los Angeles shaped my understanding of the world in profound ways. My most heartfelt thanks go to Ivan Szelenyi, chair of my dissertation committee, advisor, and mentor throughout my graduate school years at UCLA and afterward. *Köszönöm, Tanár úr!*

Gail Kligman arrived at UCLA at the best possible moment, and her advice, encouragement, home-cooked meals, as well as funny stories about her adventures in Romania and elsewhere were always much appreciated. I also would like to thank Ruth Milkman (my very first and most authentic role model for a feminist academic), as well as Carole Pateman and Donald J. Treiman, who served on my dissertation committee.

But professors are only one part of the education process in graduate school. I could not have finished this project without support, academic and otherwise, from colleagues and friends. Most important, I want to thank my closest friends and confidants, Susan Markens and Julie Press, not only for reading parts of this manuscript over and over again, for brainstorming over endless cups of tea, and for listening at all hours of the day to my worries and frustrations, but also, just as important, for teaching me about living (and eating) in America in the process. They also tried to teach me their impossible language—with significantly less success.

My work and general mental health further benefited from advice and encouragement received from the unique mix of Szelenyi-ites converging at UCLA in the 1990s: Gil Eyal, Eric Hanley, Matthew McKeever, Larry King, Eric Kostello, Caleb Southworth, and Eleanor Townsley, as well as members of my dissertation group, Manali Desai and Ellen Reese.

Reluctantly, I left UCLA in 1997 and started my job at Dartmouth College. As it turned out, I couldn't have found a more encouraging environment for continuing my research. John Campbell has been kind enough to read and comment on several chapters and versions of this manuscript. Misagh Parsa, Denise Anthony, Christina Gomez, and Deborah King also contributed with advice and encouragement, as well as their tolerance toward my long research trips to Hungary and Austria. Kimberly Albanese supplied me with orange-spice tea in addition to all sorts of other assistance, often long distance. I must also acknowledge the generosity of institutional support I received from Dartmouth College: research funds from a Burke Fellowship and two sabbatical terms provided me with resources and time to finish the revisions of this manuscript.

Friends and colleagues in Hungary, Austria, and the United States helped along the way. Dr. and Mrs. György Sugár introduced me to several of their friends who gave accounts of their participation in the underground communist movement and beyond. András Sugár shared with me his data sets, statistical knowledge, and lunches too numerous to count. Mária Hinsenkampf, from the Hungarian embassy in Vienna, arranged several appointments and interviews for me in Austria. Margaret Robinson kindly helped me understand and translate some of the more difficult German language transcripts. Two anonymous reviewers for Duke University Press provided thorough readings and sound advice.

The last paragraph belongs to my family. I owe an immense amount of gratitude to József Fiser, without whose presence (sometimes only virtual) the past ten years would have been a lot less eventful and fun. Last, but certainly not least, I wish to thank my most critical reader, Dr. György Fodor, for extensively commenting on various drafts of the manuscript and for rooting for me all along (even though I wandered about as far away from electrical engineering as I possibly could), and Vera Fodor for resigning herself to the fact that I am spending half of my life thousands of miles away. This book is dedicated to the two of them.

1. Three Generations of Women in Central Europe

My mother was Austrian and my father Hungarian. They met while my father attended medical school in Vienna. He came from a rather poor family and had five brothers and sisters but somehow managed to get a scholarship to study abroad. My mother was also a college student but she dropped out when they got married, and I was born soon afterward in 1925. The family moved back to Hungary after my father graduated and he became a doctor in B. [a rural town in southern Hungary]. My mother never went to work for pay. She raised me and my two siblings and took care of the household. Naturally, . . . we also had a live-in maid to help her, and a cook who did not live in the house but came every day. A different woman did the laundry once a week, and the children had a series of nurses, "Fräuleins" as they were called, from Austria. But my mother was ultimately in charge of the management of the household. She had the keys to the pantry and she assigned the tasks to everyone each morning. She decided what had to be cooked and sent the maid to do the shopping. She made sure that lunch was on the table every day at exactly 1 P.M. when my father came home to eat and that my sisters and I made it to the piano lessons [and] that everyone had the appropriate clothing and that all family events were properly celebrated. . . . My Austrian aunt and her family stayed with us for long stretches of time and we often visited them in the summers. My father owned an automobile, so sometimes my parents would drive to a nearby town to see a play or to go to a ball.[1]

The Austro-Hungarian Empire was officially dissolved in fall 1918 but its social, economic, and political legacies lingered on. Two of its successor states, Austria and Hungary, retained much of their common cultural, political, and social heritage for long after the declaration of their independence. In this context until the end of World War II the lives of middle-class women were quite similar in and sometimes, as in the case of Mária's mother whose life story is described above, alternated between, the two countries.

In 1949, three decades after the disintegration of the monarchy, the labor force experience of Austrian and Hungarian women was still quite similar. In both countries, about a third of all women were engaged in paid work after World War II (Benkő 1982; Steininger 1991). Some of them stayed in the labor force for all their adult lives but most only worked for a few years before they married and/or had a child and then withdrew to manage the household, sharing at least some of the same pleasures and responsibilities as Mária describes for her mother. Two thirds of the women in both countries were classified as "dependents." They were housewives who worked at home in the household and received no direct financial compensation. As a consequence, women rarely attended higher educational institutions; in 1949 only around 20 percent of all college and university students were female (*Statistisches Handbuch* 1951, 245; Oktatás 1991, 99, 102). Many, as Mária's story shows, dropped out before graduating in order to marry and start a family.

Had Mária's mother stayed in Austria, the life of her eldest daughter would probably have proceeded on much the same tracks as hers had started. In her childhood Mária dreamed of becoming a psychiatrist, but her father, who was inclined toward more traditional gender roles, talked her out of this ambition. Thus Mária attended a Catholic middle school and started a teacher's college, although she couldn't finish because World War II broke out. The war devastated this previously stable middle-class family; they lost most of their belongings to successive German and Soviet raids. In 1944, at age nineteen, Mária was married off to a man fourteen years her senior, a well-to-do and well-respected doctor from Budapest whom she had met only a handful of times before the wedding ceremony. Soon, she moved with him to his richly furnished apartment in the capital, which was a considerably larger city than Mária had ever seen.

> He treated me as if I were some sort of a wilting wildflower. I was completely locked away from the outside world, I knew nothing about what was going on in politics or in my husband's life. The wife at the time was supposed to be an ornament, plus she had to cook,

clean, and look after the children, unless they could hire someone to do it, which we couldn't because it was right after the war. I never even bought a pair of pantyhose for myself while I was married to him. He would open the door of the closet, look in and say, "You need a new bra." Then off he went to get one. Sometimes he took me with him, but that made very little difference. He would ask, "What do you think? You like it?" but I never once dared say no.

But social and political changes interfered with Mária's not particularly happy marriage, and this is where her story takes a sharp turn away from those of her female relatives in Austria. In the early 1950s, her husband, who lost his job, income, and status after the communist takeover, decided to emigrate to Switzerland. Mária, however, refused to go with him. Instead she returned to B., now a mid-sized rural town, with a two-year-old daughter but otherwise just as she came: penniless, jobless, and largely ignorant about the realities of the changing world around her. When she set out to find a job for the first time in her life she soon found out that a family member who defected to the "West" had become for the family a major political handicap, and as a result Mária could not become the schoolteacher she had hoped to be. Instead, she found work as a sales assistant in a large department store nearby. A few years later a friendly boss, against many political odds, arranged for Mária to become the head librarian in her hometown, and soon afterward she was appointed to be the director of the local community center, a job she enjoyed immensely. But this line of work required a lot of traveling and time away from home and her daughter and young son (from her second marriage), so after a while she decided to switch back to the department store but in a higher position as head of one of the major departments. In the late 1970s she was elected to be the store's trade union representative (a paid political position in state socialist Hungary), which put her in close touch with the highest management: "Initially, I didn't want any political functions, but then they talked me into it, saying that all I had to do was represent the workers. That was not true at all, as I realized later, because I was fully dependent on the manager of the store. But I still tried to fight with him for higher wages, fringe benefits, and I listened to people's problems and tried to help. I retired from this job when I turned fifty-seven in 1982. I was very, very tired, I badly needed a break."[2]

By the time Mária started her new life without her first husband she found that the expectations concerning women, the constraints present and the opportunities available, had radically changed. The Hungarian communist party, having gained full power by 1949, immediately set out to reorganize the economy and society.[3] To satisfy the party's hunger for intensive industrialization, the size of the Hungarian labor force had to be increased in the shortest possible time, and women came to be classified as an important, mobilizable contingent. This was one of the most successful campaigns in the history of the party, and as a result by the time Mária retired in the early 1980s the work experience of women in Austria and Hungary had diverged significantly. This trend is well reflected in even the most basic indicators: in 1982, 73 percent of women between the ages of fifteen and fifty-four worked for pay in Hungary, with an additional 7 percent on temporary maternity leave, raising the economic activity rate of women to over 81 percent (Koncz 1985a, 1985b). Almost all of these women worked full time, year-round, and all through their adult lives. The proportion of "housewives" in the classical sense of the term dropped from 64 percent thirty years earlier to about 5 percent in 1982 (Koncz 1985a). Some women, like Mária herself, not only participated in the labor force but even managed to gain positions of authority that would have been nearly impossible for their mothers' generation. Mária's career is a good example of the kinds of jobs women were particularly likely to achieve: positions in state administration or in service institutions, such as a cultural center, a school, or a library. When Mária moved to the department store in the male-dominated economic sphere, the post she received still accrued some authority but she was no longer the top manager, only the head of a large department. Even her political position proved to be highly typical of her gender. Women were much more likely to have political careers in the trade unions than in the more prestigious and more powerful organization of the communist party. Nevertheless, Mária and some of her contemporaries achieved degrees of authority to which neither their mothers nor their Austrian sisters could aspire.

In Austria in the same period women's labor force participation rates moved in the opposite direction: the proportion of women in paid work declined until the 1970s and only started a slow growth afterward. By the early 1980s, 48 percent of women of working age were engaged in paid work (as opposed to 81 percent in Hungary), about 20 percent of whom worked part time only (Gross, Wiedenhofer, and Vötsch 1994, 42; Rosenberger 1996; Matkovitz 1995). Most working women interrupted their careers for long stretches at a time to have and raise children. About 40 percent of Austrian women compared to 5 percent of Hungarian women were classified as housewives in 1982. Although the proportion of female students in the school system grew in both countries, in Hungary women reached equity at the postsecondary level by 1980 (*Magyarország Statisztikai Évkönyve* 1993, 287), while in Austria the percentage of women in universities at the same time stood below 40 percent (*Österreichische Hochschulstatistic* 1999, 126). If we consider the working population, the rate of educated women was significantly higher and the gender gap in education much lower in Hungary than in Austria in the twentieth-century, post–World War II generation (*Mikrozensus Jahresergennisse* 1997, 107; Census: Summary Data 1990, 25).[4]

Given the similarities between the two countries before 1949, much of this divergence can be traced to the radical transformation of social institutions carried out by the state socialist regime in Hungary. Through what processes did this transformation occur in Hungary, and what were its consequences? Lacking these radical interventions, how did women's life progress in Austria? How did assumptions about men and women modify the social order in state socialist and in capitalist societies? And, to examine the reverse side of this question: What was the effect of state socialism and capitalism on gender relations and, in particular, on gender inequality in claiming positions of authority? Are there really two (or more?) different gender regimes that characterize state socialist and capitalist societies? These are the questions I seek to answer in this book.

But we cannot stop telling the story of state socialism and capitalism in the 1980s.[5] Another two decades later, the trajectories of the two countries seem to be converging again. Women's labor force participation rates had been steadily increasing in Austria since the mid 1970s, and by 1992 close to 58 percent of working-age women (between fifteen and sixty-four years old) were in the labor force (Gross, Wiedenhofer, and Vötsch 1994, 43). At century's end, a few years after the collapse of state socialism, the proportion of Hungarian women in the workforce stood comparable to the European average at 60 percent as a result of another radical restructuring and an overall reduction in the number of workplaces (Frey 1996, 14).[6] Moreover, although the representation of women in Parliament dropped from about 30 percent to under 10 percent in Hungary after 1990, in Austria at the same time this percentage surpassed 20 percent for the first time in the country's history (Neyer 1997, 186). By the middle of the 1990s

Austria caught up in educating women as well: young women were just as likely to attend university as young men (Gross, Wiedenhofer, and Vötsch 1994, 29).

In this context, the life expectations, daily worries, and obstacles Mária's daughter, Eszter, faces are unique to post–state socialist societies, yet she also shares more similarities with members of her cohort in Austria than ever before in the past fifty years. Eszter was born after World War II and had a career that resembled neither that of her mother nor her grandmother. She became neither a housewife nor a loyal, politically correct state employee. Instead, she chose entrepreneurship when in the early 1980s the opportunities for market-oriented activities opened up in Hungary. Using money inherited from her portion of the sale of the family's large apartment, and using her earlier experience in the hotel and tourism industry, she purchased and ran a small, 24-hour food store in Budapest. The store, and later the pub she operated at lake Balaton that catered to German tourists, made a lot of money during the last years of state socialism, and she and her husband were able to travel extensively abroad. After the fall of the Berlin Wall, however, tourism from other state socialist societies declined and 24-hour private food stores proliferated, thus Eszter saw a significant reduction in her profits. Nevertheless, by the end of the 1990s she lived in a beautiful, elegantly furnished apartment in Budapest with her husband. They had no children, which was the result of a conscious decision made to allow Eszter to run her business, the couple to travel, and her husband to pursue his career as an operetta singer.

Eszter made good use of the unique opportunities of the marketizing shortage economy of the late state socialist period, and she continued her entrepreneurship after 1989 as well. Her choices and career, although enabled by the specificity of the Hungarian "second economy," were in fact not altogether different from those of many of her Austrian female contemporaries. After 1989, her worries were also similar: Could her business survive? Could she avoid unemployment? Would she get a new loan from the banks? Should she have had a family or is she happy with her choice of a successful career instead?

What causes this convergence in the life experiences of Austrian and Hungarian women workers? In fact, to what extent can we talk about a convergence at all? To answer these questions we must consider the legacies of state socialism as well as the radical social changes in both Austria and Hungary in the early 1990s. Although the focus in this book is on the state socialist period, I will briefly examine the issue of convergence in a more contemporary context in the last chapter.

How Do Gender Regimes Vary?

In this book I compare elements of the gender regimes of Austria and Hungary in the early 1980s in an effort to integrate the concept of gender into academic discussions on class structure and social mobility under capitalism and state socialism. Following R. W. Connell, "gender regimes" are understood as the "state of play in gender relations in a given institution . . . [and to include] practices that construct various kinds of femininities and masculinities," the sexual division of labor, as well as gender ideologies (1987:120). Interests, ideas, and routines that differentiate between men and women shape all social institutions. Thus markets, states, political parties, schools, the family, and so forth can all be characterized by their gender regimes, even though these are neither natural nor predetermined. Rather they are negotiated in an ongoing manner and are open-ended within certain historical, social, and economic frameworks. The character of a gender regime depends on the social environment it is embedded in, while at the same time it also shapes this environment in fundamental ways.

I examine the characteristics of the gender regimes of Austria and Hungary in a single set of social institutions, in the sphere of work, and, in particular, I explore the differences in the ways in which men and women could claim authority and move into the upper echelons of society through participation in the labor force. The intellectual ambition of this work, however, goes beyond an empirical survey of the gender regimes in the two countries. In describing these different systems of male domination I propose to contribute to four sets of literatures in sociology and feminist theory, including feminist arguments on patriarchy; discussions about the welfare state; stratification models, quantitative and qualitative, that analyze and compare systems of social advancement in capitalism and state socialism; and, finally, the expanding literature on gender relations in Eastern Europe.

There is a growing body of feminist theory that this book joins by emphasizing the negotiated nature of "patriarchy" or "gender regimes" as opposed to the image of an unchanging, deterministic, or essentialist model of male domination depicted by Marxist and radical feminists in the 1980s (Firestone 1970; Hartmann 1981). Having studied the gender regimes of Austria and Hungary in the world of work, I am struck by the accuracy of Ridgeway's (1997) image of the chameleon used to characterize male domination as it adapts to the environment in which it exists. Gendered *exclusion* from the sphere of work and politics is easily observable in both societies, but the *degree and mechanism* of this exclusion varies over time and space. The first goal of my project is to analyze these variations and thereby explore the ways in which gender regimes in stratification systems have been, and may in the future be, recreated and reshaped to fit new economic, political, and ideological interests.

In addition to practices of exclusion in effect, labor market processes in both countries have also been guided by gendered principles of *inclusion*, expressed most obviously in state policies and legal regulations encouraging some women, but not others, to work and pursue a career. To explore this aspect I look at the conditions under which state laws, legislative practices, and even policymaking assumptions and intentions enabled or facilitated a varying number of women's participation in paid work and in authority. Thus, the second set of literature I address consists of feminist analyses of state policy regimes. Interestingly enough, although there is a growing body of feminist literature on the welfare state (e.g., Orloff 1996; Sainsbury 1996; etc.), even comparative European analysis often ignores the ways in which gender was constructed in the state policies of Eastern European societies (for exceptions, see Haney 1997; Gal and Kligman 2000b), even though these countries arguably provided a great deal of welfare for their citizens in no less a gendered manner than did capitalist welfare states. My work proposes ways in which we could rethink existing models that describe the role of gender in policymaking so that they would account for state socialist social and inclusionary policies as well.

The third set of literature to which I seek to contribute consists of theories of social stratification and class under state socialism, which, as a rule, omit the concept of gender from their discussion (for example, Djilas 1957; Konrád and Szelenyi 1989; Haller, Kolosi, and Róbert 1990, etc.). Yet, as I will show, assumptions about gender and gender interests are deeply embedded in the social structures of both countries: the chances and processes of access to positions in the ruling class are different for men and women, and thus we cannot properly characterize the whole system solely on the basis of men's experience. In addition, gender is a crucial predictor of position in the social hierarchy in and of itself, and ignoring or not theorizing it produces inferior accounts of the system of social inequalities in any contemporary society.

Finally, the fourth set of literature I address is the expanding body of scholarship on women in Eastern Europe. Most writings on state socialist societies discuss Eastern Europe in isolation from other countries, particularly capitalist ones. Rarely can we find state socialist and capitalist comparisons in research designs (although for a recent exception on East and West Germany in the 1940s and 1950s, see Heineman 1999, or other work on the German unification experience), even though these social systems originated from the same intellectual background and coexisted with and influenced each other through the past fifty years. Only by comparing actually existing capitalist and state socialist societies can we uncover the differences that are the result of the specific characteristics of these social systems and can we understand what the collapse of state socialism or the move toward a unified European market might (or might not) bring.

Changes over Time and Space

Most of the analysis in this book focuses on the gender regimes in the stratification systems of Hungary and Austria in the postwar period. I want to emphasize the point that these findings are not necessarily or automatically generalizable to other institutions, to different periods, or to other state socialist or capitalist countries. On the contrary, because my argument is about the negotiated and variable nature of gender regimes I will make every effort possible to point out temporal or institutional variations in both countries. Nevertheless, the discussion of the 1980s is important as a starting point from which differences emerging at a later point in time, or elsewhere in East Central Europe, might be considered.

In the early 1980s Hungary was no more a "typical" state socialist society than Austria was a model capitalist one. Many readers will be familiar with the Hungarian experiments with "market socialism" or "the second economy" that gained the country the title "the happiest barrack of the eastern bloc," and signified its leaders' somewhat higher indulgence in political, economic, and individual freedoms. In Austria, also, we can observe a number of social institutions that sharply differentiate it from other capitalist countries, especially from those built on the Anglo-Saxon tradition. These differences range from the relative strength of the state to the rule of a long-term coalition of left-wing and right-wing political parties to the corporatist traditions represented by the Social Partners (Sozialpartnerschaft) and to the predominance and social and political significance of the Catholic Church. Generalizations have to be made carefully, therefore, because although Hungary obviously shared a number of features with other state socialist countries, just as Austria did with capitalist ones, the local contexts within which these features were expressed differed. But models are nevertheless necessary and useful for organizing our knowledge—if not for purposes of finding similarities than for uncovering contrasts, differences, and distinctions.

A Lopsided Comparison: Methodological Concerns

For those familiar with their histories, Austria and Hungary may seem like ideal points of comparison. Because of their shared historical legacies it is possible to "hold constant"—to an arguably significant degree—the effects of political institutions, culture, and tradition before 1945 and to examine the divergence of the two societies as the result of mostly recent developments. But there are some problems embedded in the nature of comparing two social systems, which even though they share a great deal of their history, are currently different in such fundamental ways. I have used both quantitative and qualitative data and analyses in this book, with each raising different but equally serious methodological questions that I would like to address here.

The dilemmas of quantitative analysis are perhaps more straightforward. In most of the ensuing statistical models I examine the individual-level, quantifiable determinants of mobility into high positions of authority. But in order to explore the differences between Austria and Hungary in the effect of, say, education on a person's chances of being a manager, one ideally would need identical models with exactly the same variables measured exactly the same way in both countries. Quite aside from the fact that there are no surveys that fully satisfy this criterion, the inclusion of identical variables is by itself problematic. Only if we estimate the same variables in the models for the two countries can we compare the size of the coefficients and decide whether the differences between them are or are not worthy of attention. It is impossible to do this in a reliable manner with models that are specified ever so slightly differently.[7] But at the same time this means that in order to measure the difference between two countries we must assume their similarity first. This is particularly poignant in the case of state socialist Hungary and capitalist Austria. Obviously, membership in a communist party is mostly irrelevant in the Austrian context, just as is ownership of major productive assets in Hungary: the much-needed assumption of similarity is clearly untenable.

What to do then? Shall we construct identical models to allow a formal comparison, or shall we stick with country-specific features in order to present correctly and meaningfully specified models? I have decided to take both routes in the following chapters, in the hope that I can maximize the benefits of both types of approaches. I start by examining the two countries separately and specify the best model I can within the constraints of the data set. This will allow an in-depth analysis of the countries on their own and the changes within them over time. Next, I run identical models for the two regions, restricting the dependent as well as the range of independent variables in order to assess cross-country differences in the use and usefulness of the determinants of most importance.

Thus, in two steps we might be able to establish comparative models that are not only statistically but sociologically meaningful. However, the problems of qualitative analysis are more difficult to overcome. Aside from the interviews I conducted in both countries, the richest source of data comes from the archives of the Hungarian communist party. In these archives are records of what the most powerful leaders of the country thought about women and their role in society: the Politburo held bi-weekly meetings, most of which were transcribed verbatim. Although important discussions were also held outside this forum, the most powerful positions resurfaced in the negotiations, in the different versions of the final documents produced, or in the volumes of (strictly classified) supporting materials submitted for each session. The archives are indeed a rich source of data, but what kind of analogous information could be found for Austria? Exactly because of the differences in the nature of the regime, there was no similarly situated and powerful political organ in Austria that could have shaped the construction of women and their role in society in as powerful a manner as did the Politburo in Hungary. The influence of the Austrian media was substantial but not comparable to that of the Politburo, especially not in the early part of the postwar period. Instead, I have used transcripts from relevant negotiations and discussions in the Austrian Parliament, but it should be noted that democratically elected legislators, especially those in opposition parties, had much less power to influence than did the fifteen-odd members of the highest and most feared executive body of the Hungarian communist party.[8]

Expressly because they were establishing and enforcing radically new principles of stratification that lacked legitimacy, tradition, and often popular support, Hungarian cadres were much more reflexive about these principles than were their counterparts in liberal democracies. Obviously, the instructions issued by the party were never carried out to the letter, and duplicity pervaded the system as Kligman (1998) persuasively argues. But the written documents, speeches, instruction manuals, and centrally commissioned newspaper articles were some, and probably some of the more significant, forces to shape social practice and ideology. For example, the formal principles of promotion (under the name of "cadre politics") were published, discussed, and modified in a number of laws, regulations, speeches, and political manuals, reflecting both the changes in the ideological commitments of the leaders as well as their response to, and perception of, the changing realities around them. No similar documents exist for Austria. Even though, in good Central European tradition, Austrian state institutions and their representatives had significant power and influence (perhaps more than their counterparts did in many other capitalist societies), those in leadership positions felt less of a pressing need to legitimate their role through repeated descriptions of the channels of promotion and social mobility than did the Hungarian Politburo. The result is a comparative dearth of documents for researchers to study.

For this reason, the comparison between Austria and Hungary has to remain lopsided; there is no point in trying to squeeze the data from one country into the preset framework of the other. Because I have more sources from Hungary I present more information on that country, but in a number of cases I nevertheless attempt a direct comparison—for example, between discussions in the Austrian Parliament and in the Hungarian Politburo. It should be noted, however, that these organizations had widely differing levels of power, style of leadership, and modes of operation, and thus these comparisons should be considered with care.

Data Sources

I have used multiple methodologies in this book because of the inherent problems in using any one set of data in such diverse contexts. For qualitative information I primarily rely on materials from the archives of the Hungarian communist party, opened up for research in Budapest in the early 1990s (Magyar Országos Levéltár, Párttörténti Intézet Archívuma; hereafter referred to as PIA). I have reviewed previously classified materials relating to the issues of the selection and evaluation of cadres and to the position and role of women in society, as well as to party membership, authority, and power. The documents I studied included transcripts of Politburo meetings between 1949 and 1989, as well as confidential reports and debates recorded and filed in various departments of the apparatus of the Central Committee and the women's organizations. Much of this research took place in the summers of 1994 and 1995. In Austria I used transcripts from sessions of Parliament in 1979 discussing the Equal Treatment Law; changes in maternity leave regulations in 1986; and the 1992 debate on the new Equal Treatment Package. These transcripts were available in the library of the Austrian Parliament.

In addition, I conducted in-depth, semistructured interviews with nineteen women managers in Hungary and fourteen in Austria, in an effort to find out how women managers themselves experienced their success and to elicit the rich and moving stories that describe the roads they had traveled to get there. These interviews do not constitute a random sample in any formal sense, but I tried to include representatives of varying age groups, social background, and position level and sector. About two-thirds of my interviewees occupied at some point in time very high-level positions, and include a spokesperson to the prime minister, a vice president of a large bank in Austria, members of the Politburo, leaders of trade unions, CEOs of textile factories in Hungary, and heads of departments in state departments (ministries) in both countries. The rest are women in lower-level managerial jobs: restaurant owners, a proprietor and manager of a fitness club, deputy managers of state departments, and chairs of academic departments (whose position and degree of power differ sharply from that of their American colleagues). I have changed names and minor personal details to mask the identities of the informants.

My most important quantitative source came from two large data sets collected by the respective statistical offices of each country. The primary Hungarian data set is from a mobility survey conducted in 1993 by the Hungarian Central Statistical Office (Hungarian Mobility Survey 1992 or Társadalmi Mobilitás Kérdőív). This data set contains information about the population over fourteen years of age, and it is a representative sample of households. I derived a sample of the population through using the weights provided in the data set. Although this simple solution does not guarantee full representativeness and opens up the possibility of undue clustering in the sample, the alternative, which would have meant including only one randomly selected individual per household, would have severely restricted the size of the data set. Therefore, I opted for simple weighting and retained the original sample size of 29,002. The Hungarian Central Statistical Office conducted similar mobility surveys in 1982, 1972, and 1962 as well, but these files are missing the crucial variable of party membership, which for political reasons was not included in the questionnaire. For this reason these data are not ideal for much of my analyses, and therefore, I constructed cohorts for 1982 and 1972 using the 1992 data set. This practice is a somewhat dubious one and calls for further explanations, which I provide in appendix A. The earlier surveys were used to cross-check the accuracy of my artificial cohorts produced from the 1992 file.

The Austrian data set is a similar mobility survey, conducted in 1982, with an N of 40,688 (*Microcensus of Austria, 1982*). Although the 1982 data set serves as the most important material for this book, I also utilized similar surveys from 1988 and 1996 that were supplied by the same statistical office in Austria. The main surveys in each country contain retrospective information about the respondents' educational history, their past and present economic and political activities and occupations, and varying amounts of data on their family backgrounds.

These three sources—archival data, in-depth interviews, and representative surveys—complement each other to shed light, from different angles, on the differences and similarities between the gender regimes in state socialist Hungary and capitalist Austria.

A Roadmap to This Book

In the next chapter I provide a theoretical framework for my analysis, elements of which have been highlighted above. I discuss the contribution of my work to current feminist theories of patriarchy, state policies, and welfare states, as well as to stratification models and theories on gender in Eastern Europe. My task in chapter 2 is to describe and contextualize my argument and to produce a framework for the comparison of the gender regimes of the two countries.

In chapter 3 I introduce the historical similarities and the present differences in the social structures of Austria and Hungary. After a very brief historical overview I describe the customary routes to positions of authority in the two countries, first by using archival materials in Hungary and interviews and personnel textbooks in Austria, and then using survey data from both countries. I focus on the 1980s but explore changes in later periods as well.

I begin in chapter 4 my discussion of the gender regimes in the two countries. First, I contrast the degree of gender inequality in the labor force, specifically in positions of authority. The key finding here is that women's exclusion and gender discrimination were more pronounced in Austria than in Hungary. At the end of this chapter I explore the question of both negative and positive discrimination as it was codified in state policies and experienced by female managers.

In chapter 5 I start the explanation of the mechanisms of women's exclusion from authority in Austria and Hungary. I study the determinants of direct and indirect exclusion: from authority itself as well as from the most important resources necessary for claiming authority. In Austria I find that women's exclusion operated primarily through economic and cultural ("symbolic") domination, while in Hungary it operated through political domination. In Hungary, access to cultural capital and a small yet noticeable reduction in the negative impact of reproductive responsibilities in the promotion process provided secondary routes for women's advancement.

Next, in chapter 6, I move away from a focus on the individual to a discussion of states and state policies. I distinguish between the ways in which women relate to the state in the two countries through an examination of the content, timing, and meaning of state policies. I rely on archival materials in Hungary and transcripts from parliamentary sessions in Austria. My argument is that in the early 1980s, the focal period of my analysis, state policies allowed women's participation only on the basis of the male norm, that is, if they acted "similar" to men in Austria, but encouraged women's inclusion as "different" and in need of special provisions in Hungary. Both policies resulted in different degrees of segregation and women's inferiority in paid work.

Chapter 7 contains a case study of state policies and political rhetoric in Hungary. I continue and expand the argument made in the previous chapters by describing the ideas and assumptions political leaders held about women, and the reasons why they constructed them as inferior political subjects. This discourse is not identical to the "official" published gender ideology of the communist party. Because it is primarily derived from classified, transcribed Politburo discussions, it provides a more reliable way of finding out why and on what basis state policies concerning women were created in the state socialist period as well as how and why they changed.

In chapter 8 I summarize my findings and discuss developments since the 1980s in both post–state socialist Hungary and capitalist Austria. Vast changes occurred in the system of stratification and in the construction of gender in Hungary after the fall of the communist party, but stability has not been characteristic of modern capitalism either. Certainly, the gender regime in the Austrian labor market and state has been modified to just as significant a degree in the last decade of the twentieth century as has the Hungarian one, although the legacies of both linger on.

2. Gender Regimes East and West

Are gender regimes significantly and systematically different in capitalist and state socialist societies? How does the construction of gender hierarchies in paid work and power vary in state socialist Hungary and in capitalist Austria? These are the central questions I address in this book. I was motivated by the dearth of both empirical and theoretical information on this topic: Theories on class and social inequalities in Eastern Europe often ignore gendered interests and practices; an omission that produces inferior accounts of the social structure, authority, and its legitimacy. And similarly, feminist theorists sometimes ignore or deemphasize the ways in which patriarchy is shaped by other social institutions in society, particularly in noncapitalist contexts. My broadest theoretical aim is to marry these two sets of theories in an effort to integrate the study of gender in the study of social relations, as well as the study of social relations in Eastern Europe to that of social relations in society in general.

My goal in this chapter is to explore whether or not arguments about authority relations and social inequalities in Eastern Europe, on the one hand, and feminist theories from East and West, on the other, provide adequate answers to the questions posed above and to identify some of the key components of the comparison between Austria and Hungary. Because I discuss first the mechanisms of exclusion from authority and then the forces of inclusion in the same sphere, I follow this division in my review and discussion of the existing literature. Yet it should be remembered that these two processes operate simultaneously, and their separation is nothing but an analytical tool that allows us to look at a phenomenon from two different angles.

Processes of Exclusion from Authority

Legal authority and cadre politics

This book is about cadres and executives, the people who are the most powerful participants in the sphere of work and politics, and it is also about the skills and resources they need to gain and maintain their leadership positions in formal organizations, such as an economic enterprise, a party office, or a state institution in state socialist Hungary and capitalist Austria. The dominant classes in capitalist and state socialist societies relied on a different combination of resources to serve as the basis of legitimacy for their rule. Although classical theories of authority are helpful in identifying some of these critical resources, they blatantly ignore gender (or masculinity, rather) as one of the most obvious sources of power and authority, and hence their accounts are necessarily misspecified.

Much of the current sociological literature uses Max Weber's notion of *Herrschaft* to describe relations of domination (Weber 1978). In Weber's description "ruling powers" need to make claims to legitimacy in order to sustain their position in the long run. The types of claims they make have a profound influence on the character of domination itself and thus on the criteria of inclusion in, and exclusion from, the dominant group. Western capitalist societies display a predominance of authority relations of the "legal-rational" type (Giddens 1971). Modern capitalist production and parliamentary democracy require the specialization of tasks; large-scale, efficient organization of independent units; and speedy processing of information on a mass scale. Capitalist exchange rests on the liberal ideology and practice of universally binding contracts among "free" individuals, honored and enforced through a web of laws and bureaucratic regulations. Authority within bureaucratic organizations, such as the workplace or the political apparatus, is achieved and legitimated through claims to formal, procedural rationality, expertise, experience, and special job-related skills (Weber 1978; Dahrendorf 1959; Giddens 1971) as well as, more indirectly, property rights (Wright 1985; Zeitlin 1987). Those at the top of the social hierarchy in capitalist societies possess high volumes of these two types of key resources: economic capital and/or expertise, experience, and skills. Authority relations in Austria, like those in other Western European societies, while retaining their own specificities, more or less corresponded to this legal-rational type.

There is less agreement about the character of state socialist authority or its dominant form of legitimacy, but there are three basic elements of contrast most scholars identify. First, in state socialist societies the relationship between the state or party authority and its subjects is based on the logic of patronage (rather than legal-rational procedures), requiring personal loyalty and trust toward the party-state (rather than making demands based on rights and written regulations or mutually agreed-on contracts) (Walder 1986; Jowitt 1987). Second, rather than technical rationality, central authorities claim monopoly over teleological knowledge, or the "historic mission," "the common good," or the "revolutionary ethos," and loyalty is commanded on this basis (Jowitt 1987; Konrad and Szelenyi 1989). Finally, the jurisprudence of state socialist authorities is wider and more diffuse: they penetrate more areas of life, not even pretending a separation of "public" and "private" (Jowitt 1987; Bruszt 1988; Böröcz 1989; Horváth and Szakolczai 1992). This kind of authority has been called "traditional," "paternalistic," or even "neotraditional" to emphasize its distinctions from the legal-rational kind and to point out its similarity, at least in some of its characteristics, to precapitalist social formations.

The dominant classes in these two types of societies possess different kinds of resources that facilitate their access to high positions of power and privilege. Pierre Bourdieu's concept of "social space" is useful for bringing these seemingly diverse phenomena—capitalist and state socialist domination—under a single analytical framework for purposes of comparison. Following Bourdieu's work (1984, 1986), let us refer to the sum of resources and power available for the reproduction of social status as a person's "capital." Members of a society own varying amounts of capital—the volume, the structure (economic, cultural or social), and the dynamics of acquisition of which then define their position in the social space of that particular society; that is, the conditions of their existence. In capitalist societies, as in Austria in the 1980s, members of the dominant class are expected to be best equipped with cultural and economic capital: these two types of resources play the crucial role in the social stratification process.

In order to apply Bourdieu's concepts to Eastern Europe some modifications are necessary, especially concerning the role of economic capital, which, after 1949, played only an insignificant part in social advancement in the region, as the communist parties abolished individuals' right to own productive assets and gradually nationalized all major forces of production. This void, however, was filled, as Böröcz and Róna-Tas (1995) or Eyal, Szelenyi, and Townsley (1998) argue, by another type of resource: social capital. The usefulness of social capital is, of course, not unique to the societies of Eastern Europe. A classic example of a particular institutionalization of this resource is nobility titles, which were essential for occupying a high social position in the stratification systems of feudal Europe as well. "Old-boys' networks" and fraternities, clubs, and societies still exist in modern capitalist societies to enhance and reproduce the privileges of its members. But Eyal, Szelenyi, and Townsley (1998) argue that this form of social capital is less strong and less usable now because the lack of formal regulations weakens its importance for the maintenance of social positions.

In state socialist Hungary, however, social capital was reinstitutionalized in a new form; nobility titles were replaced by acceptance into the ranks of the politically reliable, by admission into the circle of communist party members (Eyal, Szelenyi, and Townsley, 1998). This particular type of social capital, party membership, became essential in the production and reproduction of the social hierarchy. From here on I refer to this special institutionalization of social capital as "political capital."

In addition, cultural capital also played an important, if secondary, role in post–World War II Hungary. By the early 1970s intellectuals, mostly technical experts and economists, started to demand a place in the ruling elite. Their success did not abolish the importance of political loyalty but it did not leave it untouched either. Professionals were willing to work on attaining political capital in order to usurp some of the power held by party cadres, but they could only do so if they redefined its institutionalization. And the obverse was true also: political cadres made efforts to change the meaning of cultural capital, to blur the boundaries between the two types of resources in an effort to claim it for themselves and maintain their position in the social hierarchy.

The social space of both societies was thus structured by different types of capitals: cultural capital complemented economic capital in Austria and political capital in Hungary. Different fractions of the dominant class possessed a somewhat varied mix of these types of capitals in both countries, although in Hungary especially the boundaries between education and political resources became blurred over time. Quantitative analyses of social advancement in capitalist and state socialist societies supply evidence for these claims: education has been found to be an important determinant for social advancement in both Eastern and Western Europe (Krymkowski 1991), and political resources have been proven to have had nonnegligible effects under conditions of state socialism (Walder 1995).

What about gender?

These discussions, however, give preference to class distinctions, as did communist party leaders, and ignore significant inequalities generated along the lines of gender. Perhaps Western feminist theories can provide a better analysis.

Unfortunately, just as theories of social structure ignore gender, so too do theories of gender often disregard the analysis of the social structure in which gender regimes are embedded. For example, radical feminist theories of the 1980s understood male domination (and, specifically, women's exclusion from power and privilege) in mostly universalistic terms. Patriarchy was seen as an all-pervasive system of domination independent of class, ethnic, or other kinds of oppression. It described the power of men not primarily as employers or fathers but as husbands or individual men over women. Radical feminists argued for the difference between the essential qualities of men and women and claimed that "female culture" was suppressed and allowed little part in mainstream ideology or social practice everywhere in the world (Scott 1988).

The merit of radical feminist theory lies in its emphasis on the continuity of patriarchal outcomes. The evidence from Eastern Europe eloquently testifies to this: even in a society organized on principles quite different from capitalist ones, women's inferior position in terms of their participation in the distribution of power, privilege, and control is clearly observable. What radical feminists ignored is the systematic variability in the *processes* through which such domination comes about and in the *degree* to which patriarchal domination is realized. There are obvious similarities in women's experience in Eastern and Western Europe, yet the assumption of uniformity misses a number of stark and meaningful differences.

Gendered exclusion under capitalism

Marxist and socialist feminists have sought to correct their radical sisters' disregard for social structure and have emphasized the embeddedness of patriarchal interests in class-based oppression and in the liberal ideology of western capitalism. A number of researchers (Hartmann 1981; Milkman 1987) have shown how gendered exclusion operates to the advantage of capitalists by creating a reserve army of labor; by guaranteeing the cheap, private reproduction of the labor force; and by constructing a large market of individual consumption-oriented households. Individual men also benefit from women's relegation from paid work because it reduces the competition for positions in the workplace and allows them to enjoy personalized and unpaid sexual and domestic services.

Scholars argue persuasively that in capitalist societies women's exclusion from privileged positions in the occupational hierarchy is carried out through the construction of the workplace as a male-biased institution (Hochschild 1975; Pierce 1995), where the rules of conduct and the dynamics of the career track are based on the male experience, assuming total freedom from reproductive duties. Women's access is limited because of direct or indirect discrimination and even self-exclusion from the key resources of advancement in the capitalist labor market: skills and critical types of educational degrees, experience, job training, and credit opportunities. Both quantitative and qualitative studies on the determinants of the gender gap in authority and the "glass ceiling" identify these factors as crucial (Kanter 1977; Wolf and Fligstein 1979; Reskin and Ross 1992; McGuire and Reskin 1993). In particular, research from Austria reveals a vast difference in the educational qualifications, job experience, and work commitment of men and women all through the twentieth century (Grisold and Simsa 1992; Cyba 1991, 1996; Feigl 1986; Gross, Wiedenhofer, and Vötsch 1994; etc.).

The embeddedness of patriarchal exclusion in the dominant ideology of classic liberalism, the cornerstone of Western, democratic capitalist societies, has been identified by Carole Pateman (1989). She argues that in the new ideology and social practice emerging in Western Europe in the late seventeenth century, the division between "civil society" based on the "original contract" between free, property-owning citizens and the private household (composed of "free" men and "dependent" women and children) guaranteed the rule of men over women, albeit through novel procedures and justifications. Pateman calls this type of patriarchy "fraternal," because here men's access to women's bodies was guaranteed based on their roles as husbands and was assured by their civil association, their fraternity. The crucial point here is that women, according to the contractarians, were not considered "free individuals." They were not entitled to own property or enter into contracts in their own name, and in most cases they had no custody or decisionmaking rights over their own children. Married women's interests were subsumed under those of their husbands; they were seen as intrinsically irrational and hence "natural" dependents. As such they were relegated to the private household, directly under the rule of their husbands (Pateman 1989; Phillips 1991).

Although the ideology of liberal democracy, freedom, individuality, and rationality are still the key sources of legitimacy for authority in modern capitalist societies, a number of important improvements have occurred in the position of women in the past century. The franchise, property rights, and other regulations have allowed women's partial incorporation into the public "fraternity" of men. However, Pateman argues that such efforts are necessarily unsuccessful because the modern political order is intrinsically patriarchal.[1] The rational individual, the main building block of modern liberalism, is not gender neutral; the abstraction from gender only hides his embedded masculinity. Such incorporation can, therefore, only mean assessment by the male norm, and women would often be found wanting in this comparison.

For reasons often considered natural or biological, only men are in full possession of their own bounded bodies, a property right considered the basis of individual freedom. Women's bodies change in pregnancy and through hormonal cycles and can be legally contracted out through prostitution or surrogacy. Married women are seen as giving up claims to their bodies once they sign the marriage contract: for example, marital rape is not considered a crime in a number of countries (Pateman 1988b). Moreover, the liberal state has claims over pregnant women's bodies by retaining the right to deny (or demand a "legitimate" reason for) abortion or by holding women responsible for "feeding their fetus" properly (Markens, Browner, and Press 1997).

Western feminist theorists thus provide us with rich descriptions of the economic motives, processes, and ideological foundations of women's exclusion from power and privilege in capitalist, liberal democracies. They have, however, practically nothing to say about the form of male domination in societies that subscribed to a strict antiliberal, communist ideology and that abolished private ownership over productive assets, as well as capitalist profit, freedom of enterprise, faith, and speech, along with the very concept of "free individuals." How, then, is men's advantage in power and privilege created and reproduced in such a setting?

Local production of gender

Since the late 1980s, the universalizing trends in feminist theory have been increasingly frequently supplemented by specific accounts of gender in more geographically and historically diverse contexts, thus opening up new space for a possible answer to the question posed above (see Scott 1988). Poststructuralist feminists, in fact, emphasize the study of the local, even perhaps idiosyncratic, production of gender over the study of the framework within which such production occurs (Salzinger 1997). This approach has led to rich descriptions of gender relations in noncapitalist (or non-Western capitalist) contexts. Although little such work has emerged so far on Eastern Europe (for an exception, see Haney 1997), research from Latin America and Asia has taken greater strides toward specifying the meaning of gender (or "gender identity") and its variations (see, among others, Ong 1987; Allison 1994; Lee 1998; Freeman 1999).

Although I am not denying the importance of understanding the multitude of ways in which gender is experienced and the ongoing process of its production, my aim in this book is to focus attention on the broader context within which this happens. This context includes, following Scott (1988), both the ruling gender ideology as well as the set of social institutions (such as the state; the established and practiced rules of claiming authority; the household division of labor; state regulations about maternity; childcare; or the production of social hierarchies in general) within which gender inequality is embedded. Lee (1998) suggests that such a "heuristic framework" for the analysis of male domination has already been constructed. Indeed, this may be true for capitalist societies, but its usefulness for noncapitalist ones is one of the empirical problems I seek to explore.

Gendered exclusion under state socialism

Gender-based exclusion from membership in the dominant class was deeply integrated into the social, economic, and political structures of state socialist societies as well. Yet researchers who focus on social stratification in Eastern Europe rarely include gender in their study of social relations: they sometimes limit their research to men only (Slomczynski and Krauze 1987; Haller, Kolosi, and Róbert 1990; Luijkx et al. 1995) or if they do point out women's lower chances of social advancement (Walder 1995; Róna-Tas 1998) they do not theorize gender as a form of capital that simultaneously shapes and is shaped by the system of inequalities (for an exception, see S. Szelenyi 1998). The growing feminist scholarship from Eastern Europe (Funk and Mueller 1993; Einhorn 1993; Rueschemeyer 1998; Gal and Kligman 2000a) is more useful in identifying the specificities of state socialist gender regimes, but these studies are rarely explicitly comparative outside the region. Many East European scholars emphasize the need to establish points of comparison in order to better understand state socialist and post–state socialist gender relations, yet few have taken empirically guided steps in this direction. This is exactly the gap I hope to fill by contrasting the degree, logic, and mechanisms, as well as the dominant ideology, supporting women's exclusion from authority in state socialist Hungary and capitalist Austria.

There are three important lessons to be learned with respect to the differences in exclusionary practices. First, in my research I found that gender, or more precisely "masculinity," served as a more useful resource for access to authority in capitalist Austria than in state socialist Hungary: women experienced a higher degree of exclusion from the dominant class in Austria than in Hungary. For a number of economic, political, and ideological reasons, state socialist governments made successful efforts at reducing the direct and indirect discrimination that women experienced, thus limiting, although never eliminating, the importance of gender in the stratification process. It must be noted, however, that this process was never completed—in fact, it was probably never meant to be completed. Yet it should still be considered at least partially "successful" when compared to women's situation in the labor market in Austria.

Second, not only the degree but also the processes of women's exclusion differed. As women entered the labor force in Hungary and their presence was constructed as a necessary and unavoidable part of state socialist life, the workplace also changed—at least for women. Work hours became at least informally more flexible and shorter, and hot meals and childcare were provided at the worksites. Women's maternity leave had to be accommodated, and allowances were made for household responsibilities (such as leave for mothers when their children got sick). Women in many workplaces managed to do their shopping in their lengthened lunch break and companies regularly arranged for food and other producers to sell their goods on the factory premises. Unlike in capitalist societies, the workplace experience and even the career track were no longer based *exclusively* on the male experience.

Yet there remained a critical segment of state socialist life that was still constructed in full opposition to all that was "female": the political arena. Communist anthems and songs (and these were numerous and popular all over the region) were characteristically sung by male choirs. Indeed, the revolutionary spirit and vocabulary of the communist party, its daily practice (such as, for example, the habit of meeting after work hours and organizing weekend retreats and training programs), as well as the criteria for membership were constructed as clearly masculine. Women were allowed, even welcome, in the workplace and at universities, but their entry to political positions and their attainment of the most critical resource, political capital, was much more restricted.

Thus in both types of societies women's access to authority was blocked by their exclusion from the crucial resource necessary for successfully claiming such power: only the character of these resources differed according to what served as the central means for authority in each system of inequalities: political capital in Hungary and cultural (educational) capital in Austria. This is where we can uncover the deep embeddedness of gender in the key institutions of each society: in each a segment was restricted to men, or at least women's access was made difficult, if not by formal rules of exclusion then by a more subtle yet exclusive emphasis on the male experience.[2] As the bases of authority, power, and privilege varied in the two countries—and so did the resources, which were constructed as masculine and thus were the arenas where women's exclusion was realized. In the following chapters I will refer to the obstacles that prevented women's access to authority as "gender filters" because their implicit aim and explicit consequence was, in each case, to limit the number of women in high positions of power. These filters operated in both societies, only their location differed.

Third, we can easily trace the differences in the ideological construction of women's roles and abilities in the dominant ideologies of the two social systems, which helps in understanding how they supported the differential mechanisms of exclusion in the two countries. As I described above, in mainstream liberal ideology women were seen as "natural de-pendents": they could never achieve full individual status, which was the criterion of acceptance into the public "fraternity" of (male) citizens. In contrast, in the reformed and modernized Marxist-Leninist ideology prac-ticed by state socialist Hungary, women were depicted not as incomplete individuals but as insufficiently loyal political subjects. Women's devo-tion (in fact, women's ability to be devoted) to the communist party and the revolutionary cause was always in doubt: they were constructed not as inferior citizens but as second-class, unreliable political subjects.

Gender-based exclusion, therefore, must be seen as an integral part of the system of inequalities and the relations of authority in both Austria and Hungary. The underlying logic of women's exclusion from authority appears quite similar in the two societies, yet, importantly, its realization differed. In each country at least one social field was constructed in a way that tended to fit a male life and career experience, and this guaranteed women's limited participation in power. But the exact character of these fields varied according to (and in support of) the underlying logic of claim-ing authority in the two types of societies.

However, in order to characterize the differences in the "gender re-gimes" in the system of workplace inequalities in Austria and Hungary we cannot limit the analysis to a study of the forces of exclusion. Espe-cially under state socialism but also in capitalist societies, significant institutionalized forces propelled women toward the workplace, toward educational institutions, and even toward positions of authority. As be-fore, we must study not only the differences in the degree to which wom-en's entry into some areas of work and authority was facilitated, but also the variation in the conditions in which this participation was allowed or encouraged. In the following section I describe two additional points of contrasts between the two societies, those related to the processes and principles of inclusion.

Mechanisms of Inclusion

East Europeanists on women's participation in paid work

Researchers agree that women participated more intensively in paid work and in politics in state socialist than in capitalist societies (Heitlinger 1979; Molyneaux 1981; Einhorn 1993). Or to put this finding in a broader context: the communist party-state penetrated areas of life considered off-limits (or "private") by capitalists states, and thus simultaneously reshaped the boundaries of the "public" (Gal and Kligman 2000b).

In 1920, Lenin made the following promise to Clara Zetkin: "That is why it is right for us [the Communist Party] to put forward demands favorable to women. . . . We demonstrate . . . that we recognize [their] needs, and are sensible of the humiliation of the woman, the privileges of the man . . . The rights and social regulations which we demand for women . . . show that we understand the position and interests of women, and will have consideration for them under the proletarian dictatorship" (Zetkin 1934, 54). In a communist state, unlike in a capitalist market economy, it was not the husband's responsibility to look after his woman: this role was usurped by the community of communist party members. Such an arrangement provided important benefits for an authoritarian rule. In Hungary, as is well known, women's inclusion in the labor force eased the labor shortage of an extensively industrializing economy, and their emergence into the paid labor force enabled their direct political surveillance. As a result, women's participation in paid work and in various forms of political affairs was taken for granted in state socialist Eastern Europe.

In the first part of the twentieth century the concept of a large number of women permanently in the labor force was indeed a novel proposition. But by the early 1980s women started to join the labor market in rapidly growing numbers in capitalist societies as well. Eastern Europe was thus no longer unique because of the degree to which women came to be integrated into the labor force. Yet, if not in intensity but in the character of women's integration in what was often referred to as the arena of work and politics and in the conditions of their inclusion, there were significant differences between Austria and Hungary. These differences, just like the ones I pointed out in the previous section, follow from the very nature of the two social systems: from the differences in the basic assumptions of their dominant ideology (liberalism and Marxist-Leninism) and from the economic and political interests that provided the framework for women's integration into the sphere of work, politics, and authority in the two countries.

Citizens and subjects

The first distinction to observe concerns the differences between the relationship of the individual to the state in state socialist and capitalist societies. Indeed, the concept of citizenship is central to an understanding of people's relationship to a democratic (capitalist) welfare state. Feminist scholars, however, warn of the vast differences in the ways in which men and women relate to the state—that is, the gendered nature of "social" citizenship. Writing about the United States, Barbara Nelson (1990), for example, discusses the origins of the two-channel welfare system, where men can make claims as individual citizens, and women as dependents. Not only the number of provisions but the administration and the ideology concerning the services provided differ in the two tracks. Fraser (1994) describes male and female "subsystems" within the welfare state, where male individual-wage earners and female dependent-clients are entitled to different sorts of provisions (see also Pateman 1988a, 1989; Gordon and Fraser 1994). Although there are significant differences among capitalist countries themselves (Orloff 1996; Sainsbury 1996), the concept of individual-focused citizenship remains central to all accounts, just as does the importance of the distinction between its male and female forms.

This is not true in the East, however. Scholars argue that in Eastern Europe the very concept of citizenship was replaced by the more fitting "subject status," and not only women but men were dependent on the state for their welfare and protection. Most social rights and responsibilities accrued not on the basis of "citizenship" but on "subject status," and because work was one of them the concept of "dependence" as it is used in, for example, welfare debates in the United States cannot be applied there. Moreover, the emphasis on the individual was replaced by an emphasis on the community or the ultimate good of the international proletariat. In this context, the concept of a "two-channel" welfare state of the Western European kind is not a meaningful description. In its stead, researchers point out that the state, rather than create distinctions along the lines of gender, effected a homogenization process in social citizenship and claims making (Graham and Regulska 1997). As Verdery notes, "socialist paternalism . . . [sought] to eradicate male/female differences to an unprecedented degree, casting onto the state certain tasks associated with household gender roles" (1996, 64). Along the same lines, Kligman argues that the communist party-state "generalized the dependency relations experienced by women and by children in the context of the patriarchal family to subordinate men as well" (1992, 255). The process is reminiscent of that of a feudal lord who assumes control over his subjects, male and female alike (Bruszt 1988). Thus, although in Western Europe researchers built up the notion of citizenship that reproduces the gender divide in men's and women's relationship to the state, in the eastern part of the continent this concept was replaced by the construction of state subjects whose gender becomes less and less relevant in contrast to their loyalty and subjugation to the final authority of the party.

Indeed, as I will demonstrate, my research in capitalist Austria shows that women made claims on the state primarily as single mothers and as wives through their husbands in the early 1960s, then increasingly as wage workers themselves (although not necessarily as individual wage workers but through their membership in trade unions or other trade organizations) in the 1980s, and by the 1990s their caring work could also form the basis of social citizenship. The provisions that women as caregivers were entitled to have typically has been different from and inferior to those that could be claimed by men, much along the same lines as feminist scholars have noted in the United States.[3] At the same time, I found indications of the "homogenization process" described by previous research only for the early periods of state socialism in Hungary. Neither the concept of the citizen nor that of the homogenized subject describes correctly the ways in which women related to the state socialist party-state in Hungary. Instead, a new category has to be formulated. By the 1980s, Hungarian women related to the state primarily not as individual wage earners (which they were, of course) or individual mothers (which they also were) or through their caring work in the household (which they did just as much as women in Austria) but in a novel and uniquely state socialist way: on the basis of their membership in a socially constructed "corporate" group: "women." Indeed, this was a group that party executives singled out as one of the building blocks of society and that they saw as having shared interests and needs. This is, then, not a relationship between an individual and the state, as in capitalist societies, but between a group and the state. Claims are made not on the basis of citizenship or need but rather with reference to group membership status and the long-term goals of the larger community.

It is worthy of note that participation in public life through membership in social groups, rather than as a free individual with well-defined civil rights, was not only women's "privilege" but a general principle of state socialist societies. Aside from women, a handful of other such categories were constructed: "working classes," "youth," "party members," and, somewhat later, "intellectuals." Members of these groups were attributed with certain characteristics, specific identities, and expectations, and their advancement as well as their privileges were predicated on their acceptance of these roles and limitations. Individual rights and privileges were clearly inferior to perceived communal interests; even the language of claims making differed.[4] Perhaps an example will help to illustrate this issue. A stark expression of the difference between individual rights and prescribed roles as members of a social group was recorded in 1966, when the Politburo engaged in its first serious, post-1956 discussion of the decline of the size of the population in Hungary.[5] I discuss this example here to demonstrate both the language and the reality of "rights" and claims making on the basis of group membership. Several times earlier when the population problem had emerged, the abortion question was carefully avoided because Politburo members were afraid to evoke the Stalinist restrictive policy that provoked so much popular resistance (e.g., for 1959 see PIA 288/5/140). But in 1966, perhaps not coincidentally in the year when Ceausescu in Romania instituted his restrictions on attaining a legal abortion (Kligman 1998), members of the Hungarian Politburo also took up the issue. Although the Politburo distanced themselves from Ceausescu's solution both on political and practical grounds, several members, János Kádár the most prominent of them all, were inclined to institute restrictions. The Women's Council, in a rare show of force, rallied support behind the proabortion lobby and even used some of the Western liberal feminist rhetoric about women's rights and women's claim to their own bodies to support their position. This move profoundly infuriated Party Secretary Kádár, who at a Politburo meeting in October 1966 was quick to redirect the discourse to his own playing field: "I believe that everyone should give birth to their first child, unless there are some serious obstacles, of course. That's what I think should be in the decree. If someone has at least a rental apartment,[6] has a job . . . such a person should not be allowed to abort her first child. Now, of course, these highly emancipated women will claim that this is against their civil rights. How do we respond? *We will simply defend our position* [Megvédjük az álláspontunkat]" (PIA 288/5/406; emphasis mine). The translation "we will simply defend our position" does not fully express Kádár's discursive feat. Kádár here contrasts a discussion of women in terms of individual civil rights—the position tentatively occupied by the council's "highly emancipated women"—to that in terms of women as a group under the political domination of the leaders of the communist party. In this context individual rights (or rights as mothers or caretakers or housewives) are meaningless, what matters is the particular significance of the group of women to what the leadership perceives and designates as the ultimate goal of the community.

Making claims on the state on the basis of membership in a social group as opposed to claims as individuals or dependent wives is, therefore, one important distinction between state socialist and capitalist societies. The consequences of such constructions, however, are even more significant for identifying the contrasting characteristics of state socialist and capitalist gender regimes.

Principles of Inclusion

What did the social group status described above mean in terms of state policies encouraging or discouraging women's labor force participation in state socialist Hungary? How does this contrast to that in capitalist Austria? How did state policies define the role of the social group of women in contrast to that of dependent women? Western models of the welfare state, while they may characterize the path Austria has taken in the past twenty years, do not provide a good description for state socialist Hungary.

Model building in the field of feminist welfare state theory is often comparative. Some scholars have proposed to "gender" the existing categorization of welfare state regimes produced by Esping-Andersen (1990) (Orloff 1993, 1996) or even engender new ones (Lewis and Ostner 1994; Sainsbury 1996). These new, woman-friendly models are built, however, almost exclusively on the experience of Western capitalist societies, and I know of no explicit comparison with state socialist (or post–state socialist) states, even though the latter prided themselves on providing large measures of welfare to their citizen subjects.

Although relatively little attention has been paid to corporatist states of the Austrian kind in the Anglo-Saxon literature, Austria could effortlessly be integrated into Western feminist models of the welfare state (Cyba 1991), but it would be almost impossible to describe state socialist Eastern Europe using these theoretical constructs. For example, Sainsbury's (1996, 42) typology of gendered welfare states distinguishes between the "male breadwinner ideology" and the "individual" model of social policy. The former is characterized by a traditional family ideology, the subordination of women to the male head of the household, joint taxation, and a priority for men at work. Much of Austrian policymaking in the 1980s followed these principles (Rosenberger 1995; Scagnetti 1987). But clearly, the breadwinner model cannot be applied to describe state socialist Hungary: the male worker and stay-at-home housewife family was neither economically nor politically feasible after World War II. The family wage was abolished in the late 1940s, social provisions were increasingly tied to labor force participation, and political propaganda and police surveillance obligated all able-bodied citizens to go to work every morning. Against this backdrop, the concept of "dependence," central to recent feminist theories of the welfare state (see, for example, Fraser and Gordon 1994), must also be reworked.

But neither can we classify Hungary at the other extreme as an individual-based policy regime: social policies did not consider the genderless citizen as their basic unit. In Sainsbury's individual model, the unit of benefits, contributions, and taxation is the individual not the household; men and women receive uniform entitlement on the basis of their citizenship. None of these conditions applied to a state socialist countries where, as I argued above, even the term "individual" was abolished from the politically correct vocabulary, and women related to the state not as individuals but as members of a group, with distinct, gender-specific obligations and privileges.[7]

Therefore, in order to include state socialist societies in gender-conscious state policy models, we must reformulate the models themselves. In addition to focusing on the strengths of state efforts to *decommodify* women's work through the application of either the male breadwinner or the individual models of benefit distribution, I suggest that we examine the same phenomenon from the other side as well: the conditions on which states *encourage* women's labor force participation. After all, women have been joining the labor force in record numbers everywhere. In Austria this growth started in the late 1970s; in Hungary, in the early 1950s. But in both countries, state policies created and continuously reshaped the conditions and the principles of women's engagement in paid work. Thus I propose to add the "principles of inclusion" as a new dimension of classifying the gender regimes of state policies, an addition that should help illuminate the contrast between the gendered character of state policy regimes in the two different societies.

I turn here to feminist legal theory to explain this newly minted dimension. According to feminist legal theorists there are two general approaches to the legislation of gender equality: one based on the assumed similarity between men and women and the other on the assumed differences. The most important pieces of legislation in the United States and many other capitalist societies are based primarily, although not exclusively, on the principle of similarity (Eisenstein 1988), requiring that the law treat women in all circumstances as "similarly situated" to men. Discrimination, at least in the legal books, is eliminated and women are assumed to be able to adapt to the rules of the workplace without any specific measures designed to aid them. Women are assumed to have no specific needs or interests that would set them apart from men and that would have to be addressed separately.

But how can women, under these assumptions, enter the arena of paid work and political office and participate as equals in a space that was constructed in opposition to all that is usually considered "feminine" or "woman"? How can they successfully enter a career track that assumes no obligations outside the workplace and is based on values, hierarchies, language, and practices that are primarily associated with dominant, heterosexual masculinity? Pateman argues that women can only enter civil society if "[we] disavow our bodies and act as part of the brotherhood" (Pateman 1988b, 52). In other words, only by becoming more like men, acting like men, can women participate as equals or near equals. Paradoxically, however, as Pateman points out, this means that at the same time "we must simultaneously continue to affirm the patriarchal conception of femininity or patriarchal subjugation" (1988b, 52).

Nevertheless, this "equal" or "similar" treatment position represents a significant victory over the principle it replaced, that of the ideology of "separate spheres," which allowed men and women distinctly different legal rights and responsibilities and flatly relegated women outside the workplace to a position clearly inferior to that of men (Baker 1990; Williams 1993). But legislating "similarity" (or "assimilation" as it is also called) failed to produce gender equality, because it meant the universal application of the male norm rather than the creation of an androgynous requirement (Acker 1991). In fact, as some feminist legal theorists point out, the purportedly gender-neutral treatment of people increases male privileges in certain instances such as, for example, in alimony or custody battles where as women lost their special privileges as mothers and dependent wives in the eyes of the law, men's already strong negotiating power further increased (MacKinnon 1991).[8]

Legislation in the United States as well as in many other capitalist societies is dominated by the similarity principle, although examples of the difference idea can also be found in the treatment of women and other minorities (for a recent discussion of the feminist dilemma between difference and similarity, see Scott 1988). Most notable among these were affirmative action policies, which allowed a different treatment of men and women (or various ethnic groups) in, for example, university admissions, simply based on the gender (or ethnicity) of the applicant. Another example is the recent phenomenon of gender quotas that some political parties instituted in Western European countries such as Sweden, Norway, France, or Austria in order to increase the representation of women in Parliament. Recurring public and legal attacks on affirmative action policies and gender quotas attest to the contested nature of this approach to gender or ethnic inequalities.[9]

State socialist societies, on the other hand, relied primarily (although not exclusively) on the difference principle in a much-touted effort to create gender equality in the field of work and politics. This meant that women were considered to be distinctly differently situated than men, particularly regarding the biological difference of pregnancy but also, significantly, with regard to the socially constructed difference of women's larger share in childrearing and household responsibilities. State socialist party leaders applied the difference principle exactly in order to counterbalance these burdens. They argued that women could not fully adopt a male lifestyle and career pattern, thus special regulations and provisions were needed that applied on the basis of gender.

The innovation of this legislation lies not in the segregation of women into a separate ("other") group of social actors who need special help, but in the use of the difference principle for women's *inclusion* in, rather than *exclusion* from, the paid labor force. In previous instances, the separate spheres ideology had primarily been utilized to establish barriers in front of women's engagement in paid employment. Here, these were designed expressly to draw women into the sphere of work, although of course not exactly on the same terms as men. In that respect, in its inability to bring about gender integration and full gender equality, the difference principle produced relatively small advantages over the equal treatment method. It transformed the process and even reduced the degree of male domination, but did relatively little to eliminate its ongoing practice.

I have outlined above the key points of contrast between state socialist and capitalist gender regimes relating to an individual's access to authority, with special reference to Austria and Hungary in the early 1980s. I identified the most important differences in the degree and character of male domination and I attempted to link these differences to the system of stratification and the dominant ideology in which they are embedded in each country. These arguments are summarized in general terms below, but it should be noted that the empirical reference point of this study is Austria and Hungary in the early 1980s.

First, the degree of gendered exclusion is contrasted: relative to capitalist countries, state socialist societies reduced yet never completely eliminated gender discrimination.

Second, there are systematic differences in the mechanisms, but not in the deeper logic of exclusion across the two social systems. Women's lack of representation is achieved through blocking their entry to the key form of capital that is necessary for claiming authority, although what actually functions as this key resource varies from society to society. In state socialist countries the political field (membership in the communist party) and in capitalist Austria the cultural and economic fields (such as educational institutions and the workplace itself) were constructed as uniquely male arenas. Male domination was exercised primarily on these bases. These fields served as "gender filters" or obstacles that kept women out of higher positions in the "public sphere."[10]

Third, the ideological construction of women as not fully qualified participants in the world of work and politics must be noted in both countries. In capitalist Austria in the early 1980s this was achieved through the construction of women as dependents; that is, as second-class, not exactly rational, individual citizens. Simultaneously, in state socialist Hungary women were constructed not as irrational citizens but as incapable of full political devotion or as insufficiently loyal subjects. Both of these constructions served as the ideological underpinnings of the processes of exclusion and inclusion of the particular state socialist and capitalist type.

Fourth, women relate to the state differently in the two social systems: as individuals (wage workers or dependents) in capitalist societies and as members of an ideologically constructed, gender-based corporate group in state socialist countries. Such group membership is different from relating to the state as part of a self-organized political group (because it lacks voluntary identification and is enforced by the state), and it is also different from other, mostly class-based corporate entities that have represented workers and groups of various trades and that have had a long tradition in the region. The distinction between relating to the state as individuals or as members of the group of women have serious consequences for policymaking and for the structure of opportunities available to both women and men.

Finally, a contrast between the principles of inclusion as expressed by state policies may be observed. Capitalist policymaking has been dominated by the similarity principle: the assumption of men's and women's formal equality. State socialist policy experimented with the new form of inclusion through differences—that is, the acknowledgment of women's difference and the application of corrective measures to encourage their participation in paid work and in authority. This principle is finding its way into policymaking in Austria in the 1990s (as it did in a number of other capitalist societies in Northern Europe much earlier).

In the following pages I discuss these "mirrored oppositions" in the context of Austria and Hungary—to apply the terminology of I. Szelenyi (1978) and Stark (1986)—to at least the last four of the five points above. The mirrored oppositions provide the comparative framework for this study and allow the examination of the specific institutional manifestations of male domination in the two societies.[11] Together these propositions address several important theoretical areas. In the broadest terms, my findings suggest that theories on authority and social space are misspecified without considering gender and gendered processes. Minimally, such attention will add women's experience to the descriptive models, but in all probability it will change these models themselves because the processes that guide women's mobility (or lack thereof) may be different from that of men in a number of substantive and not simply quantitative ways.

In addition, universalizing models of patriarchy are being replaced by historically specific and comparative accounts of the processes of male domination. This study also demonstrates that the character of gender regimes varies across societies and historical periods, although male domination has never been found to be absent. Indeed, the societies of Eastern Europe are good examples of the chameleon-like character of patriarchy (Ridgeway 1997); in these societies both the degree and the practice of male domination has been transformed, yet male domination was never completely eliminated. At the same time, I argue for the necessity of not just microlevel, but also (historically specific) macrolevel, descriptions of gendered processes—heuristic devices, it might be said, to guide more locationally specific research.

Finally, the debates on the gendered nature of the state, state policies, and citizens' relations to the state draw primarily on women's experience in capitalist societies, and the inclusion of state socialist countries would profoundly reshape these models. Including a "principle of inclusion" in the study of how and under what conditions state policies encourage women's entry to the labor market will help to integrate state socialist state policy into feminist accounts of the state, welfare, and gender inequality.

3. From "K und K" to "Communism versus Capitalism": The Social Worlds of Austria and Hungary

Even a cursory walk down the streets of Vienna and Budapest reveals some of the shared historical legacies of the two countries: their geopolitical position, architecture, the presence of the Catholic Church as the dominant religion, and other similar cultural traditions and artistic or even culinary tastes. A visitor might also quickly notice the differences in the levels of economic prosperity and political climate. Where do these similarities—but also fundamental differences—come from?

The histories of what are now Hungary and Austria first crossed when savage Magyar tribes waged ransacking campaigns in the eastern part of the remains of Charlemagne's vast empire in the mid-tenth century. The Magyars were beaten back by Otto the Great at Augsburg in 955, a victory that resulted in the reestablishment of Ostmarkt (the forerunner of the German name for Austria, Österreich), the eastern territories of the Holy Roman Empire, and the restriction of the Magyars to an area farther east of this land. For centuries after the settlement of the Magyar tribes and the foundation of a kingdom, Hungary played the role of the easternmost borderland of Western civilization.

The rule of the Habsburgs began in the thirteenth century and extended to Hungary by the sixteenth, and included much of the rest of Central Europe: Austria, northern Italy, the Czech lands, Slovenia, and at times all of the Holy Roman Empire as well.[1] Not surprisingly, economic, cultural, and political development was uneven in this vast kingdom. Vienna served as the seat of the monarch and the political and cultural center for the whole region. For Hungarians, not exactly placed in the center of the empire, the monarchy provided a framework for development and some help in the ongoing fight against the two archenemies of the time: the Turks and the spread of Protestantism. But the alliance also set limits to political freedom and to cultural and economic development, especially for its peripheral states. By the eighteenth century, the progress of Hungarian industry and agriculture, in classic peripheral tradition, was to a large degree shaped by the economic needs and political considerations of the more advanced and powerful western territories of the empire, mostly in what is now called Austria and the Czech lands. Trade tariffs (for example, in 1756 and in 1779) regulated economic relations and imposed duty penalties on Hungarian exports of goods to, while encouraging industrial imports from, Austria. Hungary's role was thus seen as the producer and provider of grains and other agricultural raw materials, while its industry remained rudimentary compared to other regions in the empire. The slow progress of industry ironically meant backwardness and low productivity in agricultural production as well, not to mention that it also hindered other aspects of social progress: urbanization, education, and cultural development. As a result, Hungary was not only less developed than Austria but also differently, as well as dependent on it overall.

The Habsburg rulers built a strong, centralized state apparatus in the early eighteenth century, the traditions of which have lived on, if in different forms, in both countries. Although a number of political and educational institutions were founded on similar patterns, the dominance of Vienna in cultural, social, and political life could not be questioned. The Hungarian aristocracy spoke German at home, listened to the music of the great Viennese masters, sent their children to university or military school in Vienna, and came to shop for fashionable clothes and tableware; overall they attempted to emulate the lifestyle of their more advanced compatriots in Austria.

The relationship between the regions in the empire was not without tension, however. After one of the many unsuccessful Hungarian revolutions in the mid-nineteenth century, the relationship between the two parts of the monarchy was renegotiated guaranteeing more independence to the less-developed partner, Hungary. The ensuing period until World War I is seen as one of rapid development in most areas of the empire, yet the inequalities remained.

What was then called Austro-Hungary found itself on the wrong side in World War I and in 1918, in an effort to break up its political and economic strength and as a punishment for its military wrongdoings, the monarchy was dissolved. Mass unemployment, economic chaos, and a civil war ensued in Austria, which stabilized by the 1930s by establishing the "first republic" in the country; reluctantly, the Habsburgs relinquished their throne after some seven hundred years. Hungary lost much of its territories after World War I, which created a long-standing national trauma. Political life alternated between the extreme Left and Right: in 1919 the country experienced its first brief brush with communism, but following the failure of the Hungarian Commune the road to a pro-Nazi government seemed straight. Both Hungary and Austria participated in alliance with Germany in World War II. By 1945, Russian troops occupied all of Hungary and much of Austria as well, but withdrew from the latter a decade later while keeping a strong hold on the former. Important differences in social and economic development had existed between the two countries up to this point, yet it is here that their trajectories started to diverge in more fundamental ways.

The end of World War II landed Austria in economic chaos again. With the help of the Marshall Plan, however, and as a result of a postwar economic boom, the country soon returned to the road of rapid economic development. Political stability was achieved through a two-decade-long coalition of the two major parties after the war (the Austrian People's Party, or övp, and the Social Democratic Party, spö), which held power until 1966 (as well as during several later electoral periods). Economists call this the period of the Austrian miracle: it is characterized by the highest economic growth rate in Europe, low unemployment figures, low inflations rates, and good labor relations. The latter was and still is guaranteed through a special political arrangement, the so-called Social Partnership (Sozialpartnerschaft), which is a system of corporate representation through centralized and state-financed interest groups. All economic, social, and political decisions are negotiated by the representatives of the state, the workers, the industries, and the employers—that is, the social partners (Tálos and Kittel 1996).

Even the oil price shock of the early 1970s had a smaller negative impact on Austria than on many other countries, although both the first and the second oil crises in the late 1970s and early 1980s set back economic development and increased unemployment rates. Nevertheless, by the early 1980s Austria became a developed capitalist country with a stable democracy and a strong, traditional, corporatist welfare state (Esping-

Andersen 1990) under the decade-long rule of the Social Democratic Party in what is called the "Kreisky era." Although the country formally remained neutral and did not join NATO because of its role as the roadblock between East and West, early on it signed a free trade agreement and for all practical purposes was a full member of the European community of capitalist countries. It is this period on which I focus my analysis in forthcoming chapters.

Hungary also started the period after World War II in economic chaos. But there, with the help of the lingering Soviet soldiers and with significant domestic support, a communist government took control in 1949. The first two decades of communism were characterized by extensive industrialization, the expansion of the labor force, and a rapid development of heavy industry. The communist rule had some positive consequences: destitution and hunger were eradicated and all able-bodied people were secured a job. As a result, infant mortality declined, life expectancy increased, and social inequalities decreased overall (Szelenyi and Szelenyi 1994). But progress came with a price tag: all institutions of democracy were abolished, personal and political freedom was severely cut back, and a single and invincible communist party ruled in the name of the international proletariat. In 1956 Hungarians attempted to rebel against the communist regime, but could not be victorious against the Soviet military establishment. Several years after the revolution, however, under the leadership of Party Secretary János Kádár, Hungarians began to build their own version of state socialism with a tentative increase in market-based activities and a hesitant questioning of the role of the state as the only agent in the process of central planning. The early 1980s found Hungary at the peak of state socialism. By this time, the political and economic institutions of "reformed state socialism" were fully developed and the decline and eventual collapse still far in the future.[2] It is for this reason that the early 1980s is a good moment to study the character of fully developed state socialism of the Hungarian variety and for comparing it to the Austria of the 1980s, a stable, highly developed capitalist society.

How to Become a Manager in Hungary
and Austria

Managing an economic enterprise or a state institution is quite a different experience in a state socialist country compared to a capitalist one. Even the origin of the words denoting the holders of positions of authority in Hungary and Austria—"cadres" and "managers," respectively—reflect the differences in the systems of stratification within which they prevailed. "Cadre" is rooted in military jargon where it denotes members of a permanent army of soldiers, the core of a military group. The word "manager" (and its translations)[3] originates from "hand," and it describes the action the holder of the title is supposed to carry out: manage, lead, and execute.

More than the words, the actual routes to authority for both men and women differed significantly in Austria and Hungary. Or to use Bourdieu's terms, the types of capital necessary for social advancement varied, as did the character of the dominant classes in the two different social systems. It is important to explore this variation in order to understand how gendered exclusion and inclusion occurred within these social settings.

Cadres and managers: the self-image of the regimes

The term "cadre" retained its meaning as a member in a select, loyal, and reliable elite in communist Hungary.[4] The process of selection, education, promotion, and evaluation of cadres, or "cadre politics" as it came to be known, was considered an important part of the overall political and legitimation strategy of the communist parties. In an oft-cited speech to the Eighth Congress of the Communist Party of the Soviet Union in March 1939, Stalin emphasized the importance of cadre politics for the survival of the regime:

> Now that we have perfected our political strategy . . . party cadres, the leadership of the party and the state have gained vast importance. . . . In order to realize our political plans in everyday life, we need cadres, we need people who understand and wholeheartedly believe in our political strategy, those who can translate it into practice and would defend it, fight for its realization, and take full responsibility for it. Without such people our great plans remain on paper only. (Sztalin, 1950, 67)

A document published almost fifty years later, in 1987, very near the eventual doom of the communist party in Hungary, echoes a similar idea: "Cadre politics is an integral part of the politics of the Hungarian Socialist Workers' Party, it is an indispensable tool for the exercise of party power and for the realization of the political strategy of the communist party" (*Útmutató*, 1987, 4). Cadre politics thus meant the process of cadre selection, and as such it was one of the most important ways in which the dominant class maintained its power and restricted access to its ranks. Prescriptions for the principles of cadre politics served as the official blueprint for exclusion from, or inclusion in, this distinguished group.

These principles—that is, the requirements prospective cadres had to satisfy—were always clearly spelled out and remained essentially unchanged during the communist era. The candidate had to demonstrate the possession of three specific types of resources: political loyalty, professional expertise and leadership skills, or moral fitness.[5] Stalin and, following him, Hungarian political leaders until 1989 maintained the primacy of political loyalty in the process of selection: "The primary criteria for the selection of party cadres is political, i.e. whether the candidates are politically reliable or not" (Sztalin, 1950, 50). Hungarian political documents echoed this sentiment. For example, a 1986 report to the Politburo (PIA 288/5/962) described the criteria for access to positions of authority by arguing that "the most important criteria for selection into positions of authority are the following. 1. Clear political loyalty, Marxist-Leninist knowledge relevant for managerial duties, political knowledge, an active political life, and the willingness to publicly defend the leading role of the party and the principles of socialism." The document then goes on to list the rest of the two requirements: expertise and professional knowledge as well as managerial abilities: "2. General and professional education appropriate for the particular position, the continuous development of professional skills. 3. Leadership skills, management skills, a democratic behavior, discipline, ability to absorb new information, independence and responsibility." But although on the surface little change was perceivable, there were slight modifications in the meaning and especially the weight of the requirement of political loyalty.

Before the 1960s, having political capital in Hungary involved more than the possession of a little red party membership booklet. Reliability required a past and a family origin that would testify to credible experiences of capitalist exploitation; that is, a working-class family background and a blue-collar occupation and/or participation in the underground communist movement before and during World War II.[6] By the early 1970s, however, using the prewar parental occupation of, by now, middleaged adults as an indication of class background and political reliability seemed too ludicrous even for the Politburo.[7] Gradually, the importance of family background started to fade and party membership, in and of itself, came to satisfy the political reliability criterion. According to a large-scale internal survey of the approximately thirty thousand people on the *nomenklatura* lists of the central party organs (the highest level leaders of the country), in 1950 over 83 percent of paid functionaries could claim a working-class background, while in 1973 about 60 percent did, and only slightly more than the majority, 55 percent, in 1986. At the same time, the percentage of party members in the cadre pool increased steadily: 76 percent in 1973 and 83 percent in 1985 (PIA 288/5/962, 288/5/783). This process reflects a real change in the composition of cadres: party membership became an increasingly necessary resource and a sufficient signifier of political reliability at least at this top level.[8]

In addition to this change in the meaning of the political criterion, the importance of education (skills, a university or college degree,[9] as well as political education) increased after the 1970s. According to the surveys quoted above, in the 1950s less than half of all top-level economic and state cadres had university degrees, but by the end of the 1980s almost all of them did. Similarly in 1986, by the end of the era, almost all state-level managers graduated from college: including over 95 percent of state administrators, 93 percent of economic managers, and around 80 percent of party functionaries. This change is reflected in the discourse of cadre politics as well: young graduates, having been educated in post–World War II schools where they supposedly could not help but absorb the communist spirit, were seen as the new pool of cadres, taking over this position from working-class youth. But without political loyalty, the value of education was limited in terms of promotion, particularly until the early 1980s. This was noted in 1961 by István Szirmai, a Politburo member, in a paragraph that summarizes the criteria for promotion for much of this era: "There are a number of university graduates who we [the Politburo] would not trust with anything. But at the same time, we also know a bunch of comrades, who finished maybe four to six years of schooling, but are national level leaders, because life experience in the movement provided them with sufficient knowledge" (PIA 288/5/247).

Rarely does a dominant group state the criteria of access to its ranks as clearly and emphatically as did state socialist leaders. But these top cadres had good reason to be so explicit. These rules of stratification were radically new to postwar Hungary. Although the principles were copied studiously from the Communist Party of the Soviet Union, their insertion into Hungarian reality was unique, rapid, and literally radical (Róna-Tas

1998). Thus the new criteria for claiming authority became part of the legitimation process: inclusion and exclusion from power was meant to demonstrate the rule of the proletariat by elevating members of the working classes into positions of power and depriving the propertied class of all of its privileges. In order to retain this cornerstone of legitimacy, leaders of the regime had significant incentives to retain, continuously emphasize, and disseminate the representation of the social order described above.[10]

No such incentive existed in Austria, where the criteria for promotion were less centralized and much less vigorously codified. Nevertheless, we can catch a glimpse of the requirements from written documents of personnel departments as well as from interviews with managers themselves in a position to hire subordinates. An important distinction must be made between state bureaucracies and private enterprises. In fact, entry to the coveted position of "civil servant" in state administration was (and still is) highly restrictive and centrally regulated in somewhat similar ways as in communist Hungary, thereby testifying to the common roots of the two countries. According to the personnel managers of two large state departments in Vienna, as well as a booklet published by the Chancellor's Office that describes the 1986 law of civil service, the most important criteria of access include educational skills, special exams as well as personal qualities. University degrees have become increasingly important for gaining a managerial position in civil service in Austria, graduate degrees provide especially high standing in this society that values formal achievements. Only graduates can aspire to the highest grades of civil service in any state apparatus. But in addition to the general educational degrees, a high-level civil servant has to take special exams both before and immediately after entering his or her position. These are general, albeit difficult, exams that test knowledge about the organization of the government and the state apparatus and knowledge of work regulations and employment codes. Some positions require fluency in a foreign language, others cannot be filled without some previous experience in the field. Other than the educational requirements, only personal qualities have been listed. Reminiscent of the criterion of moral fitness in Hungary, in these documents is discussion of communication skills, willingness to work hard, ambition, and flexibility.

Aside from these formal criteria we cannot dismiss the informal importance of political capital for social advancement in Austria, although as a requirement it was rarely as widespread and clearly described as in Hungary. The term *Patreibuchwirtschaft* refers to the practice of distributing positions in the state bureaucracy to political loyals and party members (Gehler and Sickinger 1995). At least, a careful political balance between the two major parties is often struck at the distribution of the best administrative positions. Although no doubt in practice in the 1980s, this system cannot be compared to the significance of communist party membership in Hungary: it lacked the same formal legitimacy and political clout and it was even less relevant for managers outside the highest ranks of state administration. On a practical level, party membership and political affiliation have not been included as variables in any of the mobility surveys I could find in Austria, so the importance of this factor cannot be assessed in quantitative models. Nevertheless, it should be noted that my models thus fail to capture an aspect of social mobility, which is significant for at least a segment of the upper class in Austria.

The situation is somewhat different in private enterprises, where the regulations of the state and the influence of political parties are less directly instituted. (But note that even private enterprises have to abide by the rules set by the Social Partners, where representatives of the state, employers, and workers negotiate the labor contract.) The importance of educational assets is perhaps less important and less formally required in private enterprises. Personal qualities, such as ambition and loyalty as perceived by the employer, as well as experience are the most crucial factors. "I don't really care about qualifications. I would pick a person who acts like they want to take over my job in five years," claimed one of my interviewees who worked for a private news agency when I asked her about the criteria she used to pick her assistant director.

For managing one's own business, economic resources are of crucial importance: including either inheritances or loans from banks or other institutions. This latter form of access to managerial positions—ownership of one's own enterprise—was expressly prohibited in state socialist Hungary where all major productive assets were nationalized in the 1940s. As a result, private enterprises were practically nonexistent until the tentative concessions to what came to be known as the "second economy" were made in the mid to late 1980s.

In sum, the documents from the two countries testify to quite different requirements for claiming authority and access to upper-class status. Education, experience, and, in the case of private business, capital ownership and inheritance, were of the highest importance in Austria, but political loyalty and party membership, complemented by university degrees, were most useful in Hungary. These sources described the formal criteria that important representatives of the two regimes attempted to apply, or claimed to have applied. This information is important, but we must also examine how precisely these criteria were implemented in reality. To this end, I constructed quantitative models for the two countries to complement their self-image as reflected in the documents and interviews above.

Modeling access to managerial positions

A logistic regression procedure is in our case best suited for modeling access to managerial positions. The dependent variable in all models represents the respondents' chances of being in a managerial position. In most cases, this is defined as those at, or close to, the top of the organizational hierarchy in formal economic, political, or other institutions—that is, positions such as factory CEOs; chief engineers; head nurses; heads of departments and their superiors in public administration; political leaders in parties, unions, and civil organization; directors of schools and theaters; chief editors of newspapers and their deputies, and so forth. I limited my analysis to those in formal positions of authority, even though in Eastern Europe artists, freelancers, opposition intellectuals, and even sociologists have had significant indirect and informal influence on both political and social decisionmaking. I excluded this admittedly interesting social group, not only because of their small numbers but also because it is difficult to measure power and authority outside a formal institutional setting. In both countries, my analysis focuses primarily on employee managers, and unless otherwise noted I excluded those who owned and managed their land or other economic enterprise. This focus is necessary to make the Austrian group comparable to Hungarian managers, among whom, especially in the 1980s, self-employed businessmen were hardly significant in numbers.

Table 3.1 presents the distribution of all variables included in the models. According to the first rows of this table, about 4 to 6 percent of the general population held jobs that were classified as managerial in both countries in the time period under study. This indicates that I used a relatively broad definition of the term "manager," including those in lower-level positions of authority as well. About 1 to 2 percent of the population count as "top managers"—that is, those who are the top execu-

Table 3.1. Distribution of variables in the models:
Hungary 1972–1992 and Austria 1982–1996.

	Hungary (%)				Austria (%)		
	1972	1982	1988	1992	1982	1988	1996
Employee managers	4.9	5.1	5.6	6.2	4.1	3.9	5.1
Top managers	1.5	1.7	1.9	2.7	1.3	1.1	1.6
Managers in economy	4.3	4.6	5.1	5.6	3.2	2.8	4.1
Managers in state admin.	0.5	0.5	0.5	0.6	0.9	1.0	1.0
Self-employed managers	—	—	—	—	5.4	5.9	4.8
Women	50.0	49.8	49.2	48.7	36.0	39.5	42.0
Urban	71.9	73.6	74.5	76.0	35.8	38.0	37.3
Married	79.2	79.7	77.1	74.5	64.8	60.7	57.7
Postsecondary degree	7.9	10.0	11.8	13.9	2.8	6.4	8.2
University degree	4.0	3.8	4.1	4.7	—	—	—
College degree	3.3	5.5	6.9	8.4	—	—	—
Parents graduates	4.2	5.9	7.1	8.7	1.8	—	—
Upper class	8.3	7.4	6.8	6.8	6.2	—	—
Party member	10.1	9.6	9.3	8.4	—	—	—
Mean age	34.4	34.9	35.8	36.2	34.9	34.9	35.6
N	11,651	12,825	12,600	10,831	15,372	18,392	19,821

Notes: Includes economically active population between ages twenty and fifty. Urban is defined somewhat differently in the two countries due to data constraints. In Hungary, the distinction is made between villages and other settlements, in Austria the distinction is between large cities and other settlements.
Source: *Hungarian Mobility Survey* (1992); *Microcensus of Austria* (1982, 1988, 1996).

tives of enterprises of various sizes. I will occasionally present analysis of this group separately. (A full description of my samples, variables, and models can be found in appendix A.)

The archival documents and legal regulations suggest that three types of capitals might be of crucial interest in the two countries: economic, cultural, and political; with economic and cultural capital of interest in Austria, and cultural and political capital in Hungary. The quantitative data allow for the operationalization of two types of cultural capital: its institutionalized form (whether or not the respondent graduated from college/university) and its inherited, embodied version (whether or not either of his or her parents graduated from a postsecondary institution of learning). Table 3.1 presents the distribution of these and other variables in the models. Note that there is a sizable difference in the proportion of the population that completed a postsecondary education in Austria and

Hungary. University education was highly exclusive in Austria: in the early 1980s less than 3 percent of the economically active population between twenty and fifty years old graduated from college, while almost 8 percent did in Hungary. The 1980s witnessed the expansion of the education system in Austria, an important change that had happened in Hungary at least a decade earlier. In addition, the tables also provide information about the two different postsecondary tracks in Hungary: college and university. As noted before, both counted as postsecondary education but the latter was more comparable in exclusivity to university education in Austria. I will examine their effects separately.

Political capital is featured in the Hungarian models and is operationalized as membership in the communist party. This factor admittedly restricts its scope, but remember that the archival data above indicated that by the 1980s party membership came to signify political loyalty, so its representation by party membership alone, although never complete, is an acceptable alternative at least for this period. About 10 percent of the economically active population in this age group admits to membership in the communist party. This, in fact, is somewhat lower than the actual percentage of party members as recorded by the central party apparatus, a bias that is possibly due to the fact that when this survey was conducted in 1992, after the fall of the communist regime, respondents might have been tempted to deny their party membership, especially if in higher positions. This factor will, unfortunately, result in an underestimate of the effect of party membership on social advancement in Hungary.

Economic capital is operationalized, for lack of a better measure, as the main class position (occupation) of the father during the respondent's childhood. Respondents are considered to come from upper-class or upper-middle-class backgrounds if their parents owned capital or their fathers filled top-level professional jobs. Around 6 to 8 percent of the population in both countries could claim such backgrounds and are, therefore, expected to own some degree of economic capital.

The respondent is coded as holding inherited cultural capital if either of his or her parents graduated from college. In 1982, this was the case for about 6 percent of respondents in Hungary but less than 2 percent in Austria—a further indication of the differences in the educational systems of the two countries.

Except for age, all the variables in the models are dichotomous to make interpretation easier. Note that the analyses below only include the twenty to fifty year old, economically active population.[11] In the next two sections I examine the models separately in the two countries in order to include a few country-specific variables without having to worry about comparability. Then in the section following I present the reduced models and the direct comparison.

Hungary: party membership and university degrees

What types of capital are used to claim authority in Hungary in the twenty years between 1972 and 1992? Table 3.2 presents logistic regression coefficients from separate models estimating access to managerial positions at various time points in this country. The dependent variable is the main indicator of managerial position, which will be used in much of the rest of the analyses. The models generally support the claims made by party executives in their propaganda materials: political and cultural capital serve as the most useful tools for access to authority in Hungary. But this is a very quick summary of a much richer set of information embedded in these models, and it is worth exploring the details further.

The coefficients associated with party membership are positive and significant in all four years. In 1972, for example, we find that the odds of a party member being appointed are about three times larger than the odds of a nonmember ($e^{1.03} = 2.80$). There is not much change in the importance of political capital between 1972 and 1982, but we can observe a small yet significant decline by 1988 and 1992.[12] In these years, all else being equal, the relative advantage of party membership decreased from odds of a little less than 3:1 to a little over 2:1. Thus, although among those registered in the official "cadre pool" the proportion of party members increased steadily until 1987, among the lower rungs of the upper class political capital seems to have started losing some of its usefulness by the end of the 1980s.[13] At the same time, past party membership remained significant for access to managerial positions even after the collapse of the exclusive political rule of the Hungarian Socialist Workers' Party. By 1992, many of the old cadres were still in power, particularly in lower-level positions. Obviously, past political membership served as a preestablished network and as such functioned to help advancement even after 1989 (Böröcz and Róna-Tas 1995; Szelenyi and Kostello 1996).

At the same time, the importance of cultural capital clearly had been on

Table 3.2. Logistic regression coefficients (and standard errors) for model predicting access to managerial positions: Hungary 1972–1992. Dependent variable: employee managers.

	1972	1982	1988	1992
Women	−.78	−.43	−.34	−.31
	(.10)	(.09)	(.08)	(.08)
Age	.02	.03	.04	.05
	(.005)	(.005)	(.006)	(.005)
Urban	.18*	.06*	.09*	.31
	(.11)	(.10)	(.10)	(.11)
Married	.48	.64	.55	.68
	(.14)	(.14)	(.12)	(.13)
Postsecondary	1.80	2.08	2.01	1.76
	(.11)	(.09)	(.09)	(.09)
Parents grad.	.08*	−.03*	−.01*	.10*
	(.17)	(.14)	(.13)	(.12)
Upper class	.34	.29	.25*	.06*
	(.14)	(.13)	(.13)	(.13)
Party member	1.03	1.08	.85	.84
	(.11)	(.10)	(.10)	(.10)
Constant	−4.40	−4.93	−5.41	−5.75
	(.24)	(.24)	(.24)	(.26)
Chi square	637	847	854	757
N	11,333	12,672	12,469	10,537

Notes: Includes economically active population between ages twenty and fifty.
* denotes nonsignificance at p < .05 level.
Source: *Hungarian Mobility Survey* (1992).

the rise. In 1972, the odds of a college graduate to claim a cadre position stood at almost six times higher than that of a high school graduate, all else being equal. By 1988 college degrees guaranteed a slightly, although not statistically significantly, higher chance for claiming authority than in earlier years,[14] which reflects the stated desire of party executives to improve the professional qualifications of the cadre pool and to promote those with the necessary qualifications only.[15] Inherited, parental cultural capital played no significant role—net of the respondents' own achievements—in claiming authority in Hungary.

It is perhaps difficult to assess the effects of party membership and college degrees simply by looking at the size of the coefficients. But we can calculate the expected probability of various social groups using the results from the models, and these calculations would provide a more meaningful summary of my findings above. In 1982 (based on the results in table 3.2) the estimated chance of a forty-five-year-old man[16] without either cultural or political capital of making it into the upper classes of state socialist society was small, less than 4 percent. If he happened to have a college or university degree, his chances improved significantly to roughly 24 percent, while if he had no cultural but only political capital his chances stood at about 11 percent. Should he possess high levels of both types of capital, his chances of attaining a cadre status jumped to over 48 percent.[17]

One caveat must be mentioned, however. These models do not and cannot fully represent the slow blurring of the boundaries between political and cultural capital, which started in the 1980s. Occasionally, as in the case of "political education" degrees from Marxist-Leninist academies, political capital could fill the requirement of a postsecondary degree. By the 1980s party surveys show that about 10 percent of college graduate cadres possessed no other form of educational qualifications. Similarly, a regular university degree, attained after the 1950s in the new, politically loyal educational system, could serve as an indication of political savvy and reliability. For example, although the party required all cadres to participate in various forms of political training regardless of their party membership status, those with graduate degrees were occasionally excused because they were seen as having completed enough political training during the course of their regular studies. Indeed, courses on Marxism-Leninism and the history of the communist party and the labor movement, as well as on political economy and scientific socialism, were on the required curriculum of all universities. Because my models do not measure the relationship between political and cultural assets it is hard to weigh them against each other and claim a clear primacy in their importance. Suffice to say that political and cultural capital were the most important means of gaining access to authority in the 1980s in Hungary. In addition, cultural capital seems to have gradually gained more significance among managers who were not listed in the very top of the political hierarchy (i.e., those outside the *nomenklatura*). The importance of economic capital in the form of parental class inheritance is much smaller than that of cultural or political capital, although it was still relevant until the late 1980s.

Table 3.3 shows that these trends hold for top-level managers as well. I separated this group in order to discover whether or not the balance of cap-

Table 3.3. Logistic regression coefficients (and standard errors) for model predicting access to managerial positions: Hungary 1972–1992. Dependent variable: top (employee) managers.

	1972	1982	1988	1992
Women	−.90	−.59	−.73	−.87
	(.19)	(.15)	(.15)	(.14)
Age	.03	.02	.03	.05
	(.01)	(.01)	(.01)	(.01)
Urban	−.60	−.72	−.53	.03*
	(.17)	(.15)	(.15)	(.15)
Married	−.05*	.62	.81	.90
	(.23)	(.24)	(.23)	(.22)
Postsecondary	1.92	2.08	1.98	1.52
	(.18)	(.16)	(.15)	(.14)
Parents grad.	−.23*	.13*	.17*	.32*
	(.32)	(.23)	(.19)	(.17)
Upper class	.12*	.25*	−.02*	.06*
	(.24)	(.21)	(.21)	(.19)
Party member	.98	1.05	.89	.92
	(.18)	(.16)	(.15)	(.14)
Constant	−5.15	−5.28	−5.81	−6.74
	(.39)	(.40)	(.40)	(.41)
Chi square	231	334	377	409
N	11,333	12,672	12,469	10,537

Notes: Includes economically active population between ages twenty and fifty.

* denotes nonsignificance at p < .05 level.

Source: *Hungarian Mobility Survey* (1992).

ital types varied in the highest position of leadership, but the answer is that it did not. However, there are additional complications if we consider managers by the type of position they hold and separate those working in state administration from those whose job is in economic enterprises. It should be noted that the models in table 3.4 are based on a relatively small number of people (1 percent of the population in the case of state administrators), and thus should be interpreted with caution. Walder (1995; and Walder, Li, and Treiman 2000) argues that those in primarily political positions and those in not directly political positions claimed power on the basis of a slightly different set of assets in communist China. I found the same pattern in Hungary: although educational skills predominated among economic managers, political capital and university degrees

Table 3.4. Logistic regression coefficients (and standard errors) for model predicting access to managerial positions: Hungary, 1982. Dependent variable: managers in different sectors.

	Economy	State Administration
Women	−.44	−.18*
	(.09)	(.27)
Age	.03	−.03
	(.005)	(.017)
Urban	−.04*	−.22*
	(.10)	(.29)
Married	.55	2.18
	(.14)	(.92)
Postsecondary	2.07	1.56
	(.10)	(.29)
Parents grad.	−.005*	−.25*
	(.15)	(.51)
Upper class	.28*	.26*
	(.14)	(.39)
Party member	.97	1.53
	(.10)	(.28)
Constant	−4.88	−9.21
	(.25)	(1.13)
Chi square	740	102
N	12,672	12,672

Notes: Includes economically active population between ages twenty and fifty. * denotes non-significance at p < .05 level.
Source: Hungarian Mobility Survey (1992).

played roughly the same role for state administrators and for political leaders. This factor is important because it shows that the upper class is not uniform, even in a state socialist society. Although its members do own similar types of capital, the emphasis differs. Political capital is more useful for those in state and administrative positions, under the more immediate control of the communist party. In this group, party membership increased the odds of a person to gain access to a managerial position by a factor of about five, the same as that for educational degrees. Among managers in economic enterprises, controlling for all other factors, college graduation was three times more useful than party membership. An even more extreme difference between the two different segments of the upper class can be seen in capitalist Austria, as I describe below.

Austria: education and family inheritance

Table 3.5 describes logistic regression models for capitalist Austria similar to the analysis for Hungary. The dependent variable in the first column is the odds of a person being in a managerial position. I included only employee managers in the first column and present a separate one for those at the highest level of authority (column 2) as well as self-employed business and landowners in column 3.

Cultural capital is the most important type that employee managers owned, and it was institutionalized in the form of university degrees and embodied cultural capital inherited through family background. In fact, at least in this respect, there is practically no difference between lower and higher-level managers. A university degree improves a respondent's odds of success by a factor of 25, the cultural capital of his or her parents by a further 1.5, and economic capital (measured by upper-class parents) by a

Table 3.5. Logistic regression coefficients (and standard errors) for model predicting access to managerial positions: Austria, 1982.

	Employee Managers	Top-Level Managers	Self-Employed Managers
Women	−1.38	−1.99	−.14
	(.13)	(.31)	(.08)
Age	.04	.08	.05
	(.006)	(.01)	(.005)
Urban	.64	.40	−.44
	(.09)	(.16)	(.08)
Married	.31	.44*	.50
	(.12)	(.24)	(.10)
Postsecondary	3.22	2.78	−.67
	(.12)	(.19)	(.26)
Parents grad.	−.38	−.26*	−1.27
	(.19)	(.29)	(.33)
Upper class	1.11	1.05	1.83
	(.13)	(.21)	(.10)
Constant	−5.56	−8.34	−5.09
	(.24)	(.49)	(.18)
Chi square	1,344	500	509
N	15,372	15,372	15,372

Notes: Includes economically active population between ages twenty and fifty. * denotes nonsignificance at $p < .05$ level.
Source: *Microcensus of Austria* (1982).

Table 3.6. Logistic regression coefficients (and standard errors) for model predicting access to managerial positions: Austria, 1982–1996. Dependent variable: employee manager.

	1982 (reduced)	1988	1996
Women	−1.33	−1.39	−1.14
	(.13)	(.11)	(.08)
Age	.04	.05	.02
	(.006)	(.005)	(.005)
Urban	.69	.61	.39
	(.09)	(.22)	(.07)
Married	.34	.09*	.03*
	(.12)	(.10)	(.08)
Postsecondary	3.53	3.16	2.77
	(.12)	(.09)	(.07)
Constant	−5.42	−5.64	−4.17
	(.23)	(.22)	(.18)
Chi square	1,265	1,602	1,657
N	15,372	18,392	19,821

Notes: Includes economically active population between ages twenty and fifty. * denotes non-significance at p < .05 level.

Source: *Microcensus of Austria* (1982, 1988, 1996).

factor of 3. Indeed, economic and cultural capital are the most important assets for gaining authority as an employee manager in an Austrian enterprise or in state administration.

This is not the case when it comes to self-employed managers. The Austrian upper class has two distinct segments, and their forms of capital do not overlap even as much as those of the Hungarian upper class. Cultural capital is simply not an advantage for becoming a self-employed manager in Austria: indeed, those with university degrees are *less* likely to fall in this category. Economic capital, however, plays a crucial role. Obviously, inheritance is an important determinant of whether a person will or will not own their own company or land and manage it. The former group (in column 1) corresponds to the expert managerial segment of the upper classes, while the latter (column 3) includes primarily smaller and a few larger capitalists and landlords.

I followed the trends in Austria over time among employee managers in a reduced model because no information about parental background was available in the 1988 and 1996 data sets. The results (in table 3.6) are not altogether surprising: educational assets remain very important for the attainment of authority in every year. Note that by 1996 the usefulness of educational degrees declined somewhat. This may be explained, as in the case of Hungary, by a loosening of the social hierarchy and a widening of the pool of managers.

A comparison of the two countries in 1982

In light of my examination above of each country, I now turn to a comparison of the two, focusing on the year 1982. Table 3.7 summarizes the models to be compared: it includes a set of reduced models for Hungary and the already familiar 1982 model for Austria. In Hungary, I omitted the variable describing political capital in order to make the models comparable. This omission did not significantly change the size of the coefficients (compare table 3.2, column 2, and table 3.7, column 2).

The differences between the two countries are stark, and they correspond to what we would expect in a capitalist and in a state socialist society. The first point to note is the difference in the importance of cultural capital. A university or college degree multiplied an individual's odds of success by a factor of twenty-five in capitalist Austria compared to nine in state socialist Hungary in 1982. Skills and qualifications are obviously extremely useful for advancement in a capitalist society. The Austrian system of promotion is particularly well regulated and hierarchical, which is reflected in the size of this coefficient. In Hungary, several factors other than education determined an individual's chances of success.

The second difference is also not surprising: family inheritance, or economic capital, is of great importance in Austria but has no significant independent effect in Hungary. Indeed, the state socialist system, which set out to raise the proletariat into positions of authority had some success in doing away with the direct effect of parental upper-class background on high status attainment.[18] In a capitalist society, where no such efforts were made, inherited capital remained a strong predictor of a person's later success.

But could these differences between the two countries be a result of the fact that many fewer people attended universities in Austria than in Hungary, and therefore institutionalized educational capital was harder to attain and thus perhaps a more precious asset? Indeed, in 1982, about

Table 3.7. Logistic regression coefficients (and standard errors) for model predicting access to managerial positions: Hungary and Austria, 1982.

	Austria Managers	Hungary Managers	Hungary Managers (Model II)	Hungary Top Managers I	Hungary Top Managers II
Women	−1.38	−.57	−.56	−.75	−.71
	(.13)	(.09)	(.09)	(.15)	(.15)
Age	.04	.03	.03	.02	.02
	(.006)	(.005)	(.005)	(.009)	(.009)
Urban	.64	−.05*	−.06*	−.71	−.74
	(.09)	(.09)	(.09)	(.15)	(.15)
Married	.31	.68	.69	.68	.70
	(.12)	(.14)	(.14)	(.24)	(.24)
Postsecondary	3.22	2.24	—	2.29	—
	(.12)	(.09)		(.15)	
University	—	—	2.31	—	2.59
			(.13)		(.19)
College	—	—	2.16	—	2.12
			(.11)		(.18)
Parents grad.	.38	−.14*	−.13*	−.02*	−.11*
	(.19)	(.14)	(.15)	(.22)	(.23)
Upper class	1.11	.27*	.28	.24*	.23*
	(.13)	(.13)	(.13)	(.21)	(.21)
Constant	−5.56	−5.01	−4.94	−5.39	−5.24
	(.24)	(.24)	(.24)	(.39)	(.39)
Chi square	1,344	743	715	294	296
N	15,372	12,672	12,672	12,672	12,672

Notes: Includes economically active population between ages twenty and fifty. Dependent variable: employee managers; for Hungary top (employee) managers (last two columns). * denotes nonsignificance at $p < .05$ level.
Source: Microcensus of Austria (1982); Hungarian Mobility Survey (1992).

3 percent of the population age twenty to fifty had college degrees in Austria, while in Hungary over 10 percent did. Perhaps the different degrees of exclusiveness in postsecondary education accounts for the differences in the size of the coefficients. We can check this alternative hypothesis by looking at Hungary's two-tier postsecondary educational system.[19] The percentage of university graduates in the population roughly corresponds to that in Austria. In column 3, of table 3.7 I present a model that separates the impact of five-year universities and four-year colleges on the attainment of managerial status. From these models it becomes obvious

that the effect of a university degree is practically no different from that of a lower-level college degree and, most notably, even university degrees do not approach the importance of similar degrees in Austria.

Perhaps the differences we see between the two countries are due to the fact that a somewhat smaller percentage of the population is in managerial positions in Austria. Could we be describing a more prestigious group in this country? In order to test this second alternative hypothesis, I compared the base model from Austria to models about the more restricted top managerial group in Hungary (columns 4 and 5). Again, we find that the difference between the two countries both in terms of the importance of educational degrees and family inheritance remains. This indicates that the observed differences are most likely not due to the way the dependent or the independent variables are defined but rather reflect real differences in the formation of the upper classes of the two countries.

For centuries, Hungary played the role of the less-glamorous sister in the Austro-Hungarian family. In 1949, not altogether on their own accord, Hungarians tried the new experiment of state socialism, a political, social, and economic system radically different from that of prosperously developing capitalist Austria. And although some of the old traditions lived on—such as the use of the quaint Central European unit of measurement, the *dekagramm*, or the strength of the centralized state apparatus—the processes of exclusion soon took on distinctive characteristics. In Austria, in order to advance in the social hierarchy, it was advantageous to inherit some cultural or economic capital from one's family and to attend a university to gain a degree. Economic capital was rendered irrelevant by communist rule, but its void was filled by another type of capital: political loyalty in its institutionalized form. Party membership functioned not only as an indicator of political reliability but also as a passport to a large and loyal network of potentates. However, political capital had a limited effect, especially toward the end of the state socialist era, without sufficient amounts of qualification; that is, a degree from a college or a university.

As a result, a different set of people rose to upper-class positions in the two countries: their qualities were different and so was the character and legitimacy of their rule. It is within this context that we will examine to what extent and through what processes gender (masculinity) functioned as a source of exclusion from, and inclusion in, power, prestige, and privilege.

4. Exclusion versus Limited Inclusion

Did state socialism emancipate women? Or, at least, was gender inequality significantly reduced in state socialist Hungary relative to a comparable capitalist society? In this chapter I seek an answer to this question, which is as old as state socialism itself. After some initial enthusiasm for the woman-friendly policies instituted in the early history of the Soviet Union, most feminist thinkers remained skeptical about the achievements of the Marxist-Leninist emancipation project and point to lingering inequalities in paid and unpaid work, in political representation, and in everyday life. Yet, when comparing the actual experience of women working in Austria and Hungary we find significant differences in their career paths, expectations, and opportunities.

Contrast the cases of Anita, a manager in the Austrian State Department for Culture, and Judit, who held a top-level position within the Hungarian Communist Party apparatus in the mid-1980s. Both women achieved enviable success in their respective countries, but their experience of making it to the top differed in important ways: Anita describes a long process of fierce struggle against gender discrimination and exclusion, while Judit claims no such forces held her back.

Both Anita and Judit were born in the capital city of their respective countries in the late 1940s. Anita's father worked as an engineer for the Austrian army, while her mother was a homemaker who had earned an income as a fashion model before she got married and started to raise her three children. Judit's mother, in contrast, worked full time as a librarian even after Judit and her older brother were born. Neither family had serious financial concerns and both encouraged their daughters to pursue their studies. In Anita's case, her father considered it a good idea for her to study, although he did not approve of her career plans. As a descendent of a generation of soldiers and a high-ranking official himself, he did not expect his daughter to put her diploma to use. Instead, she was supposed to teach high school for a few years until she found a suitable husband and settled down to raise children and run the household. For Judit, the decision was much less complicated: by the time she graduated from high school in the early 1970s, university education for girls was fast becoming commonplace, and the option of not working did not ever cross her or her parents' minds. Everybody worked.

Both girls did well in school, graduated from university, and started to work toward their doctorate degrees. Judit received her doctorate in biology and got a job at a research institute in Budapest. She joined the communist party after graduation, partly as a career move but also, as did many of her generation, in an earnest desire to try to "reform the system from within." She worked as a researcher for several years and attended conferences and published papers in her field. She also got married, had a son, and divorced a few years later. After about ten years at the research institute, her energy and intelligence caught the eyes of her party bosses and they invited her to come work for the central party apparatus in a junior position. At first she was reluctant to accept the obvious promotion and change of careers, but she finally said yes. From there, she advanced rapidly to very close to the top of the hierarchy by the mid 1980s.

Anita defied her parents' wishes and gained a doctorate in history while working part time in a lower-level civil service job. She never married and has no children. After her graduation she applied for a better-paying job at a higher-level position. But it was the male applicant who was appointed, even though Anita was obviously better qualified. She was understandably upset about being passed over, and she wrote a letter to the State Secretary for Women's Affairs complaining about discrimination on the basis of gender. The case was investigated and her employer "got a bang on his head" (as she put it), but she herself got no revenge and, more important, no job either. In fact, she started to suspect that she didn't get the next few positions she applied for exactly because she was now perceived as a troublemaker. In a few years, however, through the husband of a friend she met at the gathering of a women's organization, she was offered the predecessor of the job she holds currently: the organization and management of a new department within a ministry (state department).

Both women achieved high-level careers in state administration, but although Anita's experience was one of constant struggle against discrimination and exclusion, Judit was handpicked and invited to her current position. Her understanding of her career advancement involves, if anything, positive rather than negative gender discrimination.

The discrepancy in the experience of the two women, and that of many other middle-class women in the two countries, is largely unexplained by the existing sociological literature. Feminist research on the region has concentrated on the similarities of women's oppression in the East and West (Heitlinger 1979; Einhorn 1993).[1] Most recent accounts depict the result of the communist emancipation experiment in a rather gloomy light, emphasizing its failure to achieve women's equality with men in terms of wages, work hours, division of labor, and levels of authority and responsibility (Siklova 1993; Einhorn 1993; Corrin 1992).[2] Although these findings are revealing in many ways, they often lack an explicit and concrete comparative dimension and thus cannot begin to isolate the potential effect of state socialism on gender relations.

Those who do compare the changes in social inequalities in the East and West usually focus solely on class reproduction and either omit women from their models altogether (Mueller et al. 1990; Slomczynski and Krauze 1987; Luijkx et al. 1995) or do not theorize about or even explore gender differences (Mach and Peschar 1990; Róna-Tas 1998).[3] The overall message of many of these studies suggests that class inequalities were not significantly reduced by the communist experiment. Yet, as the reader will see, although women's disadvantage was by no means completely eliminated, data from both interviews and quantitative surveys show an explicit reduction in gender-based inequalities in state socialist Hungary compared to capitalist Austria. By ignoring the comparison of East and West, feminist research cannot identify a *relative* change in social inequalities, and by ignoring gender, mobility research often fails to describe the vast differences in the experience of men and women in the status or educational attainment process.

The Hungarian gender regime is best described as realizing women's *limited inclusion* into authority, while Austria in the 1980s remained committed to women's *exclusion*. This is not to say, of course, that women in Hungary did not experience disadvantages, or were not in reality subject to discrimination on the basis of their gender. But the limited inclusion policy of the communist party guaranteed that at least a good number made it into middle-level and lower-middle-level positions. State socialist inclusion was segregated both horizontally (women were most often found in state administration, in trade unions, in personnel departments, in the fields of culture, health, and education, and overall in fields with lower pay and prestige) and vertically (women could rarely make it into positions at the very top of the hierarchies). Yet overall the possibility of some career advancement had been open for many women since the 1950s. This "divide and conquer" policy of the communist party may have contributed, among many other factors, to women's inability to mobilize on the basis of their gender during and after the state socialist era.

This was not the case in Austria, where a number of obvious obstacles blocked women's advancement and a career demanded an ongoing struggle against the forces of exclusion, discrimination, and gender prejudice. Just as in Hungary where the forces of exclusion complemented those of inclusion, in Austria, too, some women made it to the top. But the predominant experience of these women and of those of others in the 1980s was that of systematic, gender-based exclusion. My aim in this chapter is to highlight this broad yet often ignored difference between the gender regimes of Hungary and Austria. First I refer back to the quantitative models in the previous chapter to assess gender discrimination in both countries, then I turn to an analysis of interviews with female managers to highlight the differences in their lived experiences of positive and negative discrimination.

Inclusion and Exclusion

The contrast between limited inclusion and exclusion in the two countries is immediately evident from the survey data introduced in chapter 3. Although this data set provides no information for the precommunist period, aggregate information from statistical yearbooks suggests that women's engagement in paid work was quite similar in Austria and Hungary before World War II: about 30 percent of women were gainfully employed in both countries. By 1982, according to our surveys, about 83 percent of Hungarian women age twenty to fifty years were in the labor force compared to only 54 percent of Austrian women, while male participation was comparable in both countries. In addition, Austrian women were more likely to work part time and to withdraw from paid work occasionally.

Patterns of exclusion are perhaps even more evident when we examine women's share in positions of power. In 1982 in Hungary, 6.5 percent of male workers between twenty and fifty years of age held positions of authority, compared to 3.7 percent of women in the same age group: a male advantage of 1.6 times that of women.[4] In Austria, the respective numbers are 5.5 percent for men and 1.5 percent for women, which means that 3.6 times as many men as women held managerial jobs in the same period. Even if we take into account the unequal distribution of skills and experience between men and women, Hungarian women seem to have fared far better than did their Austrian counterparts. The logistic regression models for 1982 described in the previous chapter (see table 3.7) show that even if we control for the effect of other potentially important factors, such as education, parental background, age, and marital status, the differences estimated above between men and women remain essentially unchanged. In Austria, all else being equal, the odds associated with being a man in access to managerial jobs are almost fourfold ($e^{1.38} = 3.9$), while in Hungary the odds are less than twofold ($e^{.57} = 1.7$). In sum, women, even those highly qualified, experienced much stronger currents of exclusion in Austria than in Hungary.

These patterns are even more evident at the highest levels of managerial positions: about nine times more men (1.8 percent) than women (0.2 percent) were top-level managers in Austria in 1982, while only about twice as many men were in Hungary (2.3 percent of men compared to 1.1 percent of women) according to a simple distribution (see table 4.1). The regression models (tables 3.5 and 3.3) suggest a similar trend: the so-called glass ceiling effect seems more pronounced in Austria than in Hungary.

The Limits to Inclusion: The Glass Ceiling Revisited

The description above emphasizes the differences between Austria and Hungary through contrasting the degree of women's exclusion from authority. There are, however, a number of similarities to be noted, especially in patterns of job segregation, both horizontal and vertical.

Let us first reexamine the perhaps surprisingly small glass ceiling effect in Hungary.[5] In this respect there are probably more similarities between the two countries than can be seen in the data set above. A sample that is representative of the whole population cannot provide sufficient information about the very top of the social hierarchy, which is where women's exclusion is the most pronounced. Szonja Szelenyi (1998) has analyzed a

Table 4.1. Distribution of men and women in various managerial positions: Hungary and Austria, 1972–1996.

	Hungary (%)				Austria (%)			
	1972	1982	1988	1992	1972	1982	1988	1996
Employed								
Men	93.4	94.1	93.4	80.0	91.7	90.8	89.1	84.6
Women	77.7	82.9	82.4	70.2	45.2	53.8	57.7	60.5
All	84.8	88.2	87.6	74.9	67.3	72.3	73.3	72.5
Managers								
Men	7.0	6.5	6.8	7.3	5.9	5.5	5.4	6.8
Women	2.7	3.7	4.5	5.1	1.1	1.5	1.7	2.7
All	4.9	5.1	5.6	6.2	4.4	4.1	3.9	5.1
N	11,652	12,825	12,600	10,835	14,333	15,433	18,392	19,821

	Hungary (%)				Austria (%)			
	1972	1982	1988	1992	1972	1982	1988	1996
Top Managers								
Men	2.3	2.3	2.6	3.9	2.9	1.8	1.6	2.3
Women	0.7	1.1	1.1	1.5	0.4	0.2	0.4	0.7
All	1.5	1.7	1.9	2.7	2.0	1.3	1.1	1.6
Self-employed								
Men					6.0	5.7	5.5	5.3
Women					4.9	4.7	6.6	4.1
All					5.6	5.4	5.9	4.8
N	11,652	12,825	12,600	10,835	14,333	15,433	18,392	19,821

	Hungary (%)				Austria (%)			
	1972	1982	1988	1992	1972	1982	1988	1996
State Admin.								
Men	0.7	0.6	0.4	0.7	2.2	1.2	1.3	1.3
Women	0.4	0.4	0.6	0.5	0.5	0.2	0.6	0.6
All	0.5	0.5	0.5	0.6	1.6	0.8	1.0	1.0
Industry								
Men	6.4	5.9	6.3	6.6	5.6	4.4	4.1	5.6
Women	2.3	3.3	3.9	4.5	1.4	1.3	1.1	2.1
All	4.3	4.6	5.1	5.6	4.2	3.2	2.9	4.1
N	11,652	12,825	12,600	10,835	14,333	15,433	18,392	19,821

Notes: Includes economically active population between ages twenty and fifty.
Source: *Hungarian Mobility Survey* (1992); *Austria Microcensus* (1982, 1988, 1996).

survey of the Hungarian nomenklatura to describe the participation of women in the political, economic, and cultural elites of Hungary. She finds that women constituted about 13 percent of all top elites in the country in 1988 (S. Szelenyi 1998, 112, table 6.3). In addition, during the forty-odd years of state socialism there was never more than one woman in the ten-to-twelve member Politburo or in the similarly sized government. This means that at the top of the hierarchy, one in about ten elite members were women, which describes significantly worse odds than the 2:1 found in the nationwide survey data above. In this respect, Austria did not do worse than Hungary: in 1988, the representation of Austrian women in Parliament stood at 11.5 percent, and two women held positions in the government (13.3 percent) (Neyer 1997, 194).

Further evidence of the Hungarian glass ceiling can be found when we examine gender stratification within specific occupations, such as among school teachers, for example. Analyzing data from a survey of the population of elementary and secondary schools I found that although women were vastly overrepresented among teachers, they never reached equity among headmasters of schools. But the percentage of deputy headmasters—just one step below the headmaster—corresponded exactly to the representation of women among teachers. This is a good reflection of women's chances for gaining authority in this period in Hungary: they could make it into the chair of the second in command relatively easily, but it proved too difficult to advance to the very top.[6]

In sum, although the survey data indicated almost no difference in women's chances of advancing to managerial and top managerial positions in Hungary, we should be careful in our evaluation of this finding. If we include information for those in the highest of elite positions, we can refine the thesis on women's inclusion in authority in Hungary: women experienced less discrimination than in Austria, but their inclusion was limited to positions in lower and intermediate levels.

The limitations to women's participation are further evident in the high degree of horizontal segregation that we can observe in both countries. Women were less likely to occupy managerial positions in the most prestigious, better-paid, and more stable sectors of the economy. Consider the example of state administrators, for instance. In Hungary these jobs were underpaid and generally guaranteed lower degrees of independence, autonomy, and prestige even at the managerial level than did jobs in economic enterprises, which were somewhat further away from the watchful eyes of the party. Consequently, gender inequality was lowest in the distribution of managerial positions in the administrative field. As table 4.1 shows, by 1982 almost as many women as men held managerial positions in Hungarian state administration, especially at the middle levels of the hierarchy, which our sample is likely to capture best.[7] If we control for education, party membership status, age, marital status, and parental background, gender inequality disappears here altogether: the odds of men and women in gaining managerial positions in state and political administration was roughly equal in 1982 (see table 3.4). In positions in economic enterprises, however, women's disadvantage was multiplied: in these better paid and more highly valued occupations men's chances of advancement were approximately 1.5 times higher.

A similar (although somewhat larger) difference may be observed between state administrators and managers in industry in Austria, but, ironically, gender inequality worked in the opposite direction. More men than women were promoted to higher-level positions in the prestigious, secure, and well-paid circle of civil servants (six times as many male than female managers can be found there) compared to the less-secure and less-regulated industrial sector (three times as many men than women.) Interestingly, in Austria gender inequality was the smallest among self-employed managers. A man's odds of becoming an employee manager were about four times higher than those for a woman, while among the self-employed the gender difference in odds were merely 1.1 to 1.0 (table 3.5). Self-employed managerial jobs involve the management of small family plots or shops with just a handful of employees and are often very unstable and underpaid. Women's access was the least obstructed in this area. Note that this contrast is an excellent illustration for the socially constructed nature of occupational segregation by gender. In both countries women were crowded into positions that men were reluctant to occupy, regardless of the actual content or character of the job (Reskin and Roos 1990; Milkman 1987), although the justification for sex-typed segregation often involved references to essential male or female qualities and their association with the requirements of certain occupations.

In the first section of this chapter I argue that women experienced lower levels of exclusion from paid work and from positions of authority in Hungary than in Austria. In fact, I characterized women's experience by the term inclusion, rather than exclusion in state socialist Hungary. Yet this statement must be qualified: women's claims to authority even in the state socialist society were closely controlled, segregated, and limited.

Positive Discrimination

The concept of "positive discrimination" had been introduced in Hungary decades before it came to its dubious fame in the United States and Western Europe. In Austria, on the other hand, such gender-specific support mechanisms for encouraging women's participation in the labor force and (to a smaller degree) in authority did not come into effect until the early 1990s—exactly at the time when Hungarians officially and vehemently abandoned all such practices. The difference in the ideological commitments of the regimes to gender-based discrimination, both positive and negative, had an impact not only on the actual degree of inequality in positions of authority, but also on women's overall experience of exclusion and inclusion in the two countries.

Positive discrimination in Hungary took different forms, and its content and intensity varied over time. First, the criteria for cadre selection were explicitly not gender blind. In fact, party executives openly encouraged the nomination and appointment of women into positions of authority. Initially, explicit gender quotas were prescribed for enrollment in management and party schools that qualified the graduates to take on positions of authority, and specific quotas existed for entrance to general educational institutions as well. These quotas, however, were neither systematically constructed nor strictly enforced, and they became one of the casualties of the 1956 revolution when the term came to be associated with the grave excesses of the past.

After 1956 positive discrimination took two forms: first, the party regularly issued decrees, proclamations, and pamphlets encouraging the promotion of women, although refraining from specifying quotas; and, second, party apparatuses handpicked token women and promoted them into positions of authority in order to meet the unspecified expectations of the party decrees.

The second form was preferred for the selection of members of Parliament or other elected state and party organizations. In an interview, a young woman doctor explained to me how she became a member of Parliament in 1985. Months before the elections she was summoned to the party offices in her hospital and was told that she was the only person who fit the demographic qualities "they" (the party authorities) were looking for in a new member of Parliament: a female doctor from Budapest, between twenty-five and thirty-five years of age, who is not a party member. She had no desire to become involved in politics and had no previous political experience. But after several discussions with the party functionaries of her hospital she was intimidated enough not to be able to reject the offer. In due course, she was nominated and elected to a seat in Parliament to represent Hungarian women in her district.

Even the Politburo saw the problems associated with this practice, and members occasionally pointed it out in their discussions. As a powerful Politburo member complains: "We do not give smaller tasks to good, honest women first, the kinds of task that they are capable of carrying out, and then increase the load and finally elect them to parliament. Instead, we bring in a good peasant woman from the countryside, who has no political experience yet . . . so it's no wonder she does not make a good MP all at once" (PIA 288/5/247/). But some saw distinct advantages associated even with this process. One of my interviewees, Edina, came from a rather poor family. She experienced starvation and destitution early in her life. In 1946, at the age of fourteen, she moved to Budapest where jobs were plentiful and she found work as a carpenter's assistant. She had altogether some six years of formal schooling when the local party executive summoned her into his office and explained to her that she would be sent to party school and then appointed to a position within the party apparatus. Edina was not particularly pleased, but once admitted to the party institute she turned out to be an ambitious and hardworking student and went on to have a high-level political career. Her opinion and experience of "affirmative action" was quite different from the mainstream political opinion after 1989. She stated:

> I think it was an important thing, although nowadays this sounds like blasphemy, but I really do think it was good that according to the party resolution in the 1970s, at least 30 percent of women had to be included in every level of party leadership.[8] . . . Of course, sometimes the way this was carried out left much to be desired. But still, this meant that if earlier there had been a single token woman in a twenty-one-strong party leadership body, now there were seven. And three of those seven at least would grow to become very good leaders. I thought this was a good thing, even though women were forced into these leadership bodies. It wouldn't have happened otherwise.

There were some less-direct forms of positive discrimination also in practice. Politburo transcripts testify that Politburo members sometimes reminded each other (and through party decrees and speeches reminded the whole population) that "Comrade Kádár said that all else being equal between two people, the woman should be promoted" (PIA 288/5/140, 288/21/72/28). In this vein, no party decree could be passed that did not at least pay lip service to the issue of women's underrepresentation. Here is an example from a decree in the 1960s: "The party executive bodies should be more systematic in their efforts to promote women. This should be an integral part of their cadre recruitment work, and they should not just do it . . . before the elections, to improve the statistics" (PIA 288/5/234). Similar paragraphs appear in every one of the major party decrees on the topic, complete with statistics on the changes in the proportion of women in leadership positions as well as suggestions for the future course of action to improve the situation. In addition to this ongoing "attention"—at least on this formal, paperwork level—the party instituted a major campaign to improve the position of women in Hungarian society. This culminated in the decree of 1970 ("On the Economic, Political and Social Position of Women in Hungary"), a decade of reports, and the collection of statistics and surveys from various organizations (e.g., PIA 288/5/783). One of the major goals the decree set out to achieve was an increase in the number of women in leadership positions, and thus in response the reports addressed this question in detail (what Edina refers to above). Although the decree of 1970 did not prescribe exact numbers, at least not on paper, the party leadership still held local organizations responsible for improving their gender statistics and for considering the reasons for their lack of success. Indeed many organizations limited their activities to just that. Others, however, perhaps more threatened by party decrees, made a point of promoting women into positions of authority, if for no other reason than to "improve the statistics." As Rita, a high-level party executive explained: "They [the central party apparatus] tried to recruit women, these things did happen sometimes. They would lower the requirements a bit in order that the statistics in the reports would look better. Many of these women actually managed to grow into the task."

Indeed, most of my interviewees were conscious of the positive discrimination efforts of the party. As Olga, a fifty-nine-year-old manager of a clothing factory, noted: "I was part of every statistic, every report; I was the good example: the papers wrote about me and I gave interviews to the factory news almost every week." Even when Olga was recruited to join the party, the fact that she was a woman was significant because her participation helped boost the gender statistics that party leaders had to submit regularly to the central apparatus. "[The party leadership] kept track of me. When I joined the party, the central party-building task was to recruit college graduates ["intellectuals" or *értelmiségieket*]. So I was useful for the party cell in three ways, because I not only had a degree, but also was young and a woman."

After the middle of the 1970s, party documents testify to a significant drop in attention paid to the situation of women. No further decrees were passed on the "woman question." Although before the mid-1970s, this issue was discussed in depth at least once every six months, after 1973 the Politburo spent practically no more time arguing over the position of women or the women's movement in Hungarian society. Party leaders claimed that women had caught up with men in terms of labor force participation, educational degrees, and political awareness. Instead, a new concern emerged that was in sharp contradiction to earlier efforts to advance women's entrance into the public sphere. Worries about the falling birth rate prompted a new policy in 1985, which encouraged middle-class women to have more babies and take time off work for their families.[9] Yet, although the direct quotas and party decrees to promote women were now defunct, by the 1980s the indirect effects of these policies were starkly visible: a higher percentage of women in the workplace, at universities, and in lower-level and middle-level positions of authority as well.

Negative Discrimination

In contrast to the discussion above, one of the reasons why Austrian women had lower chances for social advancement may be found in the degree of negative discrimination they experienced on a daily basis in the labor market. Practically all of my Austrian interviewees complained about some form of gender discrimination they personally encountered. Often they identified men as the source of their problems. A café owner in Vienna, age twenty-six, stated: "Men are afraid to lose their power—this is the greatest obstacle in front of women today. I personally feel that my chances of advancement were smaller; this type of discrimination was always in the background." Another interviewee from Vienna, a fifty-three-year-old manager in education, said "I experienced discrimination during my whole career: everything took much more time. Often I was not appointed to a position because I am a woman. Men don't want to lose their sphere of power. Attitudes are all the same whether in the professional or in the private sphere."

Several informants pointed out that women were not trusted in managerial positions, were not taken seriously, and had to work harder than men to prove themselves. For example, an Austrian bank manager, age fifty-two, stated: "Whenever someone comes in, they always talk to the men in the department. No one assumes, that I, a woman, can be the boss. Once they find out though, their reaction is often positive . . . but women still have to fight harder for everything. Managerial positions are still not easily available for women." Several of my Austrian interviewees described incidents in which they were denied promotion and a less-qualified man was appointed. One of them commented, "Of course, all the board members [who made the decision] were men—I don't know what I expected. I wasn't even surprised." These positions probably reflect the influence and language of Western feminist movements: women acknowledged patriarchal oppression and saw themselves as its victims. Although they themselves may have been successful in fighting against male power, they also clearly understood the difficulties involved.

In contrast, Hungarian women's understanding of the gender discrimination they faced during their upward move in the social hierarchy was quite different.[10] Helga, the retired manager of a textile factory, for example, denied ever having experienced gender discrimination. True to her communist convictions, she chose not to believe her gender was a meaningful dimension of her social status. This was, in fact, the position typical of the older generation of cadres who grew up and internalized dogmatic Marxist teachings on the disappearance of gender discrimination under communism. Most of the older women I talked to categorically denied the importance of gender in their self-definition or life histories and most certainly did not see it as a significant political factor even after my insistence. In fact, I lost at least two potential interviewees when I told them that I was writing about gender inequality in the labor force because they insisted that they had never experienced any such thing and thus had nothing to tell me.

Younger women, or those less committed to the communist ideology, while acknowledging gender discrimination in general terms did not see it as having affected their own careers, and most certainly they did not identify men as a group as the source of their problems. For example, a sixty-two-year-old Hungarian party secretary said: "One of the reasons why women couldn't be appointed was the extra burdens they carried. They couldn't take leadership positions with all the household work they also had to do. But I didn't have any problems with being a woman on my job and that's mostly because I could do my work. That's what really mattered."

Sometimes, the women I talked to qualified their experience of discrimination even when they did acknowledge feeling it. Also, they often attributed gender discrimination to the behavior of the older generation only, and saw it as a lingering but slowly disappearing tradition from the "past." According to Judit, whose career is described at the beginning of this chapter: "I saw it mostly in the case of others: a woman had to work harder for recognition than a man. A man got rewarded for lower level achievements as well, a woman was not even expected to produce the same, high level work as a man. But this is rather characteristic of the older generation and it was mixed in with a lot of other things. Because many of these men were very nice and sweet, really, but also had this traditional view." Others attribute discrimination not to men, as women in Austria did, but to their own deficiencies, as illustrated in the following statement by a fifty-five-year-old Hungarian cadre: "Well, I really wasn't oppressed. . . . Although perhaps I could have moved a bit higher, had I been a man. Perhaps my attitude wasn't right. My male colleagues would often stay on after the work hours at the workplace and just chat or drink beers. I would most often go home to my family. And a lot of decisions were made during those beer-drinking sessions. Of course some women also stayed and they were absolutely welcome to do so."

The difference in the discourse of Austrian and Hungarian women on gender discrimination reflects not simply differences in their lived experience but also differences in the language available. It is not surprising to find elements of the ideology of Western feminism in the accounts of Austrian women, and by the same token we should not be surprised at the prevalence of communist discourse among Hungarian women. According to the latter, gender discrimination was a construct of the past and the traditional attitudes of both men and women were the reason why its elements still flourished in some areas. Women's inequality as well as their gender-specific interests were described in class terms: the language of post-1960s Western feminism was not available to verbalize the inequality experienced.[11]

In this chapter I argue that in the last decades of the twentieth century, Austrian women were subjected to higher degrees of gender-based exclusion than were Hungarian women. Survey data show that in state socialist Hungary almost all women were engaged in paid work, and gender inequality in positions of authority was *significantly smaller* than in capitalist Austria. In Austria in the 1980s, the odds of a man being hired for a managerial position, regardless of his qualifications or other characteristics, were four times higher than those for a woman of similar qualifications. In Hungary, the odds were closer to two times higher for a comparable situation. Because the two countries started out at roughly similar levels of gender inequality before World War II, much of the divergence must be attributed to the ideological and institutional changes that state socialism effected after 1947.

In accordance, women's own accounts of their careers reflect this pattern: Austrian women, even successful female managers in Austria, emphasized the processes of exclusion in their careers and gave vivid descriptions of negative discrimination they faced on the basis of their gender, while many Hungarian female cadres enjoyed the effects of positive discrimination policies that allowed them or other women promotion to high-level jobs. The state socialist emancipation project in Hungary had relative success compared to its corporatist-traditional capitalist counterpart in Austria: it achieved more equal participation—both in reality and in experience—for women at the top of the occupational hierarchy (see also S. Szelenyi 1998).

State-enforced emancipation came with a price tag, however, as numerous studies on the "triple burden" suggest (Funk and Mueller 1993; Einhorn 1993). In addition, women's inclusion in Hungary was never complete. Rather, the communist party instituted a policy of "divide and conquer" that allowed the limited inclusion of some women into positions of authority while at the same time retaining the highest and most prestigious jobs for men.

5. Mechanisms of Exclusion

From the start communist leaders set out to emancipate not only the proletariat but also the housewives of the world. Relying on terminology borrowed from the language of capitalist exploitation, early communist ideologues commented on the power that even true communist men exercised over "their" women. In a 1920 interview with German communist revolutionary Clara Zetkin, Lenin complained: "So few men—even among the proletariat—realize how much effort and trouble they could save women . . . if they were to lend a hand in 'woman's work.' But no, that is contrary to the 'right and dignity of a man.' . . . The old master right of the man still lives in secret" (Zetkin 1934, 57).

In the previous chapter I argued that men enjoyed fewer advantages in gaining elite labor market positions in state socialist Hungary than in capitalist Austria during the second half of the twentieth century. Yet regardless of the quotas and the openly enforced or tacitly understood positive discrimination policies, gender remained a powerful predictor of a person's position in the social hierarchy in both countries. In this chapter I ignore differences in degree and instead dissect the mechanisms through which women's exclusion came about in Austria and Hungary. My central argument is that although exclusion's underlying logic of male domination may have been the same in both countries, its actual manifestations varied significantly, producing two different gender regimes as well as shaping present and future systems of stratification in profound ways.

In the previous chapter I modeled the aggregate net advantages that accrued to being a man in the occupational hierarchies of Austria and Hungary. Here I want to "deconstruct" this aggregate number and explore how certain crucial social fields—specifically the most important forms of capital necessary for claiming authority—were constructed in gendered ways and how this affected the attainment and use of these forms of capital (both cultural and political) by men and women.

It is important to acknowledge the underlying similarities in the logic of gendered exclusion: women in each society were excluded from the type of capital that was the most useful for social advancement. In other words, the most important kind of capital in Hungary as well as in Austria was constructed and institutionalized in a highly gendered manner; that is, in a way that made it difficult for women to gain access. At the same time, the differences between the two countries were also striking: gender-based exclusion operated primarily through political capital in state socialist Hungary but through cultural capital in capitalist Austria. This handsomely demonstrates the chameleon-like quality of male domination (Ridgeway 1997), where appearance changes depending on the social environment. Yet, unlike a chameleon in the wild, variations in male domination themselves affect the social context in which they are found, hence shaping the future in often unpredictable ways (see chapter 8).

At the end of this chapter I introduce another type of capital (ignored by Bourdieu and others using his framework) whose gendered construction and importance in the occupational hierarchy is perhaps too obvious to note. This form of capital, which I term "reproductive capital," is the power to free oneself from reproductive responsibilities. I argue that the gendered institutionalization of reproductive capital is measurably different in the two societies, which contributes to cross-country gender differences in claiming authority. The introduction of this type of capital is a further step in the direction of dissecting the lump effect of gender in the stratification models of the previous chapter and should help to reveal more of the actual mechanisms through which gendered exclusion took place differently in state socialist Hungary and capitalist Austria.

Gendering Cultural Capital

Cultural capital played different roles in the class structures of Austria and Hungary. Not coincidentally, the gender dynamics of gaining and using educational degrees varied accordingly. In chapter 3, I explained the similarities and differences in the importance of institutionalized cultural capital—educational degrees and qualifications—in the two societies. Austrian bureaucracies required (and still do) written certificates of education not merely from universities but also from various specialized training programs as an individual advances in rank. Promotion is practically impossible without these degrees. It is thus not surprising that elite educational institutions such as the *gymnasium* (academic high school) and, perhaps more important, the university were bastions of male power well into the 1980s. Many fewer female than male students attended tertiary educational institutions in Austria and the proportion of male college graduates exceeded by far that of female college graduates in the labor market.

On the other hand, in Hungary, where advancement was at least partly predicated on seeking and finding a patron and displaying sufficient degrees of loyalty both to him and to a political cause, educational degrees played a necessary, nevertheless only supplementary, role in defining a person's place in the social hierarchy. As a consequence, in state socialist Hungary women's participation in educational institutions was not blocked: since the middle of the 1970s practically half of the postsecondary school population of students were female. Although gender segregation could be observed within educational institutions, and women dominated in teacher training colleges, in colleges of nursing and similar, often female-typed specializations, women also reached equity in law, business, and medical schools. Hierarchical segregation must also be mentioned: fewer women than men attended university but women outnumbered men in the less-prestigious four-year colleges. This distinction, however, is largely irrelevant for our purposes because college and university degrees were equally profitable for gaining access to positions of authority. The models (not presented here) indicate practically no difference in the value of the two types of degrees for social advancement at the top of the occupational hierarchy.

To provide further evidence for this cross-country difference and to gain a more sophisticated picture of women's disadvantage by controlling for other factors that might influence educational attainment, I designed a simple logistic regression model with the usual control variables of parental educational and occupational background.[1] I also included a variable to measure the age of the respondent, because older people had less easy access to the ever-expanding educational opportunities in both countries.

Table 5.1. Logistic regression coefficients (and standard errors) predicting access to postsecondary education; comparable models: Austria and Hungary, 1982.

	Austria	Hungary Postsecondary	Hungary University	Hungary College
Women	−.88	−.16	−.66	−.14*
	(.08)	(.06)	(.10)	(.08)
Age	.02	.01	−.06	−.009*
	(.006)	(.004)	(.006)	(.005)
Urban	1.03	.39	.98	.18*
	(.10)	(.08)	(.16)	(.09)
Father grad.	2.25	1.89	2.41	1.27
	(.16)	(.09)	(.13)	(.13)
Mother grad.	1.99	1.13	.77	1.20
	(.38)	(.17)	(.19)	(.20)
Upper class	1.31	.93	.64	1.00
	(.14)	(.09)	(.13)	(.11)
Constant	−4.98	−3.30	−6.47	−2.96
	(.23)	(.16)	(.29)	(.19)
Chi square	724	864	713	315
N	15,433	12,672	12,672	12,672

Notes: Last two columns: nested logit. * denotes nonsignificance at $p < .05$ level. For predicting college degree, those holding university degrees were excluded.

Source: *Hungarian Mobility Survey* (1992); *Microcensus of Austria* (1982).

Two variables describe the family's cultural capital: father's and mother's educational attainment. Both variables are expected to have positive effects on the respondent's own education. In addition, I included variables to assess the occupational background of the respondents' father, expecting to approximate the effect of economic capital on educational attainment. This is, admittedly, a very simple model, which is only intended to be used to get a picture of the relative size of the gender coefficient. For this reason, comparability is of the highest importance.

Table 5.1 displays the models for both countries, with Austria described in column 1. The first row in this column immediately points to the real barrier to women's entry to the sphere of power in 1982: the odds of an Austrian man to graduate from a university were roughly 2.5 times higher than that of an Austrian woman from a similar social background.[2] Using the predicting power of these models, the probability of a thirty-year-old man from a highly educated, white-collar family to have gained a university education in Austria stood at about 47 percent, while the chances of a woman of similar background were only about half of this, at 26 percent. One of the most important formal obstacles to authority was thus placed at the gates of elite educational institutions for women, thus a crucial gender filter operated here.

In Hungary, women were also at a disadvantage in gaining access to postsecondary certificates, but this disadvantage was much smaller than in Austria. In the same year, 1982, the predicted probability of a thirty-year old man from a highly educated, white-collar family to have graduated from college or university was 78 percent, and that of a woman of similar background was almost 70 percent. Obviously, we find a gender gap here, too, but it is much smaller than in Austria.[3]

Although Hungarian women had easier access to educational institutions, their segregation was also evident. Columns 3 and 4 of table 5.1 show that there was no statistically significant difference between the odds of men and women in gaining four-year college degrees by the early 1980s in Hungary. For higher prestige, five-year university degrees (column 3), however, the situation looked slightly different. If we separate out this more elite type of degree, which is perhaps more comparable to universities in Austria in terms of their degree of exclusiveness, we find a sizable (although still small compared to the capitalist context) gender gap in Hungary as well. In 1982, the predicted probability of a thirty-year-old woman from a highly educated, upper-class family (as in the earlier example) to hold a university degree was roughly 37 percent, while a man of similar background had a 53 percent chance. Even though both college and university degrees were similarly useful for claiming authority in Hungary,[4] the gender segregation of the postsecondary education reflected and reinforced the pattern of women's segregated inclusion into the public sphere in Hungary.

In sum, these models demonstrate that cultural capital in the 1980s, especially lower-level degrees, were relatively gender neutral in Hungary but heavily gendered in Austria. The two countries started from a similar place in the early 1950s but diverged significantly by the period under study here.[5]

Note in passing, however, that gender was practically the only ascriptive characteristic whose significance was reduced in Hungary compared to Austria. The cultural capital of the family was reproduced intergenerationally in both countries: parental educational attainment had a vast impact on the respondents' chances of getting a postsecondary education.

The families' class position—our somewhat simplistic measure of economic capital—seems marginally more influential in Austria than in Hungary. All else being equal, the odds of an upper-class father's child to attain a postsecondary degree was 3.7 times higher than those of a child from a lower-class family in Austria, but only about twice higher than in Hungary. This is the effect of the prestige and income advantages associated with upper-class position, net of the cultural capital that upper-class families are also more likely to possess.

We should point out, however, that the difference between the two countries is really quite small in this respect. Szonja Szelenyi (1998) found that state socialist educational reforms did not eliminate or even reduce the intergenerational reproduction of educational attainment in Hungary; the rules of allocation hardly changed. My research, although it is comparative across regions rather than across time periods, lends some support to this argument.[6]

Gendering Political Capital in Hungary

As we saw above, in Austria the main obstacle women had to overcome en route to a managerial position was found at the gates of elite educational institutions, especially universities. Although in earlier decades there were rules that would have excluded women from higher education, all such laws had been abolished around the end of World War I in both Austria and Hungary. Indeed, in Austria university education was free, scholarships were available, and no formal entrance exams were in place where a gender bias might have been obvious.[7] Instead women's exclusion operated in a more diffused way: parents were less likely to encourage their daughters to attend university or the academic high schools that prepared them for it. Women themselves chose to shun further education because they knew that their labor-market participation would be limited given the dominant expectations of women's role in society, which did not include education and a career. Although most of my interviewees attended university in Austria, many did so in the face of their family's objections. For example, Katharina, a sixty-two-year-old top executive in a state department, told me that she received a prestigious grant to continue her education, but when she called home to tell her parents, her mother asked her to "at least [not] sound so happy about it when you tell your father!" (whom, as both women knew, objected to her spending her youth in school). Another Austrian interviewee attributed her own success to the encouragement of her mother, whom she described as an exceptional woman who, unlike her friends' parents, understood the value of education even for girls.

These diffuse and indirect pressures were expressed in women's difficulty in gaining sufficient degrees of cultural capital. It is in this respect that Austria's contrast with Hungary is perhaps the sharpest. By 1982, in state socialist Hungary the amounts of cultural capital held by women roughly equaled, and in some cases exceeded, that of men. Because educational assets were useful for social advancement, these degrees facilitated social mobility for a number of middle-class Hungarian women. Yet gender equality in the allocation of managerial positions was never fully achieved. One important reason for this lack was women's inability to gain political capital, rather than cultural; the former being a resource that was perhaps even more indispensable for managerial success than education.

Analogous to models describing the attainment of cultural capital, I explore the process of women's exclusion from the political network of party members (i.e., party membership) through a set of logistic regressions describing the (log) odds of being a member of the Hungarian Communist Party between 1972 and 1988 (see table 5.2). These models, like those describing educational attainment discussed above, will help us understand the usefulness of being a man in gaining political capital. Although the impact of gender is of interest in these models, I controlled for the factors researchers have found important in previous studies. These factors include education, supervisory status, family background, age, size of residence, and marital status (S. Szelenyi 1987; Wong 1996). The first line in table 5.2 indicates that controlling for all these other differences, women's disadvantage was much larger in this area than in the attainment of cultural capital. In 1982, for example, a woman's odds of becoming a party member were about a third of the odds for a man of similar background. In other words, the chances of a resident of Budapest who is thirty years old, married, and a high school graduate[8] for being accepted in the ranks of the party was about 12 percent if he were a man but for a woman with a similar background the probability was only a third of this (approximately 4 percent). This fact reveals similarities to the obstacles women faced at the gates of universities in Austria. Gender is, in fact, the strongest predictor in these models of party membership—not

Table 5.2. Logistic regression coefficients (and standard errors) predicting access to Communist Party membership: Hungary, 1972–1988.

	1972	1982	1988
Women	−.97	−.88	−.85
	(.06)	(.07)	(.06)
Age	.05	.05	.05
	(.004)	(.004)	(.004)
Urban	.35	.16	.20
	(.07)	(.07)	(.08)
Postsecondary	.67	.73	.79
	(.09)	(.08)	(.08)
Supervisor	1.16	1.12	.97
	(.09)	(.09)	(.09)
Property owner	−.34	−.15*	−.09*
	(.09)	(.09)	(.10)
Upper class	−.06*	−.04*	−.07*
	(.12)	(.12)	(.12)
Married	.48	.30	.57
	(.09)	(.09)	(.09)
Constant	−4.25	−4.35	−4.69
	(.17)	(.17)	(.19)
Chi square	792	774	764
N	11,334	12,672	12,469

Note: * denotes nonsignificance at p < .05 level.
Source: *Hungarian Mobility Survey* (1992).

even educational attainment, occupation, or social origins have similarly large effects. Furthermore, in sharp contrast to educational degrees in Austria, there is only a slight decrease in the size of the gender coefficient over time; hence by 1988 the impact of gender on holding and gaining political capital did not change significantly.

The findings from these quantitatives models are clearly reflected in the party archives. Although state socialist political leaders putatively supported an increase in the number of women in the ranks of the party, there were strict limits to their good will. First, and most important, party leaders were ultimately unwilling to reorganize the everyday practice of party membership and political participation to make it easier for women who had household responsibilities to participate. They were even less likely to excuse women from the performance of these chores and to redistribute labor in the private sphere. A report to the Politburo acknowledges the problem in the 1950s: "Women do express sufficient levels of interest in participating in various political educational courses, but the time and place of many of these meetings coincides with their *gender-specific* responsibilities." (PIA 288/21/1958/12; emphasis mine). Party cell meetings were held after work in the early evening hours when women's minds were preoccupied with household responsibilities. Activists gathered over the weekend for political meetings, but again, someone had to stay at home to watch the kids and cook the Sunday meal. The party was a highly masculine institution, not merely in its often-violent revolutionary ideology and history but also in its practices and organization.

The male bias in the construction of communist party membership has historical reasons as well: the Hungarian Communist Party existed as a clandestine political movement for decades before it gained power after World War II, and the leading participants in the movement were men. The most reliable party members, at least in the beginning of the state socialist era, were those who could demonstrate that they had participated in the underground communist resistance before and during World War II. Some of the older women cadres I interviewed recounted moving stories of their own fearless battles against the local police and the army, but relative to men their numbers were few.

Livia was in her early seventies when I talked to her in 1995. She was a petite woman who grew up as the youngest of six children in a very poor Jewish family in Budapest, and she joined the social democratic youth movement at the encouragement of her brother when she was sixteen. When the war started she had to go into hiding to avoid arrest not only because she was Jewish but also because of her ongoing left-wing activities. She, like several other women, helped in the printing and distribution of anti-Nazi fliers or acted as liaisons among the underground leaders. Women were less conspicuous in this role in the streets of a city where all young men had been enlisted in the war effort.[9]

Even though Livia had learned and practiced the elaborate rules of underground operation in the social democratic party's youth section, she was arrested in 1942, tortured, and imprisoned for two years.

> They really tortured you hard . . . you needed very good nerves to last. See, I was lucky because I was a small, skinny girl and I fainted almost immediately, so they stopped beating me for a while. When they got out this equipment to give me electric shocks, one of the guards told the other to be careful not to kill me. So I knew they

wanted me alive, which gave me strength. But even though I was a really unimportant person in the movement and knew very little anyway, they still tortured me for days.

After she was released, she continued her underground work:

> I had five contacts (all women) whom I had to meet a couple of times a week. I wasn't even supposed to know their real names. I received from one of them the illegal fliers and posters and I had to pass these on and distribute them myself. I didn't know where the printing press was, I just met someone at a specified time and place and got a package from them. Then I had appointments with others for every half hour or so on different corners to pass the packages on. . . . Once I was almost caught again. I was having lunch with B. E. [another underground communist] in a café and had a bunch of fliers with me. I had no personal documentation on me at all. . . . Someone recognized me . . . and she told a Nazi policeman, pointing at me, that a communist was sitting there. Several Nazis came over to us and asked us for our documentation . . . at that point someone in the cafe started a commotion and I ran away.

But the woman she was having lunch with was arrested and not much later killed by the Nazi police.

These stories are not unique, even for the women among communist cadres of the older generation, and participation in the underground communist movement served as very useful currency for long after the war. Livia, for example, was sent to party school then to university, and after she had three children she was appointed to a very high-level leadership position in the political apparatus of the party, which she held until 1988. Yet, many more men than women were part of the underground resistance, guaranteeing men more revolutionary experience, credibility, and a network of war-tested comrades.

Aside from these historical disadvantages and the inherently male-biased everyday practice of party membership, in a less than subtle manner political executives themselves set strict limits to the number of women who were welcome among the party members. This is the process of limited inclusion in operation: women were welcome, even encouraged, but only up to a certain point. A document from 1974 demands that "the proportion of women and young people *must be further improved* among the newly accepted members. The proportion of women among those recently admitted should be around *one third*, while that of young people under thirty years of age around two thirds" (PIA 288/5/639; emphasis mine).

As table 5.3 demonstrates, the Politburo was successful in achieving a gradual increase in the proportion of female party members, but the total never exceeded one third. The data in this table were derived from internal party documents produced for the Politburo and held strictly classified until well after the collapse of the regime. Yet, the Politburo itself kept a close watch on these numbers and discussed their implications periodically. In 1950, the proportion of women party members reached almost 29 percent, but after 1956, when the party lost about half of its members, more women than men left. In 1961, therefore, the rebuilding period started with a mere 22 percent women. After this point we can observe a steady growth, and by 1972 a quarter of all party members were women, but the ratio did not reach a third by the end of the communist era.

Why this difference between the gender composition of cultural and political capital? After all, educational assets remained highly gendered in Austria, so why was this resource easier to attain in Hungary? And why not political capital? Communist leaders clearly brought about rapid and radical change in the participation of women in the public sphere. But the ways in which they could modify the social structure were based on their own and on their subjects' assumptions about gender and gendered practices: the pool of alternatives they could choose from was limited. In this sense, gender relations themselves shape the way in which social institutions are imagined and created, which, in turn, further affects and slowly modifies gender relations. The degendering of educational institutions as well as the lack of a similar process with party membership in Hungary are cases in point.

Party leaders started from the ideological assumption that private patriarchies must be abolished, women must emerge from the shelter of the family into the world of work and politics. They set out to reshape existing gender relations because they felt an ideological, economic, and political necessity to do so after World War II. Intensive industrialization campaigns in the 1950s demanded an expansion of the workforce never seen before, and called for an increasing number of laborers to fill the production lines in the mines, in factories, and in the offices. But there were important political considerations as well. Women educated in the com-

Table 5.3. Party members by gender in Hungary.

	Total Number (members and candidates)	Women (%)
1950	850,256	28.8
1951	862,114	28.7
1952	945,606	28.9
1958	416,766	—
1961	498,644	22.0
1966	584,849	22.9
1970	662,397	24.4
1972	724,350	25.7
1973	738,123	26.1
1974	754,353	26.5
1975	765,947	26.8
1976	761,184	27.3
1977	782,068	27.7
1978	797,014	28.0
1982	850,796	29.6
1988	816,622	32.1

Source: PIA 288/4/243.

munist school system were expected to be better mothers than those who did not receive the necessary ideological and scientific training.[10] This was particularly important given that bringing up children was still a woman's task, and hence the fate of the next generation depended on them. As Comrade Marosán remarked in a Politburo meeting on the tasks of the women's organization: "You did not speak enough about the education of women, even though this is very important, because children are brought up until the age of fourteen to fifteen by their parents and the school" (PIA 288/5/140). And in 1957, he added: "[Educating women] is particularly important because the wrong [political] atmosphere among children can turn into a catastrophe. We will be responsible if what happened to our young people is repeated [a reference to the role of young people in the 1956 revolution]. If we don't notice the political dangers, we will start our women[11] on a road that leads nowhere" (PIA 288/5/24). Thus women's education was seen as an important contribution to the stability of the state socialist social order, but this was not independent of assumptions about women's role in society, which was still seen as, at least to some extent, distinct from that of men. In other words, assumptions about gender shaped the opportunities provided for men and women in the new social order of communism.

It is exactly these distinct tasks performed by women in the household and in childrearing that were linked to an ideological conceptualization of women as politically less reliable and trustworthy, which in turn lead to their partial exclusion from the ranks of the party (I return to this point in more detail in chapter 7). In addition, as I argue above, the practice of party membership, designed and executed by revolutionary men, reflected a typical male organization of time: although the party acknowledges productive work responsibilities (meetings were not usually held during regular work hours) it ignored reproductive work hours because those concerns usually did not rate high on the agenda of the mostly male membership. Without the opportunity to organize outside of the boundaries of the party, there were no forces that could effectively challenge the assumptions derived from this masculine origin. Thus, exactly the same assumptions and practices concerning gender that led to the opening of the gates of educational institutions essentially closed the ranks of the communist party in front of women in Hungary.

In contrast, in Austria women's reproductive responsibilities led to a somewhat different conceptualization of the role of women in society. Political loyalty, although important, was not the main issue. Rather, women were constructed as being incapable of fully rational action and full citizenship, and education, which prepared people for both was therefore seen as unnecessary. This ideological construction of women as irrational dependents in fraternal patriarchies (Pateman 1988b) contrasts sharply with the communist manifestation of male domination, which was expressed in the view of women not as *irrational*, but as *unreliable* politically and therefore not capable of full devotion to the communist party. As Dezső Nemes, a Politburo member, argued at a meeting in 1961 when the members of this most powerful organ of the Hungarian communist party were discussing the changes in the social composition of the membership: "I agree that we have to raise the expectations [for would-be members], especially in terms of the required political activity. And moral behavior I should add. *But of course there is one group where it will be difficult to boost the requirements and this is among women.* Still, it is obvious that we have to increase the proportion of women" (PIA 288/5/227; emphasis mine).

Women thus could not achieve the level of political reliability as men, but they were still allowed, if in limited numbers, into the ranks of the party. The participation of too many women in the eyes of the Politburo would have meant the weakening of this political institution, because women's participation was never expected to be at the same standard as that of men.

Differences in the Use of Cultural Capital

As described above, gendered exclusion in Austria and Hungary was expressed differently, and this difference corresponded to the basic characteristics of the social structures and related differences in the assumptions about women and men: in Austria women's disadvantage was based on their deficiency in rationality and skills, and in Hungary on their inability to become fully loyal participants in the political circuits. But the story is more complicated than this: assumptions, practices, and interests connected with gender were not only shaped but also themselves affected by the process of stratification. Women's easy access to a certain type of capital modified the usefulness of this resource for at least women, and sometimes for men as well. The uses of cultural capital in the two countries are good points of comparison: in 1982 postsecondary degrees were relatively gender balanced in Hungary (especially if we do not differentiate between college and university degrees) but mostly male-dominated in Austria.

A new set of logistic regression models will help us evaluate how successfully men and women could apply their educational degrees toward gaining authority. As in the previous models, my dependent variable is the (log) odds of being in a managerial position in 1982. The models are the same as those presented in chapter 3, with only a few new variables added. These new terms describe the interaction between the effect of gender and education on an individual's managerial chances, or specifically, given the way the variables are coded, the additional advantage or disadvantage a postsecondary degree brings for women (as compared to graduate men).[12] The most important finding in these models is that in Austria the coefficient is positive, which indicates that gender inequality is smaller among graduates than among nongraduates (table 5.4). Women who graduate from college or university face less gender discrimination that those who do not. The opposite is true for Hungary. Gender inequality is larger among college/university graduates than among those

Table 5.4. Logistic regression coefficients (and standard errors) predicting access to managerial positions: Hungary and Austria, 1982 (with interactions between gender, education, and party membership)

	Austria	Hungary Model 1	Hungary Model 2
Women	−1.55	−.29	−.19*
	(.16)	(.11)	(.12)
Age	.05	.03	.03
	(.006)	(.005)	(.005)
Urban	.64	−.06*	−.07*
	(.09)	(.10)	(.10)
Married	.31	.66	.62
	(.12)	(.14)	(.14)
Postsecondary	3.10 ·	2.52	2.36
	(.14)	(.12)	(.12)
Party member	—	—	1.05
			(.12)
Parents grad.	.36	−.13*	−.02*
	(.19)	(.15)	(.15)
Upper class	1.10	.28	.30
	(.13)	(.13)	(.13)
Graduate (women)	.67	−.76	−.75
	(.30)	(.18)	(.18)
Party member (women)	—	—	.13*
			(.22)
Constant	5.56	5.05	4.96
	(.24)	(.24)	(.25)
Chi square	1349	761	863
N	15,372	12,672	12,672

Note: * denotes nonsignificance at p < .05 level.
Source: *Hungarian Mobility Survey* (1992); *Microcensus of Austria* (1982).

less educated, and women's returns on their educational investments are lower than that of men.

To express all this numerically, postsecondary-educated Hungarian women increased their odds of becoming managers over less-educated women by a factor of about six, but highly educated men increased theirs over less-educated men by a factor of twelve. In Hungary, a degree from a university or a college clearly enhanced a man's chances of advancing to authority more than it did a woman's chances. But the opposite tendency can be observed in Austria. Here, women's odds, once in possession of a college degree, increase thirty-eight times, while a similar degree boosts a man's (already sizable) odds by "only" a factor of twenty. In other words, education is a more useful asset in Austria, and it is particularly more useful for women.

An example can help illuminate this contrast further. Imagine a forty-year-old Austrian man, whom we will call Ludwig Schmidt. Ludwig is married and lives in Vienna, the capital of Austria, and is a wage earner. He is a smart and ambitious man, and he managed to graduate from a university even though he did not grow up in a particularly well-to-do family. Let's say that his father worked as a skilled factory worker and his mother was a housewife. Neither went to university, of course. Nevertheless, with his own degree the chances of a man like Ludwig to occupy a managerial position were quite high in 1982 in Austria: around 60 percent according to the predictions based on the logistic regression models described previously. The predicted chances of a woman of similar background, say forty-year-old Luise Schmidt, were much lower at around 40 percent. Without postsecondary education, Luise's chances would have been about 1 percent compared to 6 percent for Ludwig. Obviously, both gender and university/college education make a big difference, but education more so than gender. Educated men had almost a tenfold advantage over uneducated men, and the same factor for women was a fortyfold advantage. But the point is that the gender difference was larger within the less-educated group than the highly educated group: among college/university graduates gender discrimination seems to be smaller than among nongraduates.

In Hungary, on the other hand, the managerial chances in 1982 of the example of Lajos Kovács, a forty-year-old, married university graduate from a working-class family in Budapest, are 32 percent, while his female counterpart, Lujza Kovács, had a 15 percent predicted chance. Had neither of them attended university, their chances would have declined to about 4 percent and 3 percent respectively. A glance at these figures and a comparison to the previous set from Austria immediately show that gaining a degree helped Hungarian women's advancement, but certainly not as much as it did that of men. The chances of those without degrees to make it into positions of authority were small, but in this group there was practically no gender inequality. Among the better-educated bunch the gender gap was significantly larger. In Austria, the gender difference worked in the opposite direction. In addition, the other type of cultural capital— that inherited from one's parents—followed the same pattern in Austria.

Women who came from highly educated families reduced the level of discrimination they faced. In other words, female managers in Austria had higher levels of cultural capital: more had university degrees and many more came from families of intellectuals.

Take the example of Karina, whom I interviewed in her office in Vienna. Karina had held a series of managerial positions since the mid-1970s, including heading cultural centers for Austria in several countries around the world, as well as holding high-level positions in the Ministry of Culture. She came from a family of civil servants: both her father and grandfather served the country in civil service positions. Karina was an only child and grew up in a traditional, middle-class family in Vienna, where from an early age her parents regularly took her to the opera, to museums, and to the theater. She gained an impressive amount of cultural capital by the time she enrolled in university, where she later graduated with a B.A. in English. After further studies abroad she gained a postgraduate degree as well. In the course of our conversations she pointed out that she needed all of her qualifications, even though many of her male colleagues had nowhere near the same number. "But as a woman, you always have to do more," she said.

Because cultural capital is the most important asset used to claim authority (as an employee manager) in Austria, women had to do better than men in proving themselves in this regard. Although it was significantly harder for women than for men to attend universities, only if they did so could they start competing with men. The playing field among the highly educated was still uneven, but gaining education and outperforming men in the attainment of cultural capital made up for some of women's disadvantages.

The obverse was true in Hungary, where women were no more likely than men to have held cultural capital of either kind once in a managerial position. Women managers did not come from better-educated families, and they themselves were less likely to hold university degrees. Initially, this might have been a result of the process of counterselection. But another reason was that women managers occupied positions that required fewer credentials in the first place. Not only were these jobs lower in managerial level but, as we saw in chapter 4, women were more likely to hold political and administrative jobs requiring less formal training than, say, being a chief engineer or the head doctor in a hospital. Thus even though women were allowed to gain college and university education, this asset provided them at best with a secondary route for advancement. The usefulness of women's university degrees was lower than that of men for gaining authority. These degrees qualified a large number of women for professional jobs (the feminization of teaching, accounting, medicine, and law was much discussed in the media), but many fewer women than men could advance to the higher position of a powerful "technocrat" from this pool of "intellectuals" [*beosztott értelmiségi*].

So far we have examined women's opportunities to make use of their cultural capital in Hungary compared to Austria; and we found that in Austria, where educational assets were highly male dominated, the few women who did manage to gain university degrees could valorize them more easily. In Hungary, few experienced gender discrimination at the gates of universities, but women, even armed with a college or university degree, suffered serious discounts on the labor market.[13]

Gender and the Use of Political Assets in Hungary

What if Lujza Kovács, the forty-year-old, Hungarian university graduate, had decided to join the communist party and had been recommended and accepted by other members? Was women's political loyalty also devalued, and was it also worth less than that of men? Party membership was never a gender-balanced capital in Hungary. In the pattern of its gender distribution it rather resembled educational degrees in Austria: women made some progress but the gender gap remained consistent. Based on the example of cultural capital, instead of devaluation we would expect extra benefits for women if they managed to gain political capital.

Was women's party membership devalued, then, relative to that of men? The answer to this question can be found in column 3 of table 5.4. Unfortunately, the quantitative model does not fully support our expectations, although it does not refute them either. The models show that the interaction term for party membership and gender is positive, although not statistically (or even substantively) significant. The least we can say is that gender discrimination was not larger among party members than among the general population, even though from the previous discussion we would have expected otherwise. In other words, women who joined the party did not experience more or less discrimination than those who remained outside, or at least the level of disadvantage did not worsen as it did in the case of educational credentials. Thus, the few women who against many odds joined the communist party, attained a capital that provided some shelter from the further exacerbation of gender inequalities.

In sum, these models show that the processes of gender-based exclusion were shaped by the specific characteristics of the social structure in each society. In capitalist Austria, women were unlikely to make it to the top of the social hierarchy because they lacked cultural capital, the most important asset to become a (nonself-employed) manager. In order to be included, they had to outperform men: women in managerial positions had higher levels of cultural capital than men. They also had more economic capital; that is, they were more likely to have come from upper-middle to upper-class families.

In state socialist Hungary women had difficulties joining the communist party and thus did not gain a sufficient degree of political capital, which was crucial for social advancement in state socialist societies. They could, however, take a secondary route and gain cultural capital, which was easier to do and even encouraged by those in political power. These educational degrees, however, served women less well than they did men: cultural capital when held by a woman was devalued and therefore worth less on the career ladder (relative to men). As a result, and in sharp contrast with Austria, earlier generations of women in managerial positions especially had valuable political capital but sometimes lacked educational degrees and credentials. Female managers in Hungary were more likely to be found in positions that required lower educational qualifications but a formal testimony to political reliability.

To summarize the contrast between the two countries succinctly: the gender filter operated primarily at the gates of universities (and other elite educational institutions) in Austria, and at the entrance to party membership in Hungary. Women in both countries experienced exclusion from the form of capital most valuable for social advancement (cultural capital in Austria, political capital in Hungary). Only those who did manage to pass the filters and gain sufficient degrees of the critical type of capital could significantly improve their chances—relative to men—of social advancement.

Gender Revisited

In the previous sections of this chapter I explored the relationship between gender and cultural and political capital by explaining how each type of capital is constructed based on gendered assumptions, which in turn has consequences for the chances of men and women to possess these forms of capital as well as use them in the stratification process. It is, therefore, pointless to consider the concept of "cultural capital" without regard to its holders' gender, which profoundly influences its nature and does so in different ways in different types of societies. This argument is in line with Bourdieu's original position (1984), which holds that while gender itself does not function as a type of capital, it is a "secondary characteristic." This means that the *expression* of a class position (or the expression of a type of capital) varies with the holder's gender.[14]

In order to understand women's exclusion from authority, however, an additional highly gendered type of resource must be considered: the effect of reproductive duties (domestic work, childbearing and rearing, and unpaid caring work of all types) on a person's chances, practice, and experience of gaining and holding managerial positions. In order to capture this phenomenon within Bourdieu's framework, I will introduce and examine the usefulness of what I term "reproductive capital." Those who own reproductive capital are freed from obligations concerning the immediate reproduction of labor power—their own or that of others. Reproductive capital, just like cultural or political capital, is constructed in a gendered way—men and women own and use different amounts—but it is less broad and more specific than gender.

In order to conceptualize freedom from reproduction as a type of capital it is important to view the social organization of reproduction as mostly independent of ascribed biological qualities. In this formulation the higher the value of a person's reproductive capital, the better chance he or she has of participating in the dominant elite. Arlie Hochschild, for example, in exploring why the proportion of female full professors is so low in the academic world in the United States, argues that "the classic profile of the academic career is cut to the image of the traditional man with his traditional wife" (1975, 49). In the world of work, freedom from reproductive duties is an important type of capital, the volume of which enables the "traditional man" to build his own career. Of course, more family-oriented men may possess lower levels of this capital, either by choice or by circumstance. Similarly, women, while in general at a disadvantage, can still achieve a certain amount of reproductive capital should they choose to follow what is usually called a "male career pattern." Participating in the labor force free of reproductive burdens usually means not getting married, eschewing or postponing childbearing, or making sure in some other way—such as hiring babysitters or utilizing social provisions or self-sacrificing grandparents—that one is unencumbered by the duties associated with the "second shift."

Women without children past childbearing age, or those with older children demanding less attention, also have a higher degree of reproductive capital compared to younger women and especially young mothers. This is a potential resource that can be usefully employed in gaining advantages in the social hierarchy. Granted, women cannot fully escape the assumptions and predispositions that employers and others bring to the assessment of their career prospects, nor can they escape the social sanctions imposed on women who "act like men" (Pierce 1995). Thus women can never achieve the same degree of reproductive capital enjoyed by most men, but men who take an active part in the household also have to pay for this choice—they will be lacking the full degree of their reproductive capital so conceptualized. Indeed, ironically, several single women managers I interviewed in Austria expressed frustration at recent regulations protecting working mothers by guaranteeing extra leave and fewer work hours for those with reproductive responsibilities. They understood that these measures reduced the relative advantages their hard-earned reproductive capital (i.e., childlessness and single status) had brought them.

Cultural capital is acquired through learning, either in exclusive, formal educational institutions or in the family, whereas economic capital is accumulated through the exploitation of the productive labor of others. Just like material wealth or educational credentials, the division of labor in the household is acquired from past and present customs and is reproduced by daily practice. So is its gendering; that is, in both countries the immediate association of women with the hearth, and with babies, diapers, and milk bottles. Freeing oneself of reproductive burdens is done through the exploitation of the reproductive labor of others. Those who possess high volumes of reproductive capital enjoy the fruits of the reproductive labor of others while freeing themselves from the responsibilities, the expenses, and the work it entails. As is most often the case, husbands whose wives are responsible for childrearing and the reproduction of the families' labor power enjoy the psychological, physiological, and sometimes material advantages of having children, as well as hot meals on the table every night. But even those (men and women) who do not have children benefit from the reproductive work of others if we think of children as "public goods"—that is, as the next generation of workers and producers of technological innovations, raw materials, or services.

The point of separating the different types of capitals in Bourdieu's description of the social order is to explain the distinct class positions in the social space and the differences in the types of dominations that can be exercised on the basis of each. The power of capitalists is different from the power enjoyed by elite university professors, highly acclaimed artists, or scholars, which again is different from the power of party leaders and communist ideologues. Domination exercised on the basis of the appropriation of the reproductive work of others is also different from both. Even though the "practical or economic" and the "symbolic or cultural" types of capital are both gendered in and of themselves, freedom from reproductive duties is an additional source of power even among those deprived of any of the other types of resources: it creates distinctions among those who hold different amounts. Among the group of university professors, for example, as Hochschild described in the work I cited above, freedom from reproductive work accrued career advantages, which had little relationship to the invariably high volume of cultural capital of its holders.

Reproductive capital was a significant resource in the stratification systems of both societies, but, just as in the case of the other two types of capitals, its gendered institutionalization varied in Austria and Hungary. Specifically, a reduction of actual work hours and work discipline, along with more generous public provisions for children, produced a relative deinstitutionalization of reproductive capital (particularly for women!) in Hungary compared to Austria. Aside from the existence of a bumpy secondary route to social advancement offered through the attainment of cultural capital, this is the second most important reason why women in state socialist Hungary were more likely to be found in positions of authority compared to women of similar qualifications in Austria.

Reproductive Work and Career

Most of the managers in my sample of interviewees who had children acknowledged the career modifications required in having and bringing up children. They all employed elaborate strategies to create an acceptably harmonious balance between work and childcare. Men—husbands, partners, or grandfathers—were rarely part of the master plan. More often other women helped out: usually grandmothers or paid domestic workers.

Sometimes in Hungary, where many women shared the same difficulties, even in a middle-class suburb, communal solutions could also be arranged, as described by Lidia, a sixty-year-old party secretary: "When my children were older they had a key and came home after school, and they were supposed to warm up their lunch. The first one came home and burnt it a little, the second a bit more and it was inedible by the time the youngest got home. So I found a woman nearby whose kids went to the same school. I paid her and she cooked for all the children. In the end, it became quite a large operation, there were kids eating there from the whole block."

Without fail, all of my Austrian interviewees had hired domestic workers. Even those who lived alone at least had a cleaning woman come in once a week to tidy up their homes. Many communist cadres, much like their Austrian counterparts, also hired housekeepers. This practice had had an extensive tradition in prewar Hungary, but in a political system based exclusively on state employment it seemed an odd choice, especially when practiced by its top (female) representatives. This duality is reflected in the decision of Lidia's husband, as Lidia explains: "When the girls were small, I had some help with the housework [i.e., a paid housekeeper]. But when they became teenagers, my husband said that he was not going to bring up lazy little ladies, and he fired the housekeeper, and from then on, the girls had to help with the housework."

Another Hungarian cadre, Rita, remembers the times with some regret when she had to work late and her (oddly, male) secretary had to go pick up her son from school because the son was still too young to go home alone. Whether in the role of wife, housekeeper, grandmother, or even older daughter, it was still mostly women who did the housework.

> My husband, my mother and I do the housework together. I spend about one and a half hours daily on these things, my husband does about half an hour. (Austrian bank manager, age fifty-two)

> I do all the housework myself except for the cleaning, which is done by a cleaning lady. My partner does nothing. (Austrian restaurant owner, age thirty-nine)

> Well, I argued with him, for a while, and tried everything to get him to help out. But in the end, you don't want to have to quarrel constantly, so I just gave up and decided to do it all myself. (Austrian civil servant manager, age thirty-seven, with two children)

All Austrian women interviewees who had children saw this as a disadvantage or even as a potential threat to their careers.

> I stayed at home for seven years when my children were born, and then my mother looked after them when they started going to school. If I didn't have children, my career would have started much earlier. (Austrian interviewee, forty-eight, a civil servant)

> My profession was very important to me and this is why I waited until I was already thirty-four years old to have a child. But I didn't stay at home with him for a minute. I could never have continued my career if I did. (Austrian university professor, head of large research institute, fifty-two years old)

> Having kids slowed down my career, because I was on maternity leave for two years. (Austrian accounting manager, forty years old)

Only half of my Austrian interviewees had children, and these women described elaborate, conscious strategies they devised to combine career and work. Laura had her children early and stayed at home with them, starting her career afterward. Sabrina, as we saw above, postponed childbearing until she was more established in her career. Some, who had children mid-career, took maternity leave for a year but kept in touch with their employers and did some regular work for them. In doing this they expected to have a better chance at getting back on track when the children were older.

In addition, those who did not have any kids believed that they could not have had the same career had they decided to procreate, because, as one interviewee put it, "banking and children don't fit." When I asked childless managers how their lives would have turned out had they gotten married and had kids, they all described an alternative life, one devoid of managerial possibilities. "I would have stayed in Vienna and kept teaching high school. I probably would have stopped working when I had kids, like my mother and my sisters did," said a sixty-seven-year-old Austrian state executive.

Hungarian women, on the other hand, did not seem to experience childbearing as a similarly great detriment to their careers. One interviewee, Karola, stated, "I stayed at home for six months, then my son went to nursery school. I don't think having a child stopped me from doing anything or achieving anything." Another interviewee claims, "I never became a victim to my children." A female manager who had two children claimed that she never acted like a "real woman," stating that, "I got married twice, but I really was never into family life. I shouldn't have gotten married really. I was always much more interested in work, in creating and producing than in procreating." Finally, my only Hungarian interviewee who did not have children was convinced that having them would not have stopped her in anything.

It may be easy to dismiss this difference in Hungarian and Austrian women's attitudes toward childbearing and career as merely a reflection of the differences in gender ideology and language available to express social problems: Austrian women—especially by the 1990s when I interviewed them—were much better versed in Western feminist demands and could thus describe their disadvantage in terms that are very familiar to North American readers as well. Hungarian women did not have these tools available and thus may be seen as having bought into the communist ideology of gender equality. Nevertheless, rather than attributing false consciousness to women in state socialist Hungary, we might consider the possibility that it was indeed simply easier to combine children and a career in Hungary in the early 1980s: reproductive capital, while still significant, was a less gendered (and perhaps less important) asset here than in conservative, capitalist Austria.

One Austrian interviewee, the foreign policy editor at a national newspaper, told me that when she became pregnant in the early 1980s the personnel department had to search for the regulations about maternity benefits because this had never happened before to a person at her level of seniority. In Hungary, where most women of working age were employed in the labor force, getting pregnant would not have created such a commotion. It would have accrued disadvantages, no doubt, but through the use of parental leave policies and public nursery schools and kindergarten, and the reduction in the actual number of hours required to be spent in the labor force, the state socialist regime succeeded, to a larger degree than did its Austrian counterpart, in deinstitutionalizing freedom from reproduction as a type of capital.

Let me point out here that freedom from reproductive work is not the only type of capital whose degree of institutionalization changed after World War II. Gil Eyal, Ivan Szelenyi, and Eleanor Townsley (1998) argue that social capital, which had vast importance in precapitalist modes of production, was deinstitutionalized in capitalism but reinstitutionalized again in the form of political capital under state socialism. Similarly, economic capital was almost fully deinstitutionalized and thus lost its importance in the reproduction of the social order in state socialist societies, while it remained crucial in capitalism. We can use the same logic to compare the role of freedom from reproductive work in the class structures of Hungary and Austria. The quantitative models provide some evidence for this, although here the interpretation of the coefficient associated with reproductive capital is slightly different than in the case of cultural and political capital. Due to severe limitations in the Austrian data set, I operationalized reproductive capital as "marriage," but marriage as an expression of reproductive capital only works in interaction with gender because marriage indicates opposite tendencies in terms of reproductive freedom for men and women. Indeed, we saw that the meaning of other types of capital also varies according to the holders' gender, but here this distinction is significantly sharper. We cannot make sense of "marriage" as an indicator of reproductive capital without simultaneously considering the gender of the respondent.

With this in mind, I ran logistic regression models predicting access to managerial positions in both countries and introduced interaction terms between marital status and gender. Using information from the data sets, we can create four categories signifying different volumes of "reproductive capital": married men are expected to have the highest volume because they are most likely to have a person looking after their individual reproductive needs, while married women are expected to have the lowest. Let us compare for these four groups the chances of access to authority in the two countries.

In Austria, the chance of a forty-year old, educated man from an urban yet lower-class background (e.g., Ludwig Schmidt) to occupy a managerial position of some kind in the 1980s was, according to the models in table 5.5, about 59 percent compared to that of an unmarried man at about 46 percent. Marital status provided advantages for men in access to managerial positions. Among women, however, as expected, the opposite is true: unmarried forty-year-old educated women had a 38 percent chance of advancing to the top of the social hierarchy on their own rights, while for a married woman (and this includes only married women who are employed in the labor force) the chance is reduced to 30 percent. True to the experience of my interviewees, marriage provided benefits to men's advancement but obstacles to that of women's in Austria.

Table 5.5. Logistic regression coefficients (and standard errors) predicting access to managerial positions: Hungary and Austria, 1982 (with interactions between gender and marital status).

	Austria	Hungary
Women	−.96	.003*
	(.24)	(.26)
Age	.04	.03
	(.006)	(.005)
Urban	.63	.06*
	(.09)	(.10)
Married	.49	.80
	(.14)	(.18)
Postsecondary	3.10	2.52
	(.14)	(.12)
Parents grad.	.38	−.13*
	(.19)	(.15)
Upper class	1.09	.28
	(.13)	(.13)
Graduate (women)	.61	−.77
	(.30)	(.18)
Married (women)	−.85	−.33*
	(.28)	(.27)
Constant	−5.63	−5.15
	(.24)	(.26)
N	15,372	12,672

Note: * denotes nonsignificance at p < .05 level.
Source: *Hungarian Mobility Survey* (1992); *Microcensus of Austria* (1982).

In Hungary, a somewhat different picture emerges, again conforming to the accounts of the women who shared their life stories with me. In this country, marriage brings advantages to both men and women, and unmarried women of the same age and background are slightly (although statistically nonsignificantly) less likely to be managers than married women of similar background. For example, forty-year-old Lajos Kovács has a 37 percent chance of having managerial authority in Hungary if he is married, but his unmarried counterpart only a 21 percent chance. Compare this to Lujza Kovács's chance at 16 percent, while her unmarried counterpart is also lower at 11 percent. More female managers were married and had families in Hungary than in Austria. In other words, freedom from reproductive burdens, as defined above, was a more useful type of capital for men in their efforts to maintain their privileges in capitalist Austria than in state socialist Hungary of the early 1980s.

In this chapter I describe cross-country differences in the mechanisms of gender-based exclusion from positions of authority. The underlying logic of women's exclusion seems quite similar in the two countries: their access to the most useful type of capital was blocked in both Austria and Hungary. But the actual form of capital varied according to the logic of stratification: educational assets served this function in Austria and political resources in Hungary. Gendered exclusion was, in brief, achieved through cultural domination in Austria but political rule in Hungary.

In addition, social advancement through the possession of high degrees of cultural capital served as a secondary channel for class mobility for Hungarian women, but their educational assets were devalued and could not function as effectively as educational degrees held by men. In Austria, too, a secondary channel existed: as we saw in chapter 3, among self-employed capitalists women's disadvantage was lower than on the labor market. This means that economic capital played a somewhat analogous function to educational degrees in Hungary, at least among the petit bourgeoisie.

Finally, in this chapter I demonstrate that it is feasible and useful to conceptualize freedom from reproduction as a type of capital. Such analysis allows a more sophisticated deconstruction of the meaning of reproduction as a resource in the stratification process and an assessment of the degree to which this resource is valuable for men and for women in different types of societies. In light of this, I now turn to an examination of the state policies and regulations through which such highly gendered deinstitutionalization—limited as it may have been—was carried out in Austria and Hungary.

6. Conditions of Inclusion: Examining State Policies in Austria and Hungary, 1945–1995

The previous chapters are devoted to the ways in which men and women claimed positions of authority in state socialist Hungary and in capitalist Austria in the 1980s. Yet an analysis of the gender regimes in the labor market in the two countries is incomplete without a discussion of the framework within which women's integration or exclusion took place; that is, the construction of gender in policymaking that resulted in specific labor market, social, or welfare regulations encouraging, enabling, limiting, or even prohibiting women's participation in the sphere of work and politics. These laws and regulations are the topic of exploration in this chapter.

Neither welfare state models offered by feminists nor region-specific descriptions of Eastern Europe provide a satisfactory model for comparing policies directly affecting gender relations and, in particular, that of women's place in the occupational hierarchies of Austria and Hungary. Welfare state models by feminists do not explain the discrepancy between the Austrian and the Hungarian cases because Eastern Europe cannot meaningfully be placed on a "male breadwinner/individual worker" continuum, a variation of which usually serves as the crucial point of comparison for much of international welfare state research. State policies in communist Hungary did not, obviously, encourage the male breadwinner ideology. Similarly, targeting workers as individual citizens was alien to the ideology, intentions, and practice of communist policymakers. Not individuals but social group, and not citizens but political subjects, were the basic unit of social policy in state socialist Eastern Europe.

Scholars doing research specifically on the region often emphasize the gender-homogenization effects of large-scale political subjugation. These accounts (e.g., Bruszt 1988; Verderey 1996) do not explicitly differentiate between men's and women's relationship to the socialist state. At the same time, those who do describe the gendered nature of state policies (e.g., Gal and Kligman 2000b; Haney 1997) usually do not do so in a comparative context, hence the existing literature lacks even the conceptual framework for a capitalist versus communist analysis.

Therefore, I will start by devising new conceptual tools for the comparison of state policies targeting women's inclusion in or exclusion from the labor force in Austria and Hungary. To do so, I borrow from feminist legal theory (as well as feminist theory old and new, see, for example, Scott 1988; Pateman 1988b)[1] and propose to replace the oft-cited male breadwinner/individual worker continuum by making a distinction instead between policies based on assumptions about women's status as "similarly situated to men" as opposed to women's "difference" on the labor market.

Let me give an example to illustrate this contrast. The Pregnancy Discrimination Act of 1978 in the United States states that pregnant women should not be treated differently from any nonpregnant worker and recommends that pregnancy be handled just like any other medical condition or disability (Williams 1993).[2] Feminist scholars lobbied for this amendment to Title 7 as a response to a controversial 1972 Supreme Court ruling that upheld the natural difference of pregnancy from other medical conditions, and thus excused companies from including it in their insurance coverage (Kamerman, Kahn, and Kingston 1983). The 1978 law prohibited discrimination at hiring and promotion, put an end to mandatory maternity leaves, and prohibited firing women because of their pregnancy. The legislation assured that technically women could not be discriminated against on the basis of childbearing because the law did not consider this "affliction" substantially different from a broken arm or a stubborn spell of pneumonia. This is the "similarity principle" at work:[3] men and women, as well as the potential detriments to their labor power, are similar. Its application is a great improvement over earlier eras when pregnancy automatically excluded women from the paid workforce, let alone positions of authority. At the same time, it is obvious that legislation that ignores the gendered specificity of pregnancy and childbearing precludes any potential for positive action for new and would-be mothers.

As a result, this principle denies the need for modifications in the institutions of work and their transformation from a male-biased setting to a more woman-friendly one, because it refuses to acknowledge the socially constructed differences between the life cycle and career experiences of male and female workers.

In Hungary, as in other state socialist societies, pregnancy was handled differently. In 1967 the Hungarian Parliament passed a decree that provided a long list of special benefits for pregnant women: it required that on request they be transferred to a workplace where their level of physical exertion did not endanger their condition; obligated them to take a fully paid six-week leave prior to delivery and six months after delivery; allowed mothers (and only mothers) to stay at home for an additional two and a half years with pay to look after their children; provided job protection during and after pregnancy; and gave them special paid days off to care for a sick older child. These opportunities were open only to women and only in the case of pregnancy (and motherhood); clearly this was treated as no ordinary illness and one that was specific to women. In addition, until the late 1980s all women received the same level of compensation, unrelated to social insurance or earlier salary levels, thus reinforcing the idea of women's shared interests and separateness from men. Such applications of the "difference principle" meant women's integration into the labor force through special measures that allowed time and space for reproductive responsibilities. In that sense, the concept of work was transformed: it was acceptable to be a mother and a worker (and even a manager) at the same time, and these two roles were no longer constructed in complete opposition to one another. At the same time, these measures also reinforced the gendered division of labor—leaving women solely responsible for household and childcaring duties—and fell far short of transforming family life outside paid work. As a result, women were included in the labor force, but often segregated rather than integrated within it.

These examples serve only to illustrate the extremes of the principles of similarity and difference as applied to women's participation in the paid labor force. My argument is that at least in the 1980s, which is the focal point of my comparison, Hungarian state policies primarily operated on the basis of the difference principle, while Austrian state policies, although not at all as extreme as the example from the United States given above, veered closer to the similarity side of this continuum. This is not to argue that policymakers in either country consciously applied and decided between these two principles. Rather, only the outcome of their policymaking efforts came to point in these directions, which were in no way consciously acknowledged. Nevertheless, these national legal and legislative frameworks served as crucial factors that helped to shape the observed differences in women's participation in paid work and authority in the two countries.

In the next section I build a conceptual framework to describe in more detail the distinction I outlined above. In the rest of this chapter I explore the many historical variations exhibited in policymaking in the two countries between 1945 and 1995, which simultaneously confirm the validity of the model I discuss below while specifying it in terms of time and policymaking area.

Building a Conceptual Framework

Theoretically, four possible types of responses are imaginable to the "problem" of how to handle women's difference with respect to their participation in the public sphere, as outlined in table 6.1. I will depict each response—each state policy "gender regime"—by two types of characteristics: the degree of women's participation in the labor force and the principles or conditions on which inclusion, if it happens at all, is made possible.

As the simplest solution, women can be excluded from paid work altogether and be relegated to what is constructed outside this social acting ground. This response is described in table 6.1, where I call it "direct exclusion" (but note that it is also often referred to as the "separate spheres ideology"). Policymaking in Austria for two decades after World War II reflected this ideal, as legislation was aimed at reducing the size of the female labor force. Several gender-specific prohibitive regulations existed and practically no serious provisions were made for maternity leave or childcare. As a consequence, women's public sphere participation declined sharply; that is, the number of women involved in paid work, in education, and in politics decreased.

A second possible state reaction to the same problem of women's perceived difference is that of allowing women's inclusion in the public sphere through enforced assimilation, (termed "latent exclusion" in table 6.1). In this instance, full participation in paid work is only possible if a

Table 6.1. Framework for the comparison of Austrian and Hungarian state policies

| | Conditions of Participation | |
	Difference Principle	Similarity Principle
Inclusion in the labor force	Limited Inclusion (special measures for women in labor force)	Integration (state institutions take over reproductive work)
Exclusion from labor force	Direct Exclusion ("separate spheres")	Latent Exclusion (male norm exclusive)

male career pattern is adopted. Capitalist labor market policies in the 1970s and 1980s were closest to this category: women's inclusion was predicated on their adjustment to the male norm without an effort to change the operation and expectations of the workplace—corporations, factories, offices, or state administration. Formal regulations and laws guarantee women's equality to men, but in this case "equality to men" really means "similarity," and because women can rarely become "perfect men" they cannot compete on equal footing in the labor market. Thus the outcome is often exclusion, or at best a segregated, inferior participation, with women serving as the "reserve army of labor" in part-time, specially vulnerable positions. These politics allow women to enter the public sphere or even positions of authority if they can clearly demonstrate their distance from reproductive responsibilities. Yet the worker, especially the elite worker, is conceptualized as male, and thus women's presence is tenuous and sometimes transitory, not to mention stressful.

The third possible legislative reaction (termed "limited inclusion" in table 6.1) to the problem of women's perceived difference is the one exhibited by the Hungarian party-state from the mid 1950s until close to the end of the state socialist era. By this time, the idea that women could ever become fully adjusted to the male norm was abandoned. Women remained to be perceived as different, but this did not mean exclusion as it did in Austria in the 1950s. Rather, it allowed legislators to create female-specific tracks; that is, special policies to encourage women's entrance and participation in certain clearly specified (and often inferior) positions. For a long time, this was a new and innovative phenomenon—after all, it was the first attempt at the extensive integration of women (as women) into the public sphere. The drawbacks of this kind of inclusion soon became clear, however: difference explicitly did not mean equality, and women's jobs and career patterns paid less and accrued fewer privileges than those designed for men. Instead of being integrated into the labor force, women's participation could be better characterized as segregation.[4]

The fourth cell in table 6.1, "integration," was briefly and halfheartedly attempted by communist legislators in the late 1940s and 1950s when women's participation in the labor force became a pressing economic and ideological need. In this period, female laborers were aggressively recruited for paid work in jobs previously considered strictly male territory, such as those in the mines, on tractors and in other types of heavy physical labor. At the same time, no special provisions were offered to parents of small children and no "protective" restrictions were applied to women on the basis of their gender: women were supposed to act like men, work in the same jobs, and keep the same hours. In order to ensure women's integration, however, state-subsidized public institutions, rather than individual men or women, were designated to carry out reproductive services that earlier had been provided in the household. This is where integration came to differ from limited exclusion. The Hungarian model was short lived exactly because this latter condition proved expensive and generally unappealing to party leaders as well as to their subjects.

There is a fifth possibility, not depicted in table 6.1, because it remains the stuff of feminist dreams. The application of androgynous norms inside and outside the labor force would mean a thorough transformation of the logic of the labor market and would guarantee the possibility of combining household and paid work for both men and women without the kind of segregation that has dire consequences in terms of power, pay, and prestige. This is different from the state-centered solution of Hungary in the 1950s, because there the organization of paid work and the character of the labor force remained mostly unchanged, and only outside institutions attempted, unsuccessfully, to take over household work. In addition, these institutions were to modify women's, but not men's, work conditions and labor market experience. But as long as parents like to spend time with their children and families enjoy the intimacy of dinners together at home on a regular basis, institutionalized services alone will not guarantee an acceptable solution based on the principle of androgynous inclusion. For a real solution a deeper transformation of the organization of work (both paid and unpaid) is needed, and only a handful of countries have taken small experimental steps in this direction so far.

I have depicted above a conceptual framework to help explore the differences between policymaking targeting women's participation in the public sphere along two dimensions. That capitalist Austria and state socialist Hungary differed in terms of the degree to which women were engaged in paid work is well established in the literature. That women's participation extends to more prestigious positions within the labor force has been amply demonstrated in this book in previous chapters. Here I add a new dimension and argue that in the 1980s women's inclusion was different not only in its extent and mechanisms but also in its principles; women in Austria participated if they could adopt the male labor market norms and "act like men," while women in Hungary participated as "different from men"; that is, as members of a special social group, "women," which was targeted by gender-specific social policies.[5]

As I indicated above, this distinction most clearly characterizes the 1980s in the two countries. Let us, then, turn to an examination of the paths taken by these countries in establishing principles of policymaking and the path they have traveled since.

Historical Trajectories: Austria and Hungary, 1945–1995

Although the four different responses described above may serve as good intuitive approximations, such a schematic description is too simplistic to evaluate and particularly to compare the often-changing realities of state legislation in Hungary and Austria. In order to make a better comparison, we need to visualize historical trajectories. In the following sections I will depict both countries in three time periods—immediately after World War II, in the 1970s to 1980s, and in the 1990s—and the changes from one country to the other. Over the years in both countries substantial changes occurred that radically transformed the nature of their policymaking and, hence, gender regimes.

In addition, it is important to note that although I argue for a distinction between Hungary and Austria, at no moment could we find either society at the extremes of the similarity-difference, or even inclusion-exclusion, continuums. Rather, legislation in Austria and Hungary displayed a balanced mix of both principles, and thus my argument is merely about the presence of a *dominant* principle within a mixture of state policies. At no point should it be assumed that either principle was exclusive or that the contrast between the countries is sharper than it really is. Indeed, because of centuries of shared historical legacy in the two countries, as well as the common roots of the ideology of communism and liberalism in the philosophies of the Enlightenment, we should not be surprised to find commonalities between them. It is, however, not only possible but also useful to identify the dominating principle in each mix and to follow the changes in the trajectories of actual policymaking. This brings us closer to an understanding of the differences in women's relationship to the state and in women's position in the two societies.

Before I proceed, a word is in order on the selection criterion of the policies to be included. My aim was to collect and evaluate all state-level legislation directly or indirectly (but also not distantly) relevant to women's participation in paid work and in positions of authority in formal institutions in Austria and Hungary. I perused the text of each piece of legislation along with secondary material that discusses their relevance, and in several cases I used archival materials (from parliamentary discussions and from Politburo meetings) to reconstruct the debates that lead to their formulations. I focused primarily on maternity leave policies, labor protection laws, training programs, wage policies, quotas, and positive discrimination laws, although occasionally I considered policies in other areas as well. Obviously, no such list can ever be complete: all legislation in a country has at least indirectly some effect on gender relations. Here my efforts are directed mainly at identifying the laws and party decrees that had the greatest impact and were generally considered to be of the most importance. I list and briefly describe all the legislation I considered in appendix B, so the reader can evaluate the analysis below.

Austria and Hungary at the Greatest Distance

As many other Western capitalist countries during the fifteen years after World War II, Austria remained firmly committed to the separate spheres ideology: men's place was at work and women's place was in the house. The state made no effort to include women in the labor force; in fact, if anything, the opposite tendency was observable: a number of women who had participated in the immediate rebuilding of the country (*Trümmerfrauen*) were sent home in peace.[6] Women were not particularly welcome in other areas of the public, either. As a result of the vast number of casualties in World War II, women constituted the majority (64 percent) of the electorate, but only 9 female representatives (out of a total of 165, or

5.5 percent) were elected to the national Parliament (Rosenberger 1995). This percentage was, in fact, lower than the proportion of female representatives in Parliament in 1919, the first time women legally were allowed to be elected (Neyer 1997). Many women withdrew from the labor force after marriage and especially after having children, resulting in a visible decline in women's economic activity rates that lasted until 1970. In 1951, 35 percent of all Austrian women were engaged in paid work, while in 1970 only 31 percent were so engaged (Gross, Wiedenhofer, and Vötsch 1994).[7]

Almost none of the legal regulations of the era were directed at alleviating women's labor market difficulties and no state-level legal effort was made to encourage women's participation in paid work. In fact, the only gender-specific labor market regulation I found was intended to exclude women on the basis of "biological" difference: the international protective labor legislation (recommended by a Convention of the International Labor Organization [ILO]) was ratified in Austria in the early 1950s. This law prohibited women from performing night work in most industries and regulated their participation in a number of other occupations seen unfit for the "weaker sex." Another law enacted in 1947 reduced the retirement age for women from sixty-five to sixty, in order to "compensate," the lawmakers claimed, for hardships suffered during the war. Men's hardship apparently did not deserve the same consideration. The absence of gender-specific regulations is particularly conspicuous in the 1969 Labor Market Act, which was designed to regulate the flow and training of labor in Austria for the first time after the war, and which, nevertheless, had no specific provisions for women (Matkovits 1995).

In addition, women's representation was negligible in the Social Partnership, the coalition of employers, trade unions, and state representatives that after the war significantly influenced labor market policies in Austria. In this context, it is not surprising that the male-dominated trade unions upheld regulations that allowed differential pay scales for men and women for the same job. Thus women's crucial experience in this period was primarily that of exclusion: women were not welcome as workers, were openly discriminated against, and had very little political clout to fight against this process.

The first maternity leave policy was instituted in 1957 and extended in 1961: this was the first tangible effort on the part of the state to support married women's continued participation in the public sphere. The maternity leave policy was distinctly designed to aid women, hence it mostly reinforced the difference model: it was passed under the title Maternity Protection Law and was not available to fathers (*Status of Women in Austria* 1976). The new legislation had been preceded by ILO Convention no. 103 in 1952, which encouraged, in principle, the introduction of maternity policies. Thus after 1961 under Austrian law women could take an unpaid leave of up to a year after childbirth. Although this period did not count toward seniority or promotion, it was included in the calculations of retirement benefits, and later some financial assistance was also added. A number of women did return to work after their official leave period ended, but the lack of childcare facilities prevented many from doing so. Moreover, marriage and childbearing were more popular than ever in the postwar period: the age at first marriage dropped from 25.8 years (for the bride) in 1938 to 22.4 years in 1971 (*Demographic Yearbook of Austria* 1981), and a veritable baby boom started in the mid-1950s. The birthrate stood at around 14.5 births per 1,000 people in the population immediately after the war in 1945, but increased to 18.8 by 1963. The cohort of women born between 1921 and 1925 gave birth to 2.06 children on average, while those born between 1936 and 1940 who came to childbearing age during the late 1950s had an average of 2.33 children (*Frauenbericht* 1995).[8]

Such policies, assuming women's sole responsibilities for childcare, fit into the general framework of family laws in the 1950s and 1960s, which were built on the familiar male breadwinner model. In this period and up to 1975, Austrian legislation guaranteed women's dependent place in the home by conceptualizing marriage as a distinctly patriarchal institution. Specifically, the law allowed a husband to prevent his wife from pursuing a career of her own in case he was capable of supporting her. Women were legally bound to ask for permission from their husbands when they sought work outside the home. In addition, the law assigned different duties, responsibilities, and property rights to the two parties of a marriage. Fathers were solely responsible for all decisions made about the couple's children, and the children had to adopt his (and never her) family name and citizenship. A woman was legally bound to follow her husband in the event he moved, and she was obliged to take care of the household without laying claims to any property acquired during the union (Status of Women in Austria 1976). Elements of this principle remained intact even after 1975. For example, women were not allowed to keep their maiden names (unless they could persuade their husbands to adopt that name too) until the 1990s.

With the exception of the 1961 maternity policy, the list of relevant legislation in Austria reflects the "separate spheres" ideology and shows that women were, as a rule, not encouraged to participate in paid work. Exclusion rather than inclusion of any sort dominated Austrian labor market policies up to the 1970s.

Hungary, on the other hand, started the late 1940s in a different position. The communist party exerted efforts never seen before to include women into the labor force, using the wage system as well as centralized political pressure and propaganda to its ends. Following the ideas of Lenin and Engels (Engels 1985), the initial ideological assumption was that women should not be differentiated from men in the workforce in any way. The Constitution of 1949 proclaimed that women were entitled to the *same* work under the same working conditions as men and an earlier legislation guaranteed that women should be allowed to fill any job (Grád 1988). This is not to say that party ideologues were not convinced about the existence of physical and psychological differences between men and women, but they argued that these were simply due to the "traditional views" about women's role in society, and they expected the impending communist transformations to quickly eradicate these. Thus, women would soon join their male comrades in the mines, in the fields, and at the universities.

The intensity and the sheer number of state and party decrees in Hungary concerning women's inclusion in the labor force is especially striking compared to the situation in Austria described above. In Hungary, the major piece of legislation that should be mentioned here was passed in 1951 (Cabinet Decree 1011/1951), although a vast number of decrees and reports preceded it.[9] The 1951 legislation specifically ordered the increase of the proportion of women in the labor force, particularly in certain areas such as construction and the heavy industries. It also prescribed quotas for women in admission to vocational training programs. In contrast to Austria, no protective labor laws existed in Hungary (except for pregnant women) until the early 1960s. Quite the contrary, the women's organization of the communist party was assigned the task of recruiting more women into traditionally male occupations, such as driving tractors.[10]

In addition to labor market regulations directly targeting women, a number of more general policies also pushed women toward the labor force. The reformed wage system effectively abolished the "family wage," and after 1949 a single salary was rarely enough to support a family. Survivor benefits and widows' pensions were cut significantly; in essence, the state made it impossible for its able-bodied subjects to live on transfer income. Note that these laws came about only a few years after the end of World War II: thousands of women who had been homemakers before the war had lost their husbands and, following the cuts in widows' pensions, their daily bread. In addition, a vast campaign of job creation was launched and the recruitment process was often experienced as threatening, and sometimes even bordered on violence. And as if this weren't enough, police surveillance guaranteed that the law, which obligated everyone of working age to find paid work, was closely observed (Róna-Tas 1998). Social benefits, pensions, and medical insurance—earlier attainable through the entitlement of a spouse—were now primarily tied to personal labor force participation, thereby providing even further incentives for women to find jobs.

The mobilization of women for paid work turned out to be one of the most effective, long-term campaigns of the communist party. Although female labor force participation was on the decline in Austria and most of Western Europe, we can observe the opposite tendency in Eastern Europe. In Hungary, about 34 percent of working-age women were active wage earners in 1949, right before the communist takeover, and at the time this figure was comparable to that in Austria. Twenty years later the difference was striking: 64 percent of women between ages fifteen and fifty-five were engaged in paid work in Hungary, while practically no change had occurred in Austria (*Comparison of Socialist Indicators in Austria and Hungary* 1982).

Yet after all the initial enthusiasm of the campaign, by the mid-1950s, party leaders allowed themselves to be convinced that women were primarily qualified for work that was different from, and essentially inferior to, that of men. In 1956, for example, a report to the Politburo proposed special ways in which "women, the elderly and workers with reduced work capabilities can be mobilized for the labor force" (PIA 276/94/886). As reflected in this and in a number of other contemporaneous documents, policymakers continued to express a desire to recruit women for paid work, but they were now willing to settle for the practical solution of employing them in less prestigious white-collar occupations, which then allowed men who had filled those positions to be transferred to "more important" factory work.[11] The Politburo started to consider the problems of women's employment together with the employability of the other groups listed in the title of the report cited above. This position reflects the emergence of the idea that women's contribution to the building of the ideal communist society is usually of inferior quality.[12] A somewhat pointed exchange at a Politburo meeting illustrates the as-yet contested nature of this subtle modification in gender policies:

> In 1959, Politburo members were discussing the limits and possibilities of the employment of mothers, particularly in positions of authority. Comrade Kiss: "Of course, any woman could learn to work at the railways, but then we would need to double the number of positions there."
>
> Comrade Marosán interjects: "This is exactly the view that we have to transcend and fight against. Women seem to be able to do heavy physical labor night and day!"
>
> Comrade Kiss continues as if he hadn't heard the comment: ". . . We really tried hard to recruit women into the ranks of the police. But then the police chief showed up and said that they needed 700 women police officers instead of the 500 policemen and he asked us to increase the number of open positions. (PIA 288/5/140)

Nevertheless, at least after the early 1960s, while simultaneously acknowledging and emphasizing the difficulties involved in women's mobilization, party leaders attempted to assimilate women into at least some of the same jobs as men, and certainly with a similarly uninterrupted career pattern. For example, a proposal for reduced work hours for women was categorically rejected by the Politburo in 1951 (and later in 1969 also) (PIA 276/94/444). No maternity leave policies—aside from a fully paid twenty-week birthing leave that was in place before the war—were introduced until 1967. Instead, children were to be looked after in local nurseries, midday meals taken in the factory canteen, and dinner bought at a subsidized price fully or partially cooked in public facilities and eaten at home. Special maternity leave policies were thus not needed, except to secure a breastfeeding break for new mothers every four hours or so. In these periods mothers could go visit their children in the factory nursery and spend the allocated half hour feeding them.

Although this treatment of women assumed their original difference from men, it was seen as temporary and only a question of degree: officially women were encouraged to participate similarly as men.[13] They were expected to be Stahanovites (model workers) just like men, to strive to fulfill the plan, and they were praised in the daily papers and the central propaganda materials for exactly the same traits as were men:[14] hard work, loyalty to the party, modesty, sacrifice, and discipline.[15] The external traits of traditional "femininity" were also abolished. Women were chastised for indulging in vanity and "petit bourgeois" tastes in beauty: makeup was scorned (not to mention unavailable), nail polish seriously frowned on, and cleanliness and efficiency were supposed to have replaced capitalist consumerism. The new family laws in 1952—preceding the revision of the Austrian family law by almost two-and-a-half decades—supported the independence of women. Its proclaimed intention was to guarantee full legal equality for the partners in the marriage, allowing women to keep their birth names and dividing property, responsibilities, and obligations equally.[16]

In sum, there was a stark difference between the legislative practices of the two countries after World War II. The 1950s were characterized by the exclusion of women from the labor force in Austria, and in Hungary by their hasty and intensified inclusion. This inclusion was attempted on the basis of the similarity principle to the extent that it intended to assimilate women to the male norm, with the state committing resources, if in insufficient quantities, for this purpose.

The Development of the Politics of Difference

By the end of the 1960s the separate spheres ideology started to crumble in Austria. There were three important factors that influenced this change: the emergence of a stronger feminist movement within the context of a Social Democratic Party government, the need for more workers in the economy, and the influence of international organizations on policymaking.

Regarding the first factor, Sieglinde Rosenberger (1997, 2) argues that the independent (i.e., nonpartisan) feminist movement, which emerged in Austria in the early 1970s, was primarily concerned with fighting for issues not directly related to the labor market: for example, the legalization of abortion or legislation concerning domestic violence and marital rape. Yet, there were other significant political forces that contributed to a modification of social policies targeting women's participation in paid work. In 1966, the Grand Coalition of the Social Democratic Party[17] and the conservative Austrian People's Party ended, and after 1970, Social Democrats could exert more political influence on decisionmaking. The women's organization within the Social Democratic Party, female members of the government during the Social Democratic majority, and women's groups within the trade unions started lobbying for change in labor market policies (Rosenberger 1997).

The second, perhaps more important, factor had to do with changes in the economy. Austria experienced an unprecedented postwar economic boom, a development that required, by the 1970s, an expansion of the labor force. It is in this period when guest workers from Turkey and Yugoslavia were first invited to Austria, and women also came to be defined as part of a potential labor pool. As the labor shortage intensified, lawmakers seemed more and more willing to abandon their ideas about the traditional family and encourage wives and mothers to seek work outside their homes.

The third factor was the influence of international organizations on policymaking. For example, the ILO and the European Council (EC) noted from time to time Austria's relative backwardness compared to other European countries.[18] In some instances these organizations directly urged Austrian institutions to conduct research into the situation of women (Kreisky and Sauer 1997), but in most cases their influence was less immediate and more likely to come in the form of modest proposals. Their importance, however, is demonstrated by the fact that legislators themselves sometimes referred to the recommendations of these international agencies in their arguments for (or against) adopting certain measures in Austria. Several examples for this can be found in the parliamentary debate of the 1979 Equal Treatment Law. One representative, for instance, argued at the very beginning of the debate:

> There are international conventions that demand equal treatment. [Austria had ratified the ILO Convention 100 and the European Social Charter.] These contain control mechanisms by independent experts who examine how far these regulations have been carried out by individual national governments. Austria has received several sanctions because we violated the equal pay for equal work decree. How does this examination take place? They send out documents in several languages to the 150-plus members of the European Parliament but also to the members states. . . . So the criticism Austria received is widespread and has serious consequences. (*Nationalrat* XIV, Feb. 23, 1979).

Thus proposals from international agencies could be utilized to rally support behind certain legislative proposals in the 1970s and 1980s. Only by the 1990s, however, did the growing unifying presence of the European Union make it really difficult for Austria to stray far from the commonly accepted norm on the continent (Buchmayr, Ivancevic, and Wagner 1992; Rowhani 1989; Gutknecht 1993).

Throughout the 1970s Austrian legislation promoted women's inclusion in the public sphere with significantly more intensity than was done earlier. The 1961 maternity leave policy was the first indication of this effort, which was followed by further legislation securing some funding for childcare and kindergarten facilities in 1969 (Rosenberger 1995).

But most other legislative attempts at women's inclusion in Austria in the 1970s were characterized by a new principle—similarity—which provided no special help for women. Rather, the aim of the legislation was to revoke women's status as wards of their husbands and grant "individual" social citizenship to those who qualified, encouraging women to fend for themselves inside and outside the labor market. Not least due to the influence of international agencies such as the United Nations, which dedicated the decade of 1975–1985 to women, as well as the growing presence of a domestic feminist movement and the Socialist Party in power, Austria passed legislation in 1975 that released women from some of their oppressive family obligations and established the principle of "partnership" in marriage. A reform in 1974 of the taxation system, which had allowed individual taxation in marriage, removed the financial disincentives from married women's paid work. Property rights in marriage were modified in 1975, first trimester abortion legalized in 1974, and coeducation was enforced in all schools in 1965, including those exclusive, all-male institutions that provided the surest routes to university degrees. A new divorce law in 1978 allowed the "no-fault" separation of married partners but deprived women of the guarantee of alimony payments. These laws were novel in spirit and significant in impact, and researchers argue that they indicate the dawn of a new era in Austrian policymaking (Buchmayr, Ivancevic, and Wagner 1992).

The most significant piece of legislation, the Equal Treatment Package, which prohibited discrimination on the basis of gender and questioned the long-standing practice of differential pay schemes for men and women in private sphere jobs, was passed in 1979. The discussion in Parliament about the legislation was relatively short but clearly reflected the specificity of the Austrian labor market where collective bargaining dominates and where, consequently state legislators are reluctant to directly interfere in the workings of the economy on behalf of women, even if they admit to seeing signs of discrimination. As the Minister of Social Affairs argued: "The government does not want to exert any influence on the content of the labor contracts, as these are the result of collective bargaining and these are conducted autonomously. Neither side would be happy if Parliament tried to insert itself into the wage politics of the private sector" (*Nationalrat* xiv, Feb. 23, 1979).

The Hungarian government, of course, had no such concerns. But Austrian policymakers had another good reason not to interfere: any regulation that favored women and had costs attached might have resulted in women's further exclusion from a market that was geared almost exclusively toward men's work experience. As another representative warned by quoting a press release: "This regulation will not increase the willingness of employers to hire women" (*Nationalrat* xiv, Feb. 23, 1979). Even if legislators had wanted to, the introduction of the difference principle, special aid for women, would have had serious obstacles in a profit-conscious private economy. Thus centralized intervention, along the lines of what Hungarian redistributors could effect, was unimaginable in Austria.

Even when intervention did happen, it was meant to help women assimilate to the male norm, rather than allowing the difference principle to work. As a socialist representative urged her fellow legislators during the debate of the Equal Treatment Package in 1979: "Training will be what makes a law effective and possible. It is our common endeavor to steer girls in the male directions, toward jobs that are difficult to enter, and here we have to do more" (*Nationalrat* xiv, Feb. 23, 1979). In other words, legislators aimed at helping women assimilate as men, rather than devise and implement androgynous norms inside and outside the labor force.

In addition, the 1979 law also opened the door for legal battles, in which the Constitutional Court enforced the practice of "equal handling." In some cases, the 1979 Equal Treatment Package guaranteed new rights for men rather than women; for example, by declaring that widowers should receive a pension similar to what widows were getting, which had not been the practice earlier. This is a clear example of upholding formal equality or similarity without regard to the differential circumstances of men and women.

In contrast to Hungary, which introduced these laws in the late 1960s, protective labor legislation was abolished in 1976 in Austria: women were free thereafter to work in any occupation.[19] Other legislation in 1985 prohibited gender-specific job advertising and discrimination against women in job training programs.

The mix of policies passed in the 1970s and 1980s was dominated by the similarity principle, but seeds of the "inclusion through difference" concept were also sown. For example, unlike in the 1960s, in this period a large number of committees were formed (starting with the Equal Treatment Commission in 1979), and seminars and symposiums were arranged and studies ordered to uncover the practice of discrimination and to formulate new solutions to women's labor market difficulties. At this point, much of this discussion and research remained on the academic level or was restricted to feminist political circles and did not reach the political scene. Still, the fact that socialist legislators could claim that the 1979 Equal Treatment Package was "demanded and formulated by women" indicates that women's "difference" was becoming increasingly problematized in this country too.

In sum, the 1970s saw important changes in the gender policies of Austria: women's inclusion in the public sphere intensified, its conditions changed, and now it was based on the idea of women's assimilation as men, rather than an acknowledgment of their difference. In addition, the similarity principle, although comparable in many ways to the Hungarian policies of the 1950s, was different in one significant respect: it did not provide much help for women's assimilation to the male norm. Rather, it merely made it possible for women to play the labor market game by its mostly male-biased rules. The few women who were able to choose greater equality could now do so more than ever before.

In the meantime, Hungarian legislation headed in the opposite direction. Party leadership still utilized a number of different methods to gain control over the female half of the population by drawing them into paid labor, but by the 1960s they gave up trying to do this on the same terms as men. The new goal was to address women's limited inclusion in the public sphere and women's participation as women not as soon-to-be-perfect men. The change is evident in the following quote from a Politburo meeting in 1959, where György Marosán, a powerful member of this highest national-level party organ and usually a veritable communist champion of women's rights, acknowledges that earlier gender policies were perhaps too radical and were in need of modification: "All right, certain jobs may be unfit for women: we shouldn't send them down to the mines again, or to the bakery where the ovens are too hot, but there are positions where they could do an excellent job" (PIA 288/5/140). Other members also admit to the mistakes committed in earlier times: "I remember the times when we became world famous because we sent women into the mines and to drive the tractors. Then this approach was proven wrong" (PIA 288/5/140).

What brought about this change in policies? Johanna Goven argues that the emergence of the Western feminist movement in the early 1970s provided impetus for change in the gender policies of the Soviet Union and consequently that of Eastern Europe as well (Goven 1993a). Although I found no trace of this in the records of Politburo discussions, obviously not every discussion was documented. Nevertheless, lacking evidence to the contrary, I will describe this change as a domestic rather than an externally instigated affair precipitated by internal political and economic pressures.

One of the factors that certainly influenced the modification of labor market policies was a decrease in the demand for labor brought about by a slowing of industrial production. Already in the early 1960s we find documents that express party leaders' concerns about an oversupply of labor, especially female, unskilled labor.[20] In the 1950s the party's key labor force strategy was to channel women into clerical jobs vacated by men who moved into more prestigious, better-paid white-collar positions in the industrial sector. By the 1960s, the material, legal, and ideological obligation to work was still pushing women into the labor force, but it was becoming increasingly hard to find work for them as new five-year plans were making cuts in the speed of extensive industrialization.

In addition, the implementation of the party decrees about building more nursery schools and providing other social services such as factory meals, laundry facilities, and so forth was so slow that it led to difficulties in women's employment and thus massive political pressure against the regime. According to eye witnesses, one of the demands of the 1956 revolution was to allow women to return to their traditional roles. "No more power to uneducated peasant women!"[21] a 1956 slogan proclaimed. This seemed like a demand that was relatively easy to satisfy, particularly because another concern emerged as a consequence of the liberalization of the strict abortion law of 1953: that of the declining birth rate in the country (see Goven 1993b for more on this issue). In what turned out to be an unsuccessful effort to ease political tensions, party leaders lifted the ban on abortion imposed three years earlier by the infamous "Ratkó laws," a measure that had at least temporarily stopped the decline in birth rate. Its repeal in 1956 left party executives with no direct means to control women's fertility and thus gave them the uncomfortable vision of a shrinking population and a potential decrease in the number of young soldiers ready to fight for the communist cause. The Hungarian Politburo did not dare reintroduce abortion restrictions even though they talked about it at several meetings after 1962. Instead, a different idea was raised—with much-warranted tact:

> "It is important and also relevant here," argues Zoltán Komócsin, a Politburo member during a discussion of the declining birth rate, "that we should reinvent—of course in a subtle and realistic way—*the cult of mothers and children* in a way that would not be against our socialist principles. Naturally, given the social, political, and moral importance of the issue, we must remain within the boundaries of good taste and humanitarianism. We obviously don't want to see the posters from the Ratkó era return." (PIA 288/5/401; emphasis mine)

Emphasizing the role and duties of women as mothers and slowly building a mother cult was seen as a politically less dangerous solution to the problem of the decline in childbearing. In order to do this, however, the principle of women's integration into the public sphere had to be modified.

What exactly changed in the policymaking of the early 1960s? Certainly not assumptions about women's socially conditioned difference from men, nor even the intention of the party to keep women in the labor force. But the spectacular recruitment campaigns stopped. As a decree in the 1970s already proclaimed: "Our goal is not to *increase* women's labor force participation anymore, but rather to *improve* work (and social) conditions for those who do work" (PIA 288/21/1970/51). Yet, women were still joining the labor force in record numbers because the wage and social benefit regulations, not to mention the obligatory labor force participation laws, were still in full force. However, from the mid-1960s on, women were consciously and openly directed away from prestigious, highly paid jobs in industrial production to undervalued ones in the service sector; the principle of inclusion came to be openly controlled and characterized by segregation rather than integration.[22] As another, earlier document summarized: "The primary way of securing jobs for women is by building production facilities in the light industries and service centers as well as considering the possibility of four-hour shifts due to women's specific family circumstances" (PIA 288/21/1962/13).

Women were no longer welcome as tractor drivers or coal miners or in a whole range of other occupations (Goven 1993b). Strict protective labor legislation was introduced in 1962 and 1965 that prohibited the employment of women in a large number of highly paid blue-collar positions because the work was considered dangerous or too challenging physically. In 1967, the first comprehensive maternity leave policies were passed that allowed mothers (but not fathers) to take three years off work to look after young children. The job of the temporarily (up to three years) absent working mother was protected and a maternity allowance was paid also. In contrast to the official classification method of the ILO and of countries in Western Europe, in Hungary women were officially classified among the "economically active" population while on maternity leave. This was in part a statistical gimmick to boost female labor force participation rates without actually having to provide work for women, but it was also a symbolic gesture indicating that the leave was temporary. Indeed, women rarely dropped out of the labor force for good, but usually returned and resumed their old jobs after a few years.

In many ways, these maternity policies were quite similar to those in effect in Austria.[23] In Austria, too, maternity leave regulations were renegotiated in the mid-1970s after the legalization of abortion and the new laws provided working women with a paid leave, funded by a state fund established for this purpose and by the unemployment insurance fund. In both countries most women received a set sum (although single mothers were eligible for more money in Austria until the 1980s, and women working in agriculture in Hungary were eligible for a little less). In both countries, eligibility was tied to work status—a reminder of shared prewar traditions. Yet, there were important differences as well. Many more women took maternity leave in Hungary than in Austria, and in the state socialist country women's reentry into the workforce seemed smoother than in Austria where the proliferation of reentry programs in the late 1980s indicate the difficulty women encountered. Nevertheless, the legislation described above demonstrates that, at least with respect to pregnancy and maternity, women in both Austria and Hungary received "differentially situated status" in the postwar period.

In the peak state socialist period, however, this differential treatment principle extended to a number of other areas in Hungary as well. In 1970, the communist party ordered a thorough review of the woman question in Hungary and passed its last major decree on the topic. Although earlier, following the ideas of Engels and Lenin, women's interests were seen as synonymous with that of the (male) working class, the document "Position of Women in Hungarian Society" acknowledges women's gender-specific interests: "The theoretical basis of our 'gender politics' has only recently been established. Now we acknowledge the particularity of the situation of women and attempt to coordinate the interests of the whole society with these specific interests. While women's individual interests are, of course, primarily determined by their social class status and their occupational group, they also have other interests, which is the consequence of their specific situation" (PIA 288/5/511). This is an important statement: it is the first theoretical-ideological reformulation of the principle of women's participation in a communist society. In the 1950s women were seen as essentially "similar" to men because their only relevant social characteristic was their class position. To reflect this, even the women's organization had the same structure and tasks as that of the communist party. Now all this had to change.[24] Women were now clearly treated as a separate group with distinct roles and interests.

To explain the differences observed in men and women's desires and ambition, party leaders had earlier argued that their class-based similarity might temporarily be hidden behind "traditional attitudes" and "petit bourgeois conservatism." By the 1970s gender differences and the relevance of gender for the determination of an individual's social position were publicly acknowledged and seen as unlikely to change. Although a few paragraphs in the report suggest that the ultimate goal of women's politics is "to allow women to catch up and . . . participate in a dual-gendered economy" (PIA 288/5/511), the rest of the report is spent enumerating women's specific needs and the various measures that would be required to satisfy these.

The 1972 modification of the Constitution summarizes the by then prevailing new gender politics: the most important law of the land now promised women a right to *acceptable* work conditions rather than the same as those for men, which had been the text of the Constitution of 1949 (see Goven 1993b).

After this decade, the Politburo's interests largely turned away from gender politics. During the decade of 1970 volumes of reports had been written to evaluate the decree of 1970, but aside from the ratification of the 1979 New York Convention on gender discrimination as well as an official evaluation of the effectiveness of the 1970 legislation in 1979, Hungarian legislators stopped discussing the woman question altogether. An agreement that was acceptable for both the population and party leaders was finally reached. Thus, for lack of an economic incentive and in the name of political expediency, state socialist party leaders modified their old gender ideology and instituted the practice of inclusion through difference. Although the measures they passed encouraged women to balance work and family, their success was necessarily limited.

Postcommunism, Postindustrialism:
Austria and Hungary in the 1990s

Austria's move toward the "equal treatment principle" was tenuous, however. In the mid-1980s the political wind shifted slightly and new measures were passed that pointed toward a return to a revised difference principle. A newly emerging second wave of nonpartisan feminists, as well as women in the Social Democratic Party and in the trade unions, directed their attention to working women's issues. In accordance with the "equality principle" in use since the late 1970s, women's representatives ("contact persons") have guarded formal gender equality in the labor bureaus of each one of Austria's provinces (Rosenberger 1995). By the mid-1980s, the information gathered there along with the newly appointed women's representatives in the government dominated by the Social Democratic Party (between 1979–1983)[25] helped define women as a "problem" group and allowed feminists and women's representatives for the first time to lobby for special measures to alleviate women's labor market disadvantages. As a result, in 1985 the new Equal Treatment Package contained a number of gender-specific labor market policies, such as special training programs, informational campaigns, and job counseling for women only.

Although the ascension of the conservative Austrian People's Party to power in 1987 resulted in cuts in some of these programs, other regulations also indicate that new elements of the difference principle were slowly sneaking into Austrian policymaking. For example, in 1990, the Social Democratic Party introduced the first gender quotas in their party lists, a choice initiated, according to Rosenberger (1995), by the realization of women's increased political and electoral participation. In the same year, the national government reestablished the State Department for Women (1990) and the legislature upheld the prohibition of night work and initiated programs to promote women's specific needs in education and skills training (Kreisky and Sauer 1997). These skills training programs, proposed first by the new labor market policies in 1986, were designed solely for women, although as before they were intended to direct them toward nontraditional female trades.

Nevertheless, the similarity principle in the treatment of women on the labor market did not disappear: women's participation was still partly based on their assimilation to the male norm. In fact, the centerpiece of the Equal Treatment Package of 1992, one of the most important legislative decisions of the post-1990 period, was the equalization of the retirement age for men and women, following a 1990 ruling of the Austrian Constitutional Court, which, in the name of equality, and of course similarity, pronounced the differential pension age as violating equal treatment principles.[26]

During the parliamentary debate of the package, several legislators argued for the practice of treating women as similar to men, demonstrating the persistence of the idea of formal equality on the Austrian political scene. A good example for this came from a conservative legislator, who after someone suggested that women's representatives should be elected in companies where there was a minority of women workers, immediately retorted that in that case in companies with a minority of male workers, men's reps should also be nominated. In addition, several legislators complained about the difficulty women often face because their gender-specific responsibilities were ignored by employers. For example, representatives noted that employers would be reluctant to hire women if their work hours were reduced during pregnancy and that women would have difficulty reentering their jobs after a lengthier maternity leave. As a woman who played an important part in the formulation of the final legislation noted: "I have to say this, because I was the head of a company myself. I understand the fears of the economic sector, I myself have misgivings about [doubling the length of maternity leave]" (*Nationalrat* XVIII, Dec. 1, 1992). Several legislators cited examples of employers' disregard for women's household responsibilities and, even worse, the disadvantages and discrimination women suffer when they do care: "At job interviews the question is still asked of women, 'How do you handle your kids and marriage?' and if she doesn't respond properly that will certainly have dire consequences" (ibid.). And conservative legislators reacted strongly against the proposition that men should be obliged to partake in the reproductive tasks within the household: "Matters concerning the families are not the business of the federal government. This has to be taken care of within the family. Or is it your wish, ladies and gentlemen, that the government should dictate how many plates a man has to wash every day?" (ibid.).[27]

This proposal about a legislated obligation for sharing household responsibilities was met with furious objection from several sides and did not pass. But simply the fact that it was raised and that it received some support indicates a new era in policymaking. As does the accusation that women receive more than their fair share of the pie, as the following quote demonstrates: "People think women achieved enough, that women have been treated more than equally. That they have been preferred. It's not hard to guess which gender this group this belong to. . . . All those who think women are receiving equal treatment already, I want to invite you to look at the Social Report [an annual publication describing the status of women in Austria] just published" (*Nationalrat* XVIII, Dec. 1, 1992).

Obviously, the idea that women were receiving preferential treatment had been raised, and this by itself is an indication that steps had been taken in the "difference" direction in policymaking. Indeed, the 1992 legislation also contains many such measures. Among the important changes were an extension in maternity leave, the right of mothers to engage in part-time work until their children reached four years in age, a codification of paid leave for mothers in case their children were sick, the initiation of training programs in which women on maternity leave could participate, and the inclusion of childraising periods in the calculation of pension benefits. In 1993, the first positive discrimination policies were introduced in hiring for public sector jobs. All these measures were meant to enable women to take part in the labor force but to do so in gender-specific ways, assuming their unique responsibilities in raising children and managing the household.[28] Only a few of the legislators, mostly from the Green Party, went further, suggesting somewhat more androgynous measures such as public money spent on day care arrangements and on retirement homes, or a codification of men's household responsibilities.

Not only the content but also the style of the debate pointed toward a change in the character of policymaking, or at least a change in who and through what processes the legislation came about. The 1992 Equal Treatment Package was the result of several months-long discussions and negotiations among a group of mostly female legislators of three of the four major parties. Already in 1979, legislators claimed that the law had been formulated by women, but this was clearly more true for 1992. And not only was this legislation written by women, the fact that women and men may have had different interests in these matters was raised very clearly here. A few examples follow from arguments put forth by legislators in the debate:

> There is a difference between women speakers who were present during the creation of this package and who reported factual analysis, and the male speakers yesterday, who seem to misunderstand reality completely.

> Men's brains can introduce legal proposals that are so absurd that women simply cannot fathom them and, with the best of intentions, cannot be called advantageous for women.

> The FPÖ [Austrian Freedom Party] is not an advocate of the everyday woman, maybe that of the everyday man but not that of women.

> We [women] have reached 20 percent representation in this house, but there are very few women . . . who are [for example] advisors to the social partners. There are committees where there are no women at all. We cannot tolerate this any longer: men's committee's come together as some sort of a secret society, and there's no written record of their meetings either. . . . Women need to be represented proportionately to their numbers in society. (*Nationalrat* XVIII, Nov. 30, 1992).

Opinions here often followed party lines: Green Party members were most likely to support the difference principle and even the move toward androgynous solutions. The Social Democratic Party was the main sponsor of the legislation, and even women from the more conservative Austrian People's Party joined the coalition of women. But both men and women from the right-wing, nationalist Austrian Freedom Party strongly resisted most of the proposed measures. As one FPÖ legislator warned when discussing the part in the regulation on obligating men to share household chores: "This is the high point of this legislation: the government wants to meddle with the private sphere of the family. It attempts to undermine the family, which is the basic unit of the Austrian state. This government will force collective happiness on these families from the outside, but hopefully they won't succeed. *They didn't have success east of Austria either"* (emphasis mine).[29] (*Nationalrat* xviii, Dec. 1, 1992).

Indeed, east of Austria—the negative reference point for the Austrian Parliament—Hungarians were busy dismantling the institutions designed to elicit "collective happiness" and replace them with those meant to produce individual-level satisfaction, at least for the more fortunate. It is at this time that we can observe a convergence in the principles, albeit not necessarily in the practice or consequences, of state policies in Austria and Hungary. In the mid-1980s the Hungarian government slowly started to change its tune about gender. In part because of a persistent fear of labor surplus and unemployment, but also because of a more relaxed political atmosphere, governmental efforts to push women into the labor force grew distinctly less intense. In fact, by the late 1980s party committees started secretly to explore the question of sending women back to their homes (*Nőszövetségi dokumentumok* 1988). As mentioned earlier, increasingly less time was spent discussing the woman question in the Politburo and in the Central Committee, while, as we saw above, in the Austrian Parliament this problem received increasing attention: in the first part of the 1990s a new law on the situation of women was passed almost every year. After the fall of the communist regime, the Women's Council was disintegrated and it could not claim to represent Hungarian women any more. Following the Beijing World Congress, the socialist-led government established a Department of Women's Affairs, which, although short lived, started to play a leadership role in the representation of working women. The next, conservative government in 1998 significantly cut back on the department's privileges and resources and moved it under the Ministry of Social and Family Affairs in accordance with the new and much-publicized family ideal of a wage-earning husband and a stay-at-home mother. A central, government-backed forum for the representation of working women as a separate, "corporate" group again disappeared from the political scene.

In 1992, in another move toward the similarity principle and in accordance with the demands of the World Bank and other international financial and political institutions, the pension age for men and women was equalized in Hungary. But perhaps more important is the series of modifications in maternity policies. First, in 1985 differentiated maternity payments were introduced. Women were no longer seen as a homogeneous group, and only one particular category, that of educated, middle-class, Hungarian (as opposed to Roma)[30] women, were emphatically encouraged to have more children by the new incentives. Later, maternity leave policies were modified to grant fathers the right to stay at home with their children, should they so desire. This regulation was an indication of the relaxation of the inclusion through difference principle, even though in reality very few fathers took the leave and thus actual practice was not changed much.

But after the collapse of the state socialist political regime the move toward similarity accelerated. In 1995, maternity leave claims as universal rights were abolished, and a possible three-year leave with a very low maternity allowance was guaranteed only on the condition of financial need (Haney 1997). This meant that young women in high-level, high-paying careers could only start families by dropping out of the labor force and giving up their jobs. Women could best participate in paid work if they adopted the male career pattern and eschewed reproduction. This change in policy was the result of an increasingly conservative political-ideological environment reacting against communist gender policies. In 1998 maternity leave policies were modified again: this time in accordance with the type of family characterized by a wage-earner father, stay-at-home mother, and three children, which the new government had pronounced as ideal. Maternity leave became a universal right again and even women who were unemployed and had not worked before could take it. But in accordance with the similarity principle, women's jobs were only guaranteed for the briefest period of time (thirty days) after they returned from leave, and no training or other work-friendly measures were introduced to help them stay active in the labor force. In fact, this maternity leave represents an altogether new direction that indicates that Hungarian policymaking had come a full circle in a move toward the separate spheres ideology and women's exclusion from the public sphere through an emphasis on their differential role in childbearing and social reproduction.

Thus, while Austria started making allowances for women's difference in the labor market, Hungarians, especially in the late 1990s, were trying to revoke at least some of these measures. To some extent this move was merely a reflection of the historical trajectories of the two countries, which started out from very different legislative positions in the early 1990s, as well as the populations' perceived expectations about women's role in society. But the contradictory role of international financial institutions in influencing legislation must also be acknowledged. By the 1990s organizations such as the World Bank and the International Monetary Fund (IMF) could exert significant influence on policymaking in Hungary.[31] Specifically, the abolishment of maternity leave as a universal right was part of the austerity package explicitly required by the IMF in exchange for its continued financial goodwill.[32] But the encouragement to enforce strict austerity measures also helped cut back services that would have specifically encouraged women's labor force participation. The equalization of the retirement age, as mentioned before, was also sponsored by international financial giants. All in all, these organizations, willingly or not, seemed to be pushing Hungary toward the application of the similarity principal, thereby in some cases restricting women's privileges on the labor market.

In Austria, also, the role of international organizations was significant, although here the influence of the European Union (EU) and the ILO must be mentioned, rather than the IMF or the World Bank. In addition, the international pressure, while never uniform as the example of the pension age attests, seemed to have had the opposite effect. Austrian legislators were obviously considering their prospective EU membership when making decisions about gender policies:[33] "How does this concept [of postponing the actual equalization of pension age until well into the twenty-first century] fit in with our plans to join the EU? You know perfectly well that for the majority of EU countries the equal pension age has been realized. You know that the EU will make in the very near future the equal pension age obligatory. Then what? What happens when Austria joins the EU? And if because of the obligatory EU guidelines we'll have to violate this package—what will we tell Austrian women?" (*Nationalrat* XVIII, Dec. 1, 1992).

Aside from the retirement age and the ban on protective labor legislation for women,[34] however, social policy requirements in the EU include training for women, maternity regulations, and job reentry programs, mostly along the lines of the difference principle. But the limitations of EU pressures are also evident because a country could always ask for an "exception." As a legislator who belongs to the Green Party in Austria argued:

> I know about this discussion from committee sessions: these regulations [about postponing the equalization of retirement age] may be unsatisfactory . . . when [Austria becomes a member of EU]. When-

ever a progress emerges out of EU integration, a progress in social or labor laws, when we are under pressure, someone from the employers' side always pushes for a special break for Austria and we'll ask for an exception. This means that Austria will not have the role in the EU that we always talked about; that is, the role of a socially progressive country, a doer that will put pressure on the European community to develop further. (*Nationalrat* XVIII, Dec. 1, 1992).

In sum, in 1979 and especially in the 1990s, Austrian policymaking was clearly influenced by international pressures. These pressures came from political organizations, most importantly the EU and its related institutions. The direct effect of these organizations was limited and their policies clearly were filtered through the local political mechanisms— with some elements being used as Austrian legislators saw fit and others quietly discarded. But the organizations certainly provided ammunition for progressive women's groups in Austria, and as a result policymaking was increasingly oriented toward adding more measures that would help cater to women's differentially situated status on the labor market.

At the same time, Hungarian policymaking was under an altogether different sort of international pressure. Large financial institutions were pushing for austerity measures and a cutback on special provisions and nonmarket transfers. These measures were particularly important in the first part of the 1990s when economists saw Hungarian economic survival hinging on the loans and financial packages provided by the IMF and the World Bank. This way, and coupled with the power of conservative governments and a weak feminist movement, post-1989 policies in Hungary were making radical strides in the direction of inhibiting, rather than enabling, women's participation in an otherwise very tight labor market.

In sum, the gender regimes in Hungary and Austria can be characterized as different and ever-changing mixtures of the difference or the similarity principle of legislating women's status on the labor market. I have pointed to a convergence in the principles of state policies by the mid-1990s in the two countries: as Austria started to adopt issues such as positive discrimination, Hungarian governments were engaged in revoking the very institutions geared toward this goal.

However, the key contrast I introduce in this chapter is that between the limited inclusion through difference policies of Hungary in the late 1960s to mid-1980s and the inclusion through similarity (latent exclusion) ethos of Austrian policymaking in the 1970s and early 1980s. The Austrian policies will be quite familiar to North American readers, because most labor market policies (with the noted and much-debated exception of affirmative action programs) in the United States similarly attempt to assume women's equally situated status in the name of formal gender equity. Regulations prohibit discrimination on the basis of pregnancy and achieve this by classifying it in the same category as any other long-term disability that could, in theory, affect anybody. Austrian labor market policies differed from this only by degree: In Austria, women were also considered similarly situated to men in all respects except for pregnancy. For that contingency, specific measures were put into effect that acknowledged women's biological difference from men. But other than pregnancy and motherhood, no other differences were acknowledged between the genders that would have shaped their labor market opportunities. This resulted in laws establishing formal equality, but it also led to women's latent exclusion from prestigious positions in the labor market. Ignoring women's burdens in the household obviously did not reduce them, and thus women found it difficult to compete on a playing field that supposedly was equal to that of men, yet in reality was one of vast inequalities.

Hungarian legislators, on the other hand, happily acknowledged women's difference not only in terms of pregnancy and maternity but also with respect to their responsibilities in the household. In other words, they went one step further than legislators in Austria and allowed for women's differentially situated status not only with regard to biologically constructed difference but also socially. A number of legal regulations provided special help in allowing women to combine paid and unpaid work. Although these policies indeed drew more women into the workforce, the segregation of many into lower-prestige and lower-paying jobs seemed unavoidable.

Because these two principles are being combined in modern-day labor market policies in many Western societies, it is important to understand their operation and consequences. Perhaps the novelty of the Hungarian principle of inclusion through difference deserves special attention because in the 1990s a number of capitalist societies started to adopt elements of this principle. Of course the contexts and histories of women's inclusion differs, but some of the negative consequences may not be possible to avoid. A thorough examination of the difference and similarity principles in the otherwise quite similar countries of Austria and Hungary shows that without eliminating the male bias embedded in the institutions of work and household, neither inclusion through similarity nor inclusion through difference produces a reasonable semblance of gender equality in the labor market.

7. Difference at Work: A Case Study of Hungary

In this chapter I want to focus on a period in state socialist Hungary that I call the exercise of the difference principle. An examination of various documents from the archives of the Hungarian Socialist Workers' Party will help demonstrate how the party-state instituted and carried out this specific form of women's limited inclusion in paid work and politics. This period served as a unique and therefore interesting experiment in history. Its uniqueness is not because elements of this kind of practice had not existed earlier, they had and in fact do in a number of societies, but rather because such purposeful and centrally sanctioned application of the difference principle in the service of women's inclusion had never been tried anywhere else before or since. In a number of ways, the state socialist regime experimented with an old feminist dream: women's participation in the world of work and politics on women's own terms, taking their specific (biological or socially constructed) differences into account. But as is the case with so many other issues in state socialist history, this novel practice did not reduce but rather transformed social inequalities: it simply changed the process through which male domination and privileges in the labor force were reproduced.

In this chapter I trace the ideological underpinnings of the inclusion through difference principle as it was constructed in the discourse of the Hungarian Politburo. I show the process through which members of this most powerful party committee, the Politburo, in its transcribed discussions and writings on the woman question, constructed women as a separate, corporate social group, with special characteristics and tasks that were clearly inferior to that of men. This should demonstrate how the difference principle enabled women's participation in the public sphere and it will also reveal the limitations to such participation.

Women as a Social Group

The decrees and the practice of the communist party—the rhetoric of its leaders and the propaganda presented to the public—systematically described women as a well-defined, relatively homogeneous social group whose members had unique skills, tasks, abilities, problems, and opportunities. This was no innocent realization of biological differences but rather a highly strategic political act. Women were constructed as a "corporate group"[1] singled out as an identifiable building block of communism. This meant that women's specific, ascribed abilities were acknowledged, but unlike in Western liberal ideology such acknowledgment led not to women's exclusion from the public but rather to their inclusion, if on a selective and limited basis. Women were made to be active participants of the public sphere, but not on the same terms as men: they entered by the dubious virtue, and with the unavoidable consequences, of being a woman.

Party leaders employed a vast array of tools in the construction of women's separateness and social group status. Of these, quotas, various forms of positive discrimination policies, statistics, and a unified political representation were perhaps the most important (positive discrimination, tokenism, and quotas are discussed in detail in chapter 4). Some of these quotas certainly had some positive effect on the inclusion of women into authority, yet occasionally even members of the Politburo questioned whether party leaders were genuinely interested in this goal. As György Marosán described the practice of the selection of female parliamentary representatives before 1956: "We were only interested in having the right number of women in folk costumes in Parliament" (PIA 288/5/24).

In this context when the political will to promote women seemed relatively weak, local resistance easily sabotaged the expressed party goals. Politburo members sometimes complained openly about this, as illustrated in the following comments:

> Executives promote women not out of their internalized conviction, but only because this is the policy of the party." (PIA 288/21/1959/7)

> There are situations when husbands—who are otherwise good representatives of the party's gender politics in their workplace—consciously hinder the promotion and career building of their wives. The

reason for this is either their traditional attitudes or to secure their own personal comfort. In recent years a number of women could not be appointed because their husbands obstructed this. (PIA 288/21/ 1973/24)

There is a party secretary in the Budapest apparatus who refused to even talk to the women's representative. He passed down this responsibility. He did not understand the political significance of this at all. (PIA 288/5/140)

Nevertheless, quotas and positive discrimination policies contributed to the construction of women as a separate social group. Moreover, as a group women were seen as worthy of unrelenting statistical attention, thereby simultaneously creating and reinforcing categorization. Starting in the mid-1950s, practically all reports to party executive bodies on social, political, and labor force matters contained a breakdown by gender. In fact, very few variables were used altogether: apart from gender only class background, educational level, and age were most often included.

Party and state authorities amassed an amazing amount of strictly classified, statistical data and kept a close watch on the proportion of women in the communist party, at universities and in vocational training, in the labor force, in positions of authority, and in a number of other social situations. At least a sentence on the evaluation of the situation of women, accompanied by the usually fully meaningless but obligatory explanatory phrases, was required to be included in the discussion of most topics ranging from the social position of the working class to that of the Roma population to that of the students of party school or the cadre pool.

In addition, even the highest party organ, the Politburo, spent long hours discussing the woman question, passing decrees and requesting information on a regular basis. This was especially true for the period between the mid-1950s and early 1980s. As mentioned earlier, in this period the Politburo had the woman question, or various aspects thereof, on its agenda twenty-seven times. This may not seem especially frequent given that the Politburo met officially every two weeks and focused on two to six items each time, but in actuality it meant that with few exceptions the Politburo had a major discussion of women's issues at least once a year between the mid-1950s and early 1980s. These discussions were always preceded by data gathering and reports and discussions in supplementary party bodies such as the Secretariat or the Organizing Committee. A separate group was also established within one of the Central Committee departments overseeing the affairs of women and the Women's Council, which also gathered data and consulted on all issues concerning women. But statistics were not the only form of information gathered. Secret reports were filed on the political atmosphere among women working in various factories or living in a given city—regardless of their of their age, class, or educational backgrounds (e.g., PIA 288/21/1958/24). These reports were taken to reflect women's specific opinions about particular policies of the regime, from minor issues such as the availability of cheap shoes for children to major matters such as the cold war and military spending.

Although a much-hated exercise, specific reports on the woman question were requested from and produced by political, economic, and social organizations of every conceivable level and type. Between 1970 and 1980, approximately 110 reports were produced as a result of a 1970 decree discussing the situation of women in Hungarian society. Party secretariats of each of the country's nineteen counties (and larger cities separately), numerous large economic institutions (such as the National Savings Bank), various state departments, the youth movement and other associations (such as small cooperatives of agricultural cooperatives), universities, the police force, the military, the national trade unions, the Statistical Office, daily papers, and so forth submitted over five thousand pages of written discussion of the woman question in their fields of expertise. The social position, political interests, participation level, and the life chances of women, along with the most efficient propaganda to be employed, were discussed on these pages. Although most organizations were quite simpleminded in their efforts to toe the party line, and even copied much of the jargon propagated in the original party document, the reports nevertheless produced some useful information and, even more important, reinforced the notion of the existence of women as a separate social entity. There were only two other similar decade-long information campaigns in the almost forty-year history of the Politburo: one started in the late 1950s to assess the situation of the working class and the other concerned young people and ran parallel to that of the situation of women.

It is important to note that in these decrees, reports, and discussions the category "woman" was rarely broken down into substrata. Although the Politburo seemed keenly interested in finding out the proportion of working-class students at universities, it was never interested in the proportion of working-class female (as opposed to male) students. Except for an occasional mention of "homemakers" and "women with several children," the group of women was seen as a relatively homogeneous unit. A good example for this is the Bureau of Labor Supply, which in the 1950s produced volumes of statistics about the source of potential new workers to be recruited for extensive industrial production. Four categories were identified from which the new labor force was to be drawn: "agricultural laborers," "the youth," "workers from small private shops," and "women" (PIA 276/53/39). Here again we see "women" as a separate and seemingly homogeneous category, which is placed alongside, and not in interaction with, age, class, or occupation-based groupings. Although most of the women referred to in the documents were urban, middle-class homemakers, the female labor supply also included poor peasant women working on their family-owned plots, as well as wives of rural landlords. The reports often failed to mention the vast differences in their expectations, experience, or attitudes because the political aim was to establish and homogenize the group, rather than point out real-life variations or solve real-life problems.[2]

The single, centralized, party-controlled women's organization served as a further tool in the construction of women as a separate group.[3] It was designed to monitor the situation of, and transmit the party's policies to, all Hungarian women. Party leaders encouraged the Woman's Council to practice what they called "unified gender politics" (egységes nőpolitika), which would include all social strata of women, even those considered politically unreliable (PIA 288/5/36).

Such gender-specific political representation also contributed to the acknowledgment that women belong to a social strata to be distinguished from the mainstream male proletariat. The Women's Council served as the central organ for not only the political representation of women, but also their interests and achievements. The president of the Women's Council was an ex officio member of the Central Committee, where she talked authoritatively about issues concerning all women. After 1970, all important matters, by law, had to pass through the Women's Council and its opinion had to be heard. But note that this does not mean that Politburo members who passed final decisions actually had to listen to these opinions; in fact, the Women's Council's expressed criticism was often disregarded.

It was the Women's Council and its subcouncils that had exclusive rights to organize a celebration on March 8, the international day of women, where a member of the Politburo was delegated to greet the "other" sex.[4] The Women's Council represented Hungarian women abroad through membership in a few carefully selected international women's organizations. Most research on gender was channeled through the women's organization through their rights to administer research grants, select the appropriate researchers, and publish the results of their study. In fact, the Women's Council served as the major publishing house for publications directed explicitly at women. Between 1983 and 1988, for example, the Women's Council published some forty books on a wide variety of topics ranging from an edited volume on women in the workforce to a number of self-help books on divorce and childrearing to cookbooks and publications on skin care. The most important and profitable publication of the council was, however, a weekly magazine, which was initiated to aid the Women's Council in its quest for a "unified gender politics." *Nők Lapja* (women's journal) was a highly successful magazine, it achieved the highest circulation rate of all weeklies in the country because it was read (as its publishers hoped) by all strata of women. No other major women's journal, which would have targeted a more specialized audience, was published until 1989.

The discussion above reviews the most important mechanisms through which state socialist party leaders constructed a social group out of Hungarian women. Gender quotas, statistics, rhetoric on emancipation, and strictly channeled means of political representation all served to establish the presence of women as a separate and somewhat uniform entity in the state socialist "public sphere." What were the characteristics that members of this group shared?

Characteristics of the Group of Women

If one trait that women came to be associated with most often had to be singled out it surely would be "political backwardness." Party leaders depicted women as politically naive, less reliable, and less loyal than their male counterparts, and they attributed these qualities to women's lack of experience in the labor force and in the underground communist movement. For example, as reports to various party organs complained: "Women, who did not use to participate in public life . . . are in many ways *backward*, and do not feel capable of making use of their new-found rights and obligations" (PIA 288/21/1958/15); and "With a few exceptions, most women—because of their household responsibilities—cannot keep up with men in terms of political and professional education and in taking on managerial responsibilities" (PIA 288/21/1957/12). Another report by the propaganda department of the Communist Youth League discusses how young women should be approached through indirect political means (such as, for example, book clubs) rather than through explicitly political lectures. But, the report continues, "it has often been observed that the girls don't always understand the political lesson from the book, they are more concerned with the story itself" (PIA 288/21/1961/18).

Political leaders, and not only those at the highest levels, assumed that women's political capabilities are highly limited: "Our women are fighters, but their determination is often wasted on the wrong issues. They get excited by a few words and are willing to go to war against their own interests. . . . Our task is to teach them when and where to fight, what to do for the workers' state and for peace" (PIA 276/89/273). From these statements it would appear that women (again, a seemingly homogeneous entity with similar interests, problems, structure of experience, and type of participation) are a highly excitable bunch and their energies must be channeled by outside forces toward the proper causes.

The reports further imply that because women are less educated they need help understanding the everyday political events around them, and who better to help in this effort than their husbands? The following is from a report on a "conference of homemakers" (written for the eyes of Politburo members only): "Some women talked about husbands, who helped their wives understand the events around them. Their husbands would read out to them from the newspaper or a book and would *explain the stories too, as she was ironing or mending clothes*" (PIA 288/21/59/3).

Moreover, because women are seen as less politically aware than men, they are also considered less reliable and trustworthy and more easily influenced by the "enemy":[5] "The ideology of the counterrevolution [in 1956] is still influential among women. . . . There are many who are easily influenced by the enemy, by foreign propaganda intended to create confusion. If there is some international tension, women immediately start worrying about a war. Religiosity is more popular among women, and this has an effect on the youth as well" (PIA 288/5/140). And women have a harder time understanding the most important communist goals as well: "I was visiting the county of Szolnok . . . [and found] that the fight in the cooperative movement is more difficult to carry on among women [than among the men]. Peasants said to me that "my wife still blames me for joining the co-op" (PIA 288/5/140). In addition, women were considered unable even to appreciate the benefits the regime had brought. A Politburo member visited a party cell and recounts the following story to describe the experience: "They said that mostly women work in the factory, but it is usually men who participate in the party meetings. I asked why. They said very interesting things. These women lived and worked under capitalism, much harder than now, and still believe that it used to be better. There are a lot of them who are against our regime" (PIA 288/5/36).

These quotes illustrate that the Politburo, the most powerful political organization in Hungary, described women clearly as inferior to men, particularly in political issues. Women were considered to be more difficult to mobilize and slower to understand political initiatives. This phenomenon certainly bears similarities to the ideology of liberalism where, as I mentioned in the previous chapter, women are described as weak, emotional, and generally incapable of rational action. But if the conditions for citizenship in a liberal democracy are rationality and ownership rights, the analogy in communist discourse is devotion to the party and its teachings (Jowitt 1989). It is this devotion that qualifies a person to become an accepted member of the community. But can women achieve full devotion? Is it possible to be fully devoted to the party and to a man and one's children at the same time?

Alexandra Kollontai, for one, did not think so. It is exactly for this reason that this great Russian revolutionary and feminist encouraged women to stay single and to not let passion blind them and "becloud [their] analytical minds." One of her examples is Theresa, an ideal "new woman," for whom love is "only a brief respite on life's path." The aim of her life and its content is the party, the idea, agitation, and propaganda work (Kollontai, 1971, 64, 6–10).

Kollontai did not argue for free love on moral grounds or because she believed, as would her modern-day feminist sisters, that women should have a "right" to take ownership of their bodies and their sexuality. These words and the concept of "rights" were clearly not part of her revolutionary vocabulary. Rather, she promoted sexual freedom because she believed that love binds a woman to local and personal matters, consumes her energies, and takes her time away from more important work. In the words of Genia, the heroine of her novel *Great Love:* "I give myself without falling in love. . . . One must have time to fall in love, but I have no time. Our activities in the district have complete hold over us so that none of us have had time to think of anything else, of personal matters" (1981:113). Neither does Kollontai's main opponent, Lenin, reject her ideas based merely on moral or puritanical considerations. Instead, he acknowledges that marital, monogamous, possessive love may reduce women's energies and contributions to the party, but he argues that free sexuality will more adversely affect *men's* concentration. This, in times of an ongoing communist revolution, is unacceptable. "The revolution demands concentration, increase of forces. . . . It cannot tolerate orgiastic conditions. . . . The proletariat is a rising class. It does not need intoxication [from sex] as narcotic or a stimulus. . . . It needs clarity, clarity and again clarity" (Lenin, quoted in Zetkin, 1934, 50).

Both Lenin and Kollontai agreed, therefore, that there were problems with women's sexuality and reproductive responsibilities that might endanger the revolution, even though their solution to the problem was radically different. Kollontai recommended an end to traditional families and committed relationships. But it was Lenin's more conservative position that prevailed. Following him, Hungarian state socialist party leaders never seriously questioned the patriarchal sanctity of the family as the basic building block of society. Women's reproductive work proved still cheaper and more comfortable than the reorganization and socialization of household chores. In due course, women's sexuality was reined in. But the consequences that Kollontai predicted could not be avoided: women's attention had to be at best shared between family and community issues. This, however, did not stop party leaders from blaming women for their concentration on local matters, a task they themselves assigned them. As a Politburo member complained: "Women do not judge the technological development of the Soviet Union through rockets, but through the availability of labor-saving devices. If they find a fault, they blame the whole system immediately, not just the concrete problem" (PIA 288/21/1959/7).

Yet although it was women's reproductive responsibilities that allowed both state socialist and liberal ideologues to construct women as inferior, there was one important difference between the two major schools of modern Western political thought. Hungarian party leaders saw women's disadvantage as temporary, a result of the combination of traditional attitudes and a lack of sufficient organization and money invested in labor-saving devices. As one Politburo member argued in 1959: "Someone mentioned that motherhood is still a disadvantage [for promotion]. This will be so for maybe another twenty or even fifty years" (PIA 288/5/140). Or as one Politburo member claimed with respect to the cooperative movement quoted earlier: "I also saw [in the countryside] that fewer women participate in the cooperative movement. By the way, I see this as a temporary phenomenon" (PIA 288/5/140). Here the argument is that as soon as communism develops to its full potential, these problems will be solved, but because this particular area was given low priority, by 1959 Politburo leaders did not see it happening in the twentieth century.

Because women were labeled slow but educable, the central task of the Women's Council was to provide the necessary tools for women to catch up with the rest of society: "The aim of the political-educational work of the Women's Council is to develop the political consciousness of women,[6] to widen their horizon, awaken their desire for self-education and culture. With all this we intend to transcend the cultural backwardness of women and help them become good soldiers for the progressive cause, and thus secure the conditions for emancipation" (PIA 288/5/36). But women seemed to have needed education in more mundane areas as well: "I think one of the tasks of the Women's Council is to teach women how to live their lives in our society. There are a lot of unused opportunities in the field of culture and sports as well. For example they could discuss issues about how to balance the household budget" (PIA 288/5/140). This was perhaps an exaggeration. In fact, although party leaders agreed that women's emancipation had not been fully realized, they praised women for the vast steps they took in the "right" direction. The following quote from the 1970 party decree on the situation of women in Hungary congratulates women on the road they traveled at the same time that it acknowledges their failure to become fully equal to men. A somewhat underhanded compliment follows: "While women were mostly attracted to the regime through their emotions, intuitively now they are also conscious devotees" (PIA 288/5/511).

In sum, party leaders considered women politically inferior to men and as more likely to be religious, less experienced in the labor movement, and more prone to outside influences. But they did not blame women's inborn abilities for their political unreliability. Rather, women's reluctant devotion to the party was seen as a result of a lack of experience and political training. Thus, in order to be accepted as credible members of the political community, and to gain a chance for important positions of authority, women had to go through an extensive process of self-criticism and reeducation.

Women's Tasks in the Public Sphere

Women had not only specific characteristics but also clearly defined tasks and a related social position distinct from that of men. Although they were, of course, expected to participate in the labor force and in political life, the functions assigned to them differed significantly from those assigned to men. In a discussion about women's new social role after the 1956 revolution, a Politburo member expresses the general sentiment: "There are a number of tasks outside state and party politics that we can only get women to carry out. . . . *Local politics is women's task.* They should visit the hospital, check to see if there is a good road in the village, if they have child care centers, what the schools are like, how well the food store is supplied" (PIA 288/5/24). And as a rejoinder, another member adds: "For years, the women's organization was organized on the pattern of the party. We must avoid such mistakes in the future. The women's movement should pay more attention to family issues, . . . to the protection of children, schooling, [and] education, and should employ methods like tea parties and sewing or cooking courses. It should focus on '*trivial*' *chores*" (PIA 288/5/24, emphasis mine). Trivial chores, indeed. Note also the shift from an organization that used to operate as a (mostly male) party organ to one specially designed for the particular responsibilities and interests of women. As these and numerous other documents testify, local politics, caretaking work, education, and childcare were the tasks assigned to women in the public sphere, as well as in the household, of course. Previously, we saw how women were depicted as less fit for political participation, but certainly educable. These "trivial chores" were designed to provide this education both for them and for the next generation.

Thus, even though women were expected to be full participants in the public sphere, there was a clearly delineated set of tasks they were supposed to carry out. And this assignment was not significantly modified later either. In a 1970 Politburo meeting Rezső Nyers graciously suggests that "in our society there are a number of tasks we can safely assign to women. . . . *[Women] are particularly adept at social welfare jobs.* Of course, they don't have a good view of the whole picture. . . . I think women should be entrusted with more of the upbringing of children. And of course, the management of the household. . . . I believe women are better at these struggles" (PIA 288/5/509). Note again the linguistic means used in this quote to describe a group distinct from one's own: the use of the personal pronoun "we" as it stands in opposition to "women." Clearly this and many other similar instances show that members of the Politburo thought of women as an entity at once homogeneous in some important respects and yet distinct from themselves, and, more important, that under this assumption they passed decrees that had real-life consequences.

As it was so often emphasized that women belonged to a separate social group, it was natural that their interests in the public sphere should be represented through the Women's Council, whose leaders, as mentioned above, always participated at Politburo meetings when a relevant issue was discussed. In these meetings the Politburo held the Women's Council directly responsible when women did not behave according to the Politburo's plans, when the gender quotas could not be filled, when women did not produce enough children, or when they did not seem enthusiastic enough about attending party schools or getting vocational training. But the task of the Women's Council was also clearly separated from that of the leaders of the party, indicating the gap between women's and men's responsibilities: "The women's council should explore [the tasks mentioned earlier by one Politburo member] . . . For example, they should strive to achieve issues such as that [female] ticket vendors and other service personnel should behave *more politely* toward the customers. Then *we* [the predominantly male party leadership] will fight on their behalf, so they would not be abused [by the also predominantly male management of the given enterprise]" (PIA 288/5/140). Here the division of labor between the male communists and women is made even clearer. Women are encouraged to work on "smiling," and men will then do the "fighting." This should clearly be in everyone's best interest, given women's political ignorance and naïveté.

Women were assigned specific tasks in the public sphere, much in accordance with their duties in the household and their assumed inexperience in the field of politics and labor. But the tasks women were supposed to do were not only different from but also inferior to those carried out by men.

Limits to Women's Advancement

There are several indications that the division of tasks was not completely unintentional. For example, the quotas set for women's participation in the party as well as in positions of authority were somewhere around 30 percent, or a third of all positions. This is very far from equality understood in conventional terms. In an interview in 1995, a top-level party executive, Mrs. J. Orbán, argued that the goals described in the Central Committee Decree of 1970, whose aim was to achieve women's equality in positions of authority, had been realized because by 1980 about 30 percent of leadership positions in the party and state apparatus were held by women. Based on decades of experience in the party apparatus, she considered this perfectly satisfactory and as fulfilling the goal of women's emancipation.

The highest council of party leaders shared Orbán's position. The annual reports on the social composition of party membership showed that the proportion of women never exceeded a third of all party members, and although the Politburo occasionally agonized over the low representation of workers or of young people among the members, women's participation was never considered at length, and a general satisfaction was often expressed.

In a number of documents, top-level party cadres identify the limits to which women are allowed to participate on the political scene. Note, for example, this report from a Politburo meeting in March 1953: "The proportion of *women is too high in certain fields* and in some positions. For example, 46 percent of all party instructors, 65 percent of all instructors in three-to-six-month-long courses, and 40 percent of the employees at local party apparatuses are women" (PIA 276/53/116). Interestingly enough, already a job with 40 to 60 percent of positions filled by women is considered overrepresentation. A similar hysteria erupted in the late 1980s when the proportion of university students in law and economics passed 50 percent.

Limitations to how far women can proceed and when they can do so are evident not only in cadre recruitment but also in the labor force. In 1960, when during the discussion of the Second Five-Year Plan the possibility of unemployment was raised, János Kádár made it clear that of the two groups, women and youth, most likely to be threatened by joblessness, it is women who should be disadvantaged (PIA 288/5/182). He claimed that it was "theoretically [read politically] necessary" that young people should have priority over women; women's participation in the labor force is conditioned on the abundance of jobs. Similar threats to women's labor force participation—otherwise cherished by Politburo members—resurfaced every time there was a danger of excess labor.

In addition, women were not necessarily entitled to good-quality jobs and they were expected to be satisfied with whatever was available, even if it were deemed second rate and insufficient for men. Consider these words from a top-level Politburo member at a meeting in July 1959: "We often receive requests from various rural cities that they need help establishing a factory where a lot of women could find work. Unfortunately only very few of these requests can be granted. But we should definitely start thinking about what kind of work we could provide to rural women, *work that is not very high quality*, but would still provide a living" (PIA 288/5/140). Here the Politburo member explicitly argues that the jobs the state should provide for women need not pay very well or even be particularly rewarding. Women have to work outside the household and participate in the public sphere if the opportunity arises, but their inferior, second-class position in this situation is taken for granted.

The situation for young women was especially marginalized, as illustrated by János Kádár's comment recorded in 1966:

"We are having a lot of problems with youth nowadays. We have talked about shop assistants and other people involved in retail jobs. They say that the wages are too low. But in my opinion it does not have to be much higher at all. Rather perhaps we should introduce a system where young women, between fifteen and twenty, who have no particular skills or qualifications would come and work in retail for four to six hours a day. They would work here for a while and then they would be replaced by another bunch of young women. *They will never make here as much as in the mining industry.*" (PIA 288/5/394).

Kádár here acknowledges that women's work does not provide as much as a man's job (in, for example, the mining industry). But such wages are seen as sufficient for women, especially women who are likely to start their families at the same time. In other words, women must participate in paid work as part of the political education process but they obviously are not supposed to participate like men. Segregation is not only acceptable but also encouraged and centrally legitimated.

And, ultimately, it was clear that the Politburo had the final authority over how far women could venture, as stated in a meeting in July 1959: "The state upholds the right to appoint exclusively party members to certain positions. . . . *Similarly, we uphold this right with regard to the nomination of men*" (PIA 288/5/140).

In the previous chapter I discussed two different principles of state policies directed at the inclusion of women in the sphere of work and politics. According to the similarity principle women are only allowed to enter the public sphere if they "disavow their bodies" (Pateman 1988b) and adjust to the male norm. The difference principle, on the other hand, would guarantee women's inclusion even under conditions different from those of men.

The specifically state socialist legacy should be observed in the combination of the difference principle with the aggressive, state-centered promotion of women's labor force participation. But although Hungarian party leaders claimed that only local resistance inhibited women's full emancipation, there is clear evidence that shows a deliberately and centrally assigned second-class status to what was often called the "weaker sex." Women in Hungary had to pay the price for the acknowledgment of their difference: their inclusion was limited, segregated, produced inferior privileges, and was predicated on the shortage of labor and the continued goodwill of party leaders. A specifically communist construction of women's inferiority emerged: women were described not as second-class citizens but as less-reliable, not sufficiently devoted, defenders of the communist cause.

8. Convergence in the Twenty-First Century?

I set out at the beginning of this book to investigate gender differences in accessing positions of authority in Hungary and Austria, and, more broadly speaking, the characteristics of state socialist and capitalist gender regimes in paid work and occupational mobility. Before World War II the occupational and educational structures of Austria and Hungary (as well as women's positions within these structures) displayed much similarity, although Austria was more developed and was significantly better positioned in the world capitalist market than Hungary. It was in 1945 that their real divergence began, in terms of both political culture and economic priorities.

After World War II, Austria rapidly joined the Western European community of capitalist states. It soon became a developed democracy while simultaneously holding on to its Central European, corporatist, conservative traditions. The principles of stratification remained intact for several decades after World War II: access to authority was guaranteed through the possession of productive assets (for capitalists and landowners) and cultural capital in the form of elite educational degrees (in the case of managers and top executives.) Both the cultural and economic embodiment of family inheritance remained important: it assured the steady reproduction of social status from generation to generation. In Austria, a deeply Catholic country, women's role in society remained primarily tied to the household until the 1970s, when economic need and political pressure pushed some women into the labor force and into universities.

Hungary, on the other hand, started on a different path. After the communist takeover in 1949, formal democracy was replaced by the dictatorial rule of the communist party. The newly emerging upper class relied on the use of political (rather than economic or cultural) capital to exercise domination and maintain and reproduce their privileged positions. Although over the years skills and training regained some of their earlier significance in the process of social mobility and began to serve as a secondary route to upper-class status, the importance of political loyalty and reliability never ceased. The communist party radically reformed women's position in society as well: economic, political, and ideological interests led to a wholesale recruitment of women into the labor force and into educational institutions from the late 1940s onward.

The gender regimes that emerged in the stratification systems of these two societies varied significantly. Gender operated as a source of exclusion in both countries, but the degree, process, and hence the character of its institutionalization varied. The contrast between Austria and Hungary demonstrates both the perseverance of patriarchal domination in modern-day societies as well as its flexibility and adaptability.

In what follows I will summarize my arguments by briefly describing Austria's and Hungary's different types of gender regimes; that is, the different ways in which domination was exercised on the basis of gender under state socialism and capitalism. I conclude by exploring some of the longer-term consequences of the two types of gender regimes for gender equality in high-level paid work, especially in light of the rapid social transformations in both countries at the end of the twentieth century.

Austria in the 1980s: Gender Regime in a Corporatist, Capitalist Welfare State

In the early 1980s, a typical married, middle-class Austrian woman spent much of her adult life as a homemaker and mother, and she depended on her husband (or on the state through her husband's citizenship entitlements) for her financial well-being. She probably graduated from an academic high school but did not attend university. Even if she did spend several years working outside the home, she quit her job upon marriage or at the birth of her first child and returned to the workplace only decades later.

In Austria in the early 1980s social mobility for women was almost exclusively attainable through marriage and through the successful career of the husband, and this state of affairs was seen to follow naturally from women's perceived differences from men. Gender difference was understood as a primarily biological trait related to childbearing and to women's "natural" predisposition to emotional rather than rational action. As a consequence, women's participation in the community of equal, rational individuals was questioned, and their dependent status was postulated as necessary and indeed optimal. Legislators, the media, and the law saw women primarily not as wage workers but as the natural wards of their husbands and as (past, present, or future) caretakers of children and the elderly. Labor market policies and workplace or career requirements were, therefore, built on the assumption of a male career supported by the reproductive work of a stay-at-home wife.

As is the case everywhere, not all women were "lucky" enough to find a dependable husband, and others chose to ignore the expected gender distinctions altogether. For these women paid work became possible on the condition that they adopt the norms designed for male individuals and thus eschew childbearing, or that they take care of their reproductive duties using their own financial, intellectual, and emotional resources. This situation, which follows from the male bias embedded in the organization of work and career in capitalist societies, as well as from the very assumptions on which the concept of the individual is built in liberal-capitalist ideology, did not change much even when labor shortages demanded women's increased participation in the labor market. Although state regulations made some allowances for women's childbearing duties, they did not alter the fundamental conditions of women's participation in the "fraternity of men," which required the acceptance of "similarity" in order to achieve more gender equality.

Authority in formal institutions was thus defined as an almost exclusively male responsibility and privilege. Gender distinctions were institutionalized in labor and marriage laws, as well as in everyday workplace regulations. As such, being a man proved to be a valuable resource used to effect women's large-scale exclusion from authority. At the same time, however, it also allowed groups of women to formulate demands on the basis of their gender and understand in gendered terms the discrimination they faced on the labor market.

Austrian men in the 1980s claimed formal authority in economic enterprises and state institutions on the basis of economic and cultural capital. Indeed, the latter, in the shape of university degrees and other certificates of training, became a crucial resource for managers who exercised their authority as employees of state or even privately owned companies and administrations. Aside from direct exclusion from the labor market, women's lower representation in positions of authority was due to their difficulty in gaining access to these elite educational institutions. Here no formal criteria of selection existed that directly filtered out women, but as a result of more subtle forms of discrimination and self-exclusion women did not reach equality in postsecondary education in Austria until the early 1990s. Male domination operated through the exclusion of women from the most important resource necessary for claiming authority: in a legal-rational bureaucracy like Austria, cultural capital served this function.

The few women who did gain valuable cultural capital (and also were willing or able to minimize domestic responsibilities) significantly improved their relative chances for upward mobility in the Austrian labor market. Yet, overall, in the 1980s women's experience in Austria can primarily be described as exclusion from authority and can be characterized by the paradoxical requirement of having to adjust to a male norm yet also face discrimination, even when abandoning the classic patterns of women's traditional life cycle.

Hungary in the 1980s: Gender Regimes in a State Socialist Society

Compared to women in Austria, by the 1980s Hungarian women were significantly more successful in claiming at least lower-to-intermediate levels of authority. As the two countries followed similar paths until World War II, the social institutions of state socialism are likely to account for this divergence.

In Hungary the inclusion of women in paid work was defined as an ideological, political, and economic necessity. Following Engels's footsteps, Marxist-Leninist party ideologues understood women's emancipation through work as analogous to that of the emancipation of the working classes. Politically, abolishing the control of husbands over women and drawing all subjects under the direct surveillance of the party-state seemed highly desirable. And because mothers had a vast influence on the development of the future generation, their identification with the state socialist system turned out to be nothing less than a political imperative.

In economic terms, extensive industrialization demanded a rapid increase in the number of workers, especially those doing physically demanding labor. Central planners soon realized that women were the ideal candidates to replace men in white-collar clerical occupations so that the men might be moved to better-paid and more prestigious occupations, thereby easing the labor shortages that emerged in the early 1950s.

Thus women's participation in paid work was defined as a condition to the success of the state socialist regime—as an integral part of its overall political and economic goals. It is not, however, the "fraternity of men" that women were thus demanded to join. Instead, women were expected to contribute to the "common good" defined by a central authority that had a monopoly over setting goals, defining tasks, and allocating privileges. Women, like men, became subjects in their own person (not just as extensions of their husbands) within the realms of this communist, yet patriarchal rule.

Yet state socialist policymakers also had to respond to the problem of women's "difference"; that is, to popular views about (and popular interests tied to) women's primary responsibilities in childrearing and the household. As a response, policymakers redefined women's widely understood inferiority in two ways. First, rather than as a biological trait, they now described it as socially constructed and derived from the "traditional views" of the population. This new conception did not lower the significance of women's "difference," but it did open up the distant possibility of eradicating the notion through educational and political campaigns.

Second, and more important, in the process of constructing women as subjects (rather than as household dependents) policymakers introduced the idea of women's inferiority within this subject status. Or, more generally, communist ideologues and policymakers replaced the concept of the male-biased individual with that of the no less male-biased subject. But of course the embedded primacy given to the male experience was expressed somewhat differently. Although in many other societies pregnancy and childbearing were seen to damage women's "rationality" and individuality, in Hungary childbearing and household chores were considered to tie women to local rather than national and international issues. Women were not seen as less rational than men but rather as less able to devote themselves to the communist cause, given that their primary allegiance was supposed to go to their offspring. Women therefore could never be fully trusted. And rather than the capacity to act rationally it was the capacity to be loyal, reliable, and devoted to the communist cause that served as the cornerstone of full subject status—that is, of privileged participation in paid work and authority.

Nevertheless, communist policymakers managed to reconcile the inferiority of women and the need for their education and control through paid work. They did this partly through a redefinition of the world of work by placing less emphasis on productivity and by creating shorter work hours, or to put it more broadly, by deinstitutionalizing freedom from reproductive responsibilities as a form of capital within the workplace and the career track. In the process, however, communist policymaking constructed women as a group of laborers with special needs and also with special responsibilities and privileges. Thus they included women as workers and as subjects of the state but simultaneously acknowledged and reinforced their difference, which resulted in women's participation in paid work in a highly segregated and mostly inferior manner.

The actual processes of exclusion also differed in Austria and Hungary, although not in its overall logic. In state socialist Hungary, authority was ultimately claimed on the basis of political capital, those lacking the trust of the central authorities had little chance of making it into the ruling elite. As a consequence, male domination was exercised most effectively in and through the political field. Politics, and political loyalty itself, were constructed as primarily masculine arenas: women could never be completely trusted. From this women's underrepresentation among holders of institutionalized political capital (party membership) seemed to follow, which in turn led to their exclusion from equal participation in state socialist authority. Hungarian women thus experienced inclusion into authority, although only in a segregated and limited fashion: they were encouraged to take lower-level managerial responsibilities but were summarily excluded from the top of the social hierarchy. Nevertheless, the "divide and conquer" policy of the state socialist regime and the comparative advantage of women in Hungary relative to Austria (always the reference point for political dissent) successfully prevented the formulation of interests along the lines of gender during and for decades after state socialism.

Moving into the Twenty-first Century

Monumental changes occurred in both Hungary and Austria in the last decade of the twentieth century, and these changes once again seem to be bringing women's labor market experience in both countries closer to each other. Yet, these processes are difficult to understand without assessing the historical legacy of state socialism and post–World War II capitalism in the two countries. In this book's final section I want to foreshadow some of the changes that have occurred in gender inequality in authority, and more broadly in the labor force, in the two countries and to point out the important linkages between these recent developments and the historical legacies of the second half of the twentieth century.

Researchers have paid more attention to the radical changes that occurred in women's social position after the collapse of state socialism in the East than the relatively less spectacular changes in the West. Specifically, most scholars expected to see a steady growth in gender inequalities on the labor market after 1989, in particular in high-level positions in Hungary. Indeed, there were a number of good reasons to expect this.

First, social inequalities measured by other important dimensions such as class and ethnicity grew perceptibly after 1989. In this context, the expectation that inequalities among men and women should also increase is quite logical.

Second, women are in a more vulnerable position than men in the labor markets of Western capitalist societies, thus if Eastern Europe is heading in the much-desired, Western capitalist direction, it makes sense to expect a similar situation to unfold here as well. Although in Hungary women's education and labor force experiences have been equal to, or at least very closely approximating, those of men, women could still be perceived as less-valuable laborers given their responsibilities in the household. Women, even while engaged in full-time work, have always been, are still expected to, and still expect themselves to perform most of the household chores and childrearing tasks in the family. As a consequence of the demands of this role, women are often seen as inferior and less-reliable workers than men, and are expected to be more likely to quit, be absent, and expend less energy than men. In this context an employer driven by the profit motive may be reluctant to hire a woman and be more likely to lay her off first, once the principle of hoarding labor is replaced by that of economic efficiency.

Third, state regulations regarding women's employment also changed. Even though the Politburo in the late 1980s had secretly started to explore the question of reducing the size of the female labor force, no explicit measures were taken at that time. In fact, policies advocating women's paid work remained in force, as did maternity leave legislation, subsidized daycare centers, and factory lunch programs. Many of these benefits, however, came to an end with the collapse of state socialism. Maternity policies, once a universal right, were turned into a means-tested provision, and even more important, job guarantees disappeared.[1] It was no longer a legally enforced expectation of women (or of men, for that matter) to work. Factories, short of money, closed daycare centers all over the country and cut back on other subsidized service facilities. Other state policies, most notably the legality of first trimester abortion, although challended in Parliament, remained in force.

Fourth, not only were some of the policies advocating women's participation in the labor force revoked but a serious ideological backlash against women's paid work burst into the public discourse soon after 1989. Along with many other institutions of state socialism, the concept of women's emancipation was challenged and right-wing governments popularized a conservative gender ideology about women's proper place and role in 1990 to 1994 and again between 1998–2002.

International surveys taken at the time showed Hungarian women expressing more conservative gender ideologies than their Western sisters: many more women in Hungary claimed to want to be stay-at-home mothers than did women in England, Germany, or Austria (Tóth 1990).

In the face of all these threats to women's independence no legitimate political institution emerged that would have been able to fight for (or at least represent) women's interests. The old state socialist women's movement survived the regime change but lost much of its financial resources and all of its credibility in the eyes of Hungarian women. Feminist movements sprang up but remained small, disorganized, and marginalized.

For all these reasons, it is not surprising that researchers feared a growth in gender inequalities (Einhorn 1993; Petrova 1993). However, at least the first decade in the immediate aftermath of the state socialist era in Hungary did not fully bear out these expectations. Even though women's labor force participation rates declined, so did those of men. In fact, the degree of men's overrepresentation in wage work remained almost constant, and several other indicators suggest that although everyone's position has deteriorated women were not especially disadvantaged. Maria Frey (1996), for example, points out that the gender gap in wages actually declined by about 15 percent after 1989. Women's participation in educational institutions remained high: about 56 percent of postsecondary degrees were awarded to women in 1996 (Magyarország Statisztikai Évkönyve 1996). Tables 3.1 and 3.3 support findings from elsewhere about a slow growth in the proportion of women in managerial positions (Frey 1996). Thus, in a number of important respects, gender inequality did not increase sharply in the labor market of post–state socialist Hungary (see also J. Szalai 2000).

Yet, if we take seriously the legacies of state socialism, these findings should not come as a surprise. The generation of women who grew up between 1945 and 1990 with the expectation of a full-time, life-long career still express pride in their work and in their participation in the labor force, as do their daughters who saw their mothers go to work every day. A representative sample of the population (ages twenty to fifty for our purposes) shows that 61 percent of women, but only 54 percent of men, claim to be proud of their occupations. In addition, the majority of women (66 percent) said that they found their jobs interesting; felt that they were helping others with their jobs (74 percent); or thought that their jobs were "socially useful" (78 percent). There was no difference (substantive or statistical) in the response of men and women to these questions. In other words, it seems that women in Hungary did not altogether lose their interest in work, conservative gender ideology notwithstanding. If we go beyond simple pronouncements about "overemancipation" we find that most women draw satisfaction from their paid jobs and do so to a degree similar to their male counterparts.

In addition, as a result of the particular nature of the economic transformation process, women in Hungary found themselves, at least temporarily, in a more advantageous position on the labor market than did men. By 1996, the unemployment rate among women (in the age twenty-to-fifty cohort) climbed to 8.8 percent. Admittedly, this was a shocking change from the state socialist era, where official unemployment rates were close to zero.[2] But men's unemployment rate in the similar cohort stood at 12.2 percent in 1996. This is a significant gender difference, but to women's advantage. There are a number of reasons for this discrepancy which I discuss in more detail elsewhere (Fodor 1997). Suffice here to say that during the state socialist period, women were overrepresented in the "nonproductive" service sectors, and thus it is here that they were found after the collapse of regime. But the privatization and "rationalization" process hit factories first: most were inefficient, using old machinery to produce goods that could only be sold on the (now defunct) Soviet market. Most of the jobs, which were eliminated in the first five years of post–state social-ism were male-dominated ones, primarily blue-collar positions in the heavy industries and in construction. In the survey mentioned above, about the same percentage of men and women told interviewers that they no longer work because they were fired. But over twice as many men (29 percent) as women (14 percent) said that they had stopped working be-cause their jobs had disappeared (calculations by author from Omnibusz 1997, using the age twenty-to-fifty cohort).

In Austria, also, we can observe the combined effect of the past decades and the radical changes in the early 1990s. In line with the trends in other European countries, the gap between men's and women's labor force par-ticipation has decreased over the years: women are claiming an increas-ingly large piece of an otherwise shrinking labor market pie. In fact, by the middle of the 1990s there was practically no difference between women's labor force participation rates in Hungary and Austria, and this con-vergence was due just as much to a decline in Hungary than to an increase in Austria. In addition, the expansion of the Austrian postsecondary edu-cational system that began in the late 1970s resulted by the 1990s in a growth in the overall percentage of people with university degrees and a decline in the gender gap in educational attainment. The proportion of women in managerial positions increased also, although by the late 1990s Austrian women's representation still had not reached that of their Hun-garian counterparts in the early 1980s.

Paradoxically, therefore, the changes in women's labor market posi-tions were in the past decade or so larger in Austria than in Hungary. Neither country achieved gender equality by any definition, yet the steps taken by Austrian women seem enormous. In this respect, and in the future course that Hungary might take, the influence of international organizations must be observed. Even though Austria joined the ranks of the European Union (EU) only in 1995, preparations for the formal signing of the document started much earlier and Austria had had to demonstrate that its national legislation and policies in force did not violate European standards. Even at the legislative debate of the 1979 Equal Treatment Package, contributors cited the need to conform to EC and ILO regulations as a reason for and the impetus behind the introduced initiative.

In 1979, the most immediate international reference points were the EC and the ILO. But as Austria moved closer to membership in the EU, its direct and indirect influence grew. The opinion of researchers on the effectiveness of EU directives on women's position in national economies is divided. Most agree that in principle, at least, EU policies are impressive (Duncan 1996; Egan 1998; Mazey 1998; Ostner and Lewis 1995). In most cases, as in Austria, EU policies are more favorable to working women than are the national-level regulations (Mazey 1998). Even though the effectiveness of "superstate feminism" (Hoskyns, quoted in Duncan 1996, 400) has been questioned, in Austria, at least, the support (direct or indirect, real or perceived) provided by these international organizations to local feminist efforts seems important for women's participation in paid work and politics.

In sum, then, women have been gaining grounds in the public sphere in Austria, even though it is an arduous and slow process. In Hungary, on the other hand, rather than slowly expanding, opportunities are contracting for all. Women do not seem particularly to be losing ground, at least not immediately after the transition. The legacy of state socialism lingers on: women are still likely to be employed, are reluctant to function merely as housewives, and have increased their representation in educational institutions and in managerial positions. Much of this stability or small decline in the gender gap is not due to a major improvement in women's positions, but should be seen as a result of the decline in the position of men. Nevertheless, the fact that women are not victimized, as researchers expected in the immediate aftermath of the state socialist regime, is an indication of women's ability to survive on the newly emerging labor markets and in a newly emerging gender regime that promotes women's similarity to rather than difference from men. Yet, ironically, as the previous chapters attest, it was exactly the "differential treatment" of state socialists in past decades in Hungary that prepared women for their relative success in the capitalist labor markets.

An examination of the gender regimes in state socialist Hungary and capitalist Austria reveals two very different histories of women's integration into the labor force. Indeed, there are stark differences in both the degree and the mechanisms of male domination in the two social systems. Yet, this story also demonstrates the similarities in the two countries, the most notable of which is that without eliminating the male bias embedded in the very depth of the institutions of work, authority, and politics, gender equality can never be reached.

Appendix A. Data Sets, Samples, and
Definition of Variables

Samples

For the quantitative analysis in this volume I used data from the *Microcensus of Austria* for 1982, 1988, and 1996 (collected by the Austrian Statistical Office in Vienna) and the 1992 *Hungarian Mobility Survey* done by the Central Statistical Office. The data sets contain representative samples of households for each year and in each country.

For Austria, I used different surveys for each time point I study in this book. For Hungary, however, I used a single data set to simulate cohorts for earlier periods. Using cross-sectional data for a longitudinal argument warrants a long explanation, especially because the Hungarian Central Statistical Office had conducted similar mobility surveys in 1982 and 1972 as well. There was, however, one important, and not quite innocent, omission in those previous years: information on party membership was not included in the questionnaire. For this reason, I was forced to limit my usage to the 1992 data set, where this singularly important variable is available. If the 1992 data set is weighted to produce a random sample of the population, then it is fair to assume that it is also a reasonable representation of the population in 1982. Of course, the 1992 survey will have missed people who died in the ten-year period between 1982 and 1992 and thus are not included in the sample. To alleviate this problem I limited my selection to individuals between the ages of twenty to fifty for the analysis in each year. Restricting the upper age limit reduces the influence of the differential mortality rates in different social groups. Nevertheless, the results for 1972 are more tenuous than those for 1982, and they should be interpreted with care. Because of the differences in the probability of dying, younger people, women, those living in urban environments, and those with better economic resources are somewhat overrepresented in the earlier "virtual" samples.

Given that a 1982 sample does exist, I was able to do cross-checks. When I ran reduced models and compared the output for "my" constructed cohort for 1982 and the "real" cohort from the original survey, very few differences were found. This should give us confidence in the reliability of the 1992 data set as applied to 1982.

The Construction of the Dependent Variable: Managers

The dependent variable in almost all the models presented in this book is an individual's chance of becoming a manager. How do we define "managerial position," then? I have selected and examined a group of people at the top of the social hierarchy and in a position of formal authority; that is, those with the highest levels of power over decisionmaking in a number of social arenas. As mentioned in chapter 3, I excluded intellectuals without formal office even though the influence on decisionmaking of some of the better-known freelance thinkers might have been significant. Unfortunately, however, their power and prestige was too difficult to assess and measure.

But even this restricted concept has a number of different meanings and operationalization possibilities. Eric Olin Wright (1997), for example, uses three dimensions—decisionmaking authority, sanctioning authority, and formal managerial positions—to assess the gender gap at the top of the occupational hierarchy. McGuire and Reskin (1993) also combine three dimensions—formal position, supervisory level, and supervisory authority—to analyze predictors of the authority level of respondents. Although I do not have such detailed measurements at my disposal in the surveys on Hungary and Austria, it is comforting to know that even those who did use different dimensions did not find major discrepancies across their measurements. Wright, for example, argued that country variations in the gender gap in authority along the different types of authority dimensions were small, and each measurement separately told quite a similar story. These findings allow me to focus on a single dimension of authority—formal position in the occupational hierarchy—and still promises to capture much of the information necessary.

I operationalized "formal position of authority" by using occupational classifications in both countries. The most important managerial category so derived, and the one I primarily focus on to compare Hungary and Austria in each of the chapters, omits two potentially important groups: self-employed managers and blue-collar shop floor supervisors. Because self-employment was significantly more prevalent in Austria than it was in state socialist Hungary in the early 1980s, I decided that for the sake of comparability I had to limit my analysis to "employee managers." In separate country models, however, I also compared self-employed and nonself-employed managers within Austria.

In the Hungarian survey a very detailed variable is available that describes a person's position in the occupational hierarchy in over sixty separate categories, so I was able to fine-tune my classification in this area. In Austria the available information was much more aggregated, and I had to rely exclusively on job titles, which were classified in a somewhat idiosyncratic Austrian system. Unfortunately, in neither country were explicit questions asked about the person's actual role and power in the occupational setting. In both Hungary and Austria, however, the people selected were white-collar managers supervising the work of others or having a significant influence on the labor process. Examples of these individuals would include principals of schools and kindergartens; factory managers and their deputies; department heads and their deputies in state, government, or economic organizations; chief engineers; directors of factory branches; store managers, etc. About 4 to 6 percent of the twenty-to-fifty-year-old working-age population falls into this category, which I call "position of authority" or "manager" in the two countries, with somewhat fewer individuals in this category in Austria (4.2 percent in 1982) than in Hungary (5.1 percent in 1982).

For Hungary I constructed four measures of managerial status. First is the general managerial category as defined above. About 5 percent of the economically active population between twenty and fifty years of age could be classified here in 1982. In addition, I selected out those in the highest positions of authority and called this group "top managers." About 2 percent of the population was classified in such highly powerful and lucrative positions; these people are doubtlessly the top fragment of the ruling elite. In addition, I was able to distinguish between managers who have powerful positions in the economic sphere from those in the political/state administration sphere. The former group is larger at about 4.6 percent of the population, while the latter is small (0.5 percent). This distinction is still important because I expect the two groups to claim authority on slightly different grounds: economic managers probably possess higher levels of cultural capital, while state and political leaders should claim power mostly on the basis of political loyalty.

In Austria, I also constructed several measures of managerial status, but these are slightly different from those I defined for Hungary. I differentiate between the general managerial category, which describes those in middle-level and higher-level managerial positions in bureaucracies (about 4 percent); a subgroup of the general category, which includes those at the very top (about 1.3 percent); and a group of self-employed managers who run their own businesses and have at least one employee (about 5.4 percent). It is also possible here to distinguish between those managers active in state administration and those in economic enterprises.

Operationalizing the Independent Variables

I have used the following independent variables in my models: gender, age, party membership, postsecondary education, marital status, urban or rural location of job, class background of father, and educational background of both parents. Age is coded in years, while the rest of the variables are dichotomous, yes/no variables.

Although most variables are defined in a rather straightforward fashion, I must attach a short explanation about the class background of the respondent. My aim was to distinguish upper-class from middle-class respondents, thus I defined upper-class background as that of a family that owned a significant amount of land or other productive assets, or where the head of the household held a high-level managerial occupation. This variable thus includes both capitalists (in Austria and prewar Hungary) and high-level and highly paid professionals as well. Because the point is to use this variable as information on the economic capital of the respondent, such conflation is acceptable.

Finally, a note on the urban or rural character of the location of the job is in order. Unfortunately it was impossible to define urban environment similarly in the two countries due to the differences in the coding of the location in the two surveys. Hence "urban" includes much smaller settlements in Hungary than in Austria: those with a population of at least fifty thousand. In Austria, only large cities qualify as "urban." Thus although the urban-rural distinctions are important within each country, it is not possible to compare them across the two countries.

Appendix B. Chronology of Legislation Targeting or Affecting Women

Austria

1918   Voting rights granted for women, women first participate in elections of 1919

1920   Legal gender equality included in the Constitution

1947   Age limit for retirement for women reduced from age sixty-five to sixty (remains sixty-five for men)

1950   ILO Convention on prohibition of night work for women is ratified; women cannot work at night except in the industries of health, sanitation, culture, entertainment, education, transportation, and tourism (in 1992, this prohibition was reinforced by the Constitutional Court)

1952   ILO Convention no. 103 is ratified; the principle of providing maternity protection and leave is accepted, but no practical applications are offered

1953   ILO Convention on Protective Labor Legislation for Women is ratified, but is reexamined and abolished in 1976

1957   Federal protective legislation for mothers is passed with the following provisions: women can take six months unpaid maternity leave; cannot be fired before and after birth; must take eight weeks leave before birth; must be transferred to less-strenuous work (all provisions on condition of medical examinations)

1961   Maternity leave extended to one year: unemployment insurance pays income for those eligible, and period does not

	count in promotion, seniority, or bonus but does count toward retirement
1965	Coeducation enforced in all-male elite schools
1966	First female member of government is elected. A division of Women's Affairs in the Ministry of Social Affairs is established, but has little effect until the 1970s
1969	Promotion of Labor Market Act regulates training and encourages active labor force policy. Although act contains no direct mention of women, it makes them eligible for training programs on the basis of financial need, regardless of marital status and husband's income
1974	Maternity cash benefits raised: lump sum, adjusted automatically (extended to adoptive mothers in 1976)
	Tax system changed from being based on household to based on individual
	First trimester abortion legalized
1975	Novel principle of partnership in marriage introduced in the new Family Law: women do not need husband's permission to work; children belong to both parents equally
1976	Protective labor legislation for women withdrawn
1978	Divorce law makes no-fault divorce easy but deprives women of alimony
1979	Equal Treatment Law prohibits discrimination in labor market in private sector; differential pay scales for men and women abolished
	Women representatives appointed (Women's Secretariate) in Bundeskanzleramt and in Ministry of Social Policy; gender-specific political representation only until 1983
1980	Widow's pension issue discussed in Constitutional Court (men to be eligible, not women only)
1981	Women defined as "problem group" in labor market policies. No specific measures for women passed during this period of high unemployment
1982	Legislation raised for optional parental leave for fathers (but law not passed until 1989–90)
1983	Women's Secretariate eliminated
1985	Gender-specific job advertisements deemed unconstitutional; linguistic equality in job descriptions is called for

First gender quotas established in Social Democratic Party: women representatives in Parliament to be 15 percent (women's representation passes at 10 percent in 1986 for the first time in Austrian history)

1985–89   Equal Treatment Package finally to include specific measures for women, including training for nontraditional occupations, as well as retraining. Guarantees no discrimination in decisions for promotion and overtime, extra income, etc.

mid-1980s   Progressive labor market policies established to help create jobs for women (state financing provided initially until job becomes part of labor market)

1989   First serious criminal law reform to deal with violence against women and rape in marriage

1989–90   Maternity leave for fathers established; reemployment subsidy paid by government to help women return to labor force

1990   School books reexamined to excise traditional gender stereotypes

Maternal leave to become parental leave, although women have primacy; leave extended from one to two years

Constitution Court rules equal retirement age for men and women to be adopted by 2028 (passed as law by Parliament in 1992)

Ministry for Women's Affairs established (transformed from Women's Secretariate); special ombudsperson established for discrimination issues (position existed since mid-1970s but its effectiveness increased significantly in the early 1990s)

1992   Prohibition upheld on night work for women (except in a few industries)

1992–94   Equal Treatment Package to include equal treatment laws in public sector; antidiscrimination laws, damages if discriminating, positive policies to encourage women's employment. Government subsidies given to companies if women employed with aim of at least 45 percent in all positions (if less than 45 percent, women preferred). Women must be granted part-time work after giving birth.

Burden of proof for discrimination cases reversed. Laws established against sexual harassment

1994   "Daughters can do more!" Training program established for girls to prepare them for labor market and help them choose nontraditional jobs

1995   Women can retain birth name in marriage (decided in 1975 but not in effect until 1995)

European Court considers automatic preferential treatment contrary to equality principle

1996   Parental leave renegotiated: reduced to eighteen months (from two years) for women, but can be two years if father takes at least six months. Positive encouragement for fathers to stay at home with babies

Hungary

1948   Gender equality proclaimed in law

1949   Constitution guarantees similar work conditions for men and women, although differential retirement age is upheld. Constitution pronounces work an obligation for all Hungarian Women's Democratic Alliance (MNDSZ) (the first official procommunist women's group) established

Late 1940s   Gender quotas in parliamentary and local "elections" introduced

1949–51   Propaganda materials and wage and social policy force women to enter labor force

1951   New labor law describes quotas for women's participation in labor force and training. Also provides protection for pregnant women and upholds twelve weeks for fully paid maternity leave

1952   Family law: aim is women's equality in family; allows women to keep birth name in marriage

1953   Abortion ban upheld and enforced

Women's organization abolished; women's issues dealt with within other party institutions

Labor laws: protective legislation for pregnant women only

1953–56   Taxes on childless couples introduced

1956   Abortion ban repealed

Revolution demand: return women back to household

1957	New women's organization established: Magyar Nők Országos Tanácsa (Hungarian Women's Council)
1960s	Educational system in Hungary is reformed: expansion results in the inclusion of women (especially in lower-level colleges)
1962	Protective labor legislation introduced: women banned from many physically challenging jobs
	Maternity leave extended to twenty weeks
1965	Second set of protective labor laws established; restricts even further the number of occupations available to women
1967	Maternity leave regulation established: three-year paid leave for working women. All women receive lump sum. Eligibility is twelve months in labor force before birth of child, or full-time student status
1970	Party decree stated in "Position of Women in Hungarian Society": encourages promotion of women into positions of authority; demands better-quality childcare facilities and more household devices for women; demands yearly progress reports from organizations
1972	Constitution modified: women entitled to working conditions similar to those for men
1979	Party decree established for the evaluation of the decade-long campaign for women's equality
1980	New York Agreement ratified as a general decree against sex discrimination
1982	Protective labor legislation upheld
1985	Maternity leave policies modified, introduced. First year leave at 80 percent of pay; additional two years at set rate. Differentiation among women established
1992	Maternity leave turned into means tested rather than universal right
	Gradual equalization of pension age for men and women begun
1998	Maternity leave again established as universal right

Notes

1. Three Generations of Women in Central Europe

1. Abridged and summarized from my interview with Mrs. F. (Mária) in 1994 for this project. Names and a few minor details have been modified to guarantee anonymity (Thanks to Erika Varsányi for research assistance.) The interviews were conducted in the summers and winters of 1992 through 1998 in Austria and Hungary. I used snowball sampling, looking in both countries for managers in various positions and mostly in the age group over forty-five years old. The interviews took about two hours each and most were taped and transcribed. I asked each respondent about their family backgrounds, career paths, current marital and family circumstances, and their experiences of and opinions about gender discrimination. Overall, I conducted thirty-three interviews (nineteen in Hungary and fourteen in Austria).

    Note that all translations in this volume are mine unless otherwise indicated.

2. Retirement age for women at the time was fifty-five years in Hungary (sixty years for men).

3. Its name before 1956 was Magyar Dolgozók Pártja (Hungarian Workers' Party) and after 1956 it was Magyar Szocialista Munkáspárt (Hungarian Socialist Workers' Party). All through this book I refer to both as the Hungarian communist party, (or simply, the communist party) a name that indicates the party's long-term ambitions and historical and ideological legacy rather than the reality of its practice. I chose this terminology for its brevity and familiarity.

4. In younger Austrian generations the rate of college attendance became roughly equal among men and women by the late 1990s (Gross, Weidenhofer, and Vötsch 1994, 29), but gender differences in the educational attainment level of the overall working population linger.

5. There is much controversy over the correct terminology used to describe the social organization of Eastern European societies between 1949 and 1990. Throughout this book I refer to the countries and their social and economic regimes as "state socialist" in accordance with other recent work on this subject. Yet I will describe the political ideology of policymakers and the party as "communist" to signify its proclaimed intentions as well as its ideological and historical legacies.

6. This percentage is calculated for women between fifteen and sixty-four years of age; that is, the working age defined according to the European standard. In Hungary, women's retirement age has traditionally been lower at fifty-five, and only started gradually to increase to sixty-two after 1992. The labor force activity rate for women in the fifteen-to-fifty-four year group was 71 percent in Hungary at the same time, which is higher than the percentage presented above, but there is no comparable number available for this age group in Austria or the European Union. Nevertheless, the tendencies are quite clear, especially because a further drop in the rate of women's labor force participation can be observed between 1992 and 1995 (Frey 1996, 13–14).

7. The formal test of difference would have to be carried out in a single model through interaction terms for each variable and each country.

8. Important negotiations were held in other party organizations as well—for example, in the Executive Committee (Intéző Bizottság), whose sessions were not transcribed or recorded. But because many Politburo members were present at both meetings, we could reasonably be sure that most positions were indeed represented at the Politburo sessions as well—although sometimes this information has to be read between the lines.

2. Gender Regimes East and West

1. In fact, some feminists go even further and argue that "univocal sovereignty" as it exists in liberal democracies is itself patriarchal because, due to its indivisibility, it is unable to incorporate embodied "difference" of any kind (Jones 1993).

2. I do not want to claim that there is an essential male (or female) experience. Rather, given that the distribution of labor in the household is practically invariant in the two social systems, my point is that male-biased institutions do not take into account women's (not at all biological, yet still very pressing) household responsibilities.

3. Recent efforts at alleviating some of these distinctions should be noted. For example, since the early 1990s mothers bringing up children can count the years spent away from the labor force as part of their working years when calculating pension or social security benefits.

4. Corporate groups in Austria operate under a somewhat similar logic, providing a marvelous illustration of how a long-standing East Central European tradition can be recreated in two such different forms in Austria and Hungary.

Yet corporate groups were never constructed along gender (or age) lines in Austria but always along class and status, and thus their relevance here is marginal.

5. In an effort to increase the pool of soldiers and laborers for the communist cause, abortion was expressly prohibited under the Stalinist Rákosi government in Hungary by a 1953 decree (PIA 276/53/108). In actual fact, abortion had been illegal earlier as well, and ironically the 1953 decree *reduced* the punishment for various forms of termination of pregnancy. But little of the word of the law had been enforced previously, so in essence it was this 1953 legislation that instituted a strict prosecution of abortionists and their clients as well as a close scrutiny of women of childbearing age. These efforts resulted in a sharp increase in the birth rate between 1953 and 1956, as well as much public hatred toward the political regime.

In what was probably an effort to ease the mounting political tension, the Rákosi government legalized abortions in June 1956, five months before the revolution. Fearing political opposition, the post-1956 Politburo did not dare to touch this law for a full decade and a half (see, for example, the Politburo discussion in 1962 in PIA 288/5/267).

6. Renting an apartment was rather inexpensive in Hungary because rental units were almost all state owned and subsidized. The difficulty lay in gaining access to a title of a rental because apartments were scarce, especially in large cities. If an individual had claims to a rented apartment, he or she could "sell" it for significant amounts of money—an illegal but widespread practice. Therefore, renting an apartment in Hungary meant more than in capitalist countries—indeed, in a way it was a sign of financial stability.

7. Similarly, Fraser argues that "the family-wage ideal was inscribed in the structure of most industrial era welfare states" (1994, 591). This normative framework was obviously replaced by something altogether different by the mid-1950s in most state socialist societies, while it lingered on in Western Europe and in North America.

8. Recently, feminist theorists have started to question the usefulness of the similarity principle and have suggested alternative, asymmetrical models of gender equality (Littleton 1991; MacKinnon 1991; Scott 1988), Littleton's "acceptance model," for example, acknowledges socially constructed (as well as biological) differences between men and women but argues for legislation that would make these differences costless. This approach, however, is much contested because potentially it opens the way for an essentialist treatment of women's difference and, as MacKinnon argues, "doesn't give women the dignity of the single standard" (1991, 86).

9. Positive discrimination policies are widely challenged in the United States and elsewhere as well. In Europe, for example, in 1995 the European Court pronounced positive discrimination illegal.

10. The term "public sphere" introduces much controversy in the feminist literature. In addition, its uncritical use to describe the societies of Eastern Europe

has been persuasively questioned (Gal and Kligman 2000b). Nevertheless, I occasionally use the concept, but strictly as shorthand for "paid work and political office."

11. Following I. Szelenyi (1978), David Stark (1986) applies the concept of "mirrored oppositions" to a study of internal labor markets in state socialist and capitalist economies. The function of an internal labor market—just like that of male domination—is broadly similar in both types of societies, but its institutional conditions and embeddedness differs. The framework helps provide a way to understand the broad similarities and the specific differences in social institutions in state socialist and capital societies and as such is a useful tool for my analysis.

3. From "K und K" to "Communism versus Capitalism": The Social Worlds of Austria and Hungary

"K und K" is the popular name for the Kaiserliche und Königliche Gesamtmonarchie, the Dual Monarchy.

1. Note that in English texts the name "Habsburg" is sometimes spelled "Hapsburg." I will use the Central European spelling.

2. Researchers often differentiate between two periods of state socialism in Hungary. The first extends to the mid-1960s and is sometimes called "classical (Stalinist) model of socialism" or "consolidated socialism," while the second extends from the mid-1960s to 1989 and is referred to as "reform socialism" (Eyal, Szelenyi, and Townsley 1998; S. Szelenyi 1998). Most of the research in this book focuses on the latter era, although references to earlier periods will be made occasionally.

3. In German, the term "manager" is often used, or the translation *Leiter* or *Führer*. In Hungarian, the word *káder* was indeed the official term, although *vezető* (leader) was also used. The latter comes from the verb "to lead."

4. In practical usage, the term "cadre" denoted not only party but also state functionaries and all leaders in general (sometimes even potential leaders, as in "cadre pool") in the communist regime.

5. The third criterion was added as an afterthought. It was conveniently obscure and rarely enforced. The following is an example of the application of this criterion: In a 1962 Politburo meeting members were discussing the nomination of a man for a very high position of authority. János Kádár remarked: "He is a hardworking man alright . . . but we can't appoint him because his family life is in such a mess." Another member, the person who put forth the original nomination replied: "Oh, no, he cleared that up, he got a divorce." But Kádár was not satisfied with a simple divorce. "Since when does *that* constitute a solution?" he asked. "Now what should we do with him? You want us to attend his second wedding?" (PIA 288/5/255). But the person got the appointment anyway. Much of the discussion about morality remained at this level and did not usually hinder advancement.

6. Not only was a person's own occupation relevant for the evaluation of his or her political reliability, but so was that of his or her family of origin, spouse, and other relatives. In fact, the family information was sometimes considered more important than the actual class position of the person involved. This is the principle that allowed Jenő Fock, then prime minister to Hungary, to argue at a Politburo meeting in 1972 that his daughter (an engineer in her forties) should really count as having a "working-class" origin and consciousness based on his own ten years in a factory job some forty years earlier. By this time, and probably all through the adult life of his daughter, Fock had been a top executive of the communist regime—most notably he had been prime minister or deputy prime minister for fifteen years. Curiously enough, this seemed irrelevant in identifying the "real" class background of his daughter (PIA 288/5/592).

7. A new statistical category was suggested to amend this problem: instead of using the prewar occupation of the parents, the Politburo considered focusing on the current occupation of the parents. This, however, raised further problems of intergenerational mobility; most notably, it did not allow cadres themselves to claim preferential treatment for their children on the basis of their own occupation, because they themselves did not count as blue-collar workers anymore. In addition, counting cadre parents as not belonging to the working classes ruined the carefully monitored proportion of working-class representation in a number of fields. For example, in 1963 the Politburo expressed some unhappiness over the percentage of working-class children among those admitted to university, which was only 37.4 percent. On further examination, they decided that the introduction of a different statistical category was in order: the first (not 1938 and not current) occupation of the parents (or the nominee himself or herself). If as a youth a person ever worked as a manual laborer, even if only between college and high school or for the summer holidays, his or her original occupation was recorded as blue-collar worker. This meant that older cadres, who by the 1970s had been in positions of power for a quarter of a century, could still claim the potential political capital associated with a working-class first occupation if they ever earned an income as apprentices or laborers (see the example of Prime Minister Jenő Fock above). This clever trick also increased the proportion of working-class children in the 1963 college freshman pool to 46 percent (from roughly 37 percent), and the Politburo was satisfied (PIA 288/5/293).

8. The importance of party membership was to be found not only in the need to express political loyalty: a party booklet also indicated membership in a relatively closed elite. Party members had access to classified information, starting from simple everyday matters, such as the increase in the price of a food item, to more important issues such as changes in party policies and directions. It was useful for a person in a position of authority to be a member not only *before* they were appointed, but also *while* in office, otherwise he or she was left out of an important information channel that in itself helped main-

tain his or her position by advising its holder ahead of time of forthcoming shifts in party policy and a change in the officially accepted road to communism. The importance of this aspect of party membership is clearly demonstrated by the fact that party membership did not fully lose its predictive power in explaining access to privileges even by 1993, four years after the disappearance of the communist party from the political scene (Böröcz and Róna-Tas 1995).

9. In Hungary, there were two distinct channels of postsecondary education: universities and colleges. The former took about five years to complete and provided more academically oriented and more prestigious training, while the latter lasted three to four years only and concentrated on less-theoretical types of knowledge. I will rarely distinguish between these two in this book, because from the point of view of access to managerial positions there was practically no difference in their usefulness. Unless I note otherwise, the term *postsecondary training* will refer both to college and university education.

10. Simultaneously they were also forced to respond to challenges both from outside and inside, perhaps the most successful of which was the increasingly intensive demands to share power by members of the technocratic intelligentsia (Lengyel 1996; I. Szelenyi 1982; Szalai 1990).

11. I chose to exclude inactive members of the population in both countries, because my key dependent variable assumes participation in the labor force. It would bias the results significantly if I included those who do not work for pay and thus have no chance of being promoted to a formal position of authority. As mentioned above, had I included the inactive population in both countries, the differences between Hungary and Austria would have been even more pronounced.

12. For 1992, communist party membership is coded "yes" (1) if the person was the member of the Hungarian Socialist Workers' Party in 1989. Obviously, after 1989 the significance and meaning of party membership changed enormously. The fact that our models reflect this only slightly shows the slowness of elite change as well as the importance of the network characteristics of communist party membership in Hungary.

13. The effect is so small, though, that it could easily be due to the post–state socialist political bias concerning party membership that I discussed above. Although members of the *nomenklatura* (special list of top leaders) could hardly deny their earlier political involvements, managers in lower-level positions were more likely to succeed in doing so. Thus the changes we see in these models could merely be the result of bias due to self-reporting.

14. I used discrete time event history analysis to assess the statistical significance in the changes in the most important predictors in both countries. I will not present the output from these models here, but these event history models are the sources of the interpretation of changes over time.

15. The real surprise (although this is not strictly relevant for our discussion, which primarily focuses on state socialism) is the declining effect of cultural

capital after 1989, when at least some researchers expected a significant rise in the importance of skills and qualifications (Nee 1991). This is a puzzling finding, which has been reproduced in other data sets as well, and thus cannot easily be attributed to random variation. There are two possible explanations. First, the percentage of private business owners increased significantly by 1992 in Hungary, and they are less likely to have high-level degrees from universities. Business owners are difficult to identify in the 1992 data set and are thus not excluded. Second, it is also possible that the predetermined nature of the social structure loosened in the first five years after the collapse of communism, thus weakening the effect of all formal variables that had been used to measure social advancement.

16. Let us assume also that he is married, lives in a large city, and does not have upper-class or college-graduate parents.

17. There is no significant positive interaction between political and cultural capital, and thus the possession of both has no more significance than the two added together.

18. Recent mobility studies question the effectiveness of the communist regime in abolishing the significance of social background in status attainment in Hungary (S. Szelenyi 1998). My findings are somewhat different. This discrepancy could be due to the fact that as opposed to most mobility studies, I focus on a single outcome category at the very top of the social hierarchy. In the process of the attainment of managerial status, my models show a significant contrast between Hungary and Austria. My argument is, therefore, made in relative terms: *compared* to Austria, the importance of parental capital seemed to have been smaller in state socialist Hungary.

19. As noted before, college and university degrees must be distinguished in Hungary. Most college degrees took four years, although some required only three. University degrees took longer, usually five to six years, and were considered more prestigious and focused more on theoretical rather than practical knowledge.

4. Exclusion versus Limited Inclusion

1. Some early feminists (e.g., Simone de Beauvoir) occasionally praised the communist experiment, although their discussions were largely based on ideological commitment rather than actual empirical research.

2. For an exception, see S. Szelenyi (1998).

3. In addition, their argument is somewhat ambiguous: although some researchers argue that the link between family background and class position was indeed looser in communist than in comparable capitalist societies (Haller, Kolosi, and Róbert 1990), others find little or no such systematic differences (Mueller et al. 1990).

4. It should be noted that hereafter all analyses refer only to the twenty-to-fifty year-old, gainfully employed population. Because this latter condition re-

stricts the circle of women more in Austria than in Hungary, if we were to calculate the same percentages for the whole population we would find even larger differences between the two countries.

5. The concept of the glass ceiling (i.e., the observation that women's access to top-level positions is more difficult than to lower-level ones) is well known in the North American literature (Kanter 1977; Reskin and Ross 1992; Albelda and Tilly 1999), although Wright et al. (1995) found no evidence for it in a comparative survey of several European countries and the United States.

6. I would like to thank András Sugár for allowing me access to this data set.

7. Note that this pattern holds at the top of the social hierarchy as well. In the 1988 Hungarian nomenklatura, 5.3 percent of the economic elite compared to 17.6 percent of the political elite were women (S. Szelenyi 1998, 112).

8. This was a tacit understanding among party executives; I could not find it written in the actual decree.

9. The Politburo was already alarmed enough by population statistics in 1973 to attempt to restrict access to abortion and to consider a revitalization of a campaign popularizing motherhood. Members passed the appropriate law, but its implementation was, by and large, sabotaged by local resistance. The 1985 legislation indicates a change in the direction of lawmaking, moving from placing restrictions to changing incentives. This move can be seen as the culmination of population control efforts that started in the late 1960s and early 1970s.

10. My interviewees themselves were all in managerial positions, and given their success they might have been the lucky few to avoid experiences of discrimination. Yet the contrast with Austrian managers in similar positions stands. In addition, in a 1993 survey of the general population I found that a negligible number of people claimed to have experienced gender discrimination in Hungary, even though a few did claim discrimination on the basis of their ethnicity or political convictions. In other words, the experience of no gender discrimination is not limited to the higher echelons of power in Hungary.

11. Note that my argument is certainly true for middle- and upper-middle-class, educated women—a relatively small, albeit important, stratum—but the experience of women working in blue-collar, male-typed factory jobs might have been different. Class differences were not at all negligible among women even in supposedly classless Hungary.

5. Mechanisms of Exclusion

1. This model choice was partly driven by data limitations for Austria. But for Hungary, where the data allow more tricks, I tested a much larger model that included variables describing the residence type, party affiliation of parents, and property status of the families. These larger and more carefully specified models yielded essentially the same gender coefficients that concern us here.

2. The odds of women are calculated by exponentiating the logistic regression

coefficient: $e^{-.88} = .41$. Women's odds compared to that of men's are .41:1. The odds of men are found by exponentiating .88, the coefficient for women with the opposite sign, which is about 2.4.

3. The gender gap declined through the years in both countries. But although by 1988 the odds of having a college degree were about the same for working men and women in Hungary, the gender coefficient was still negative and statistically significant in Austria for the same year.

4. One exception is the highly feminized college degree in nursing or in elementary school teaching. These degrees were unlikely to qualify their bearers for high positions of authority except as headmasters or head nurses, of which there are relatively few positions. But a number of different types of college degrees in state administration, finance, or technology were often no less feminized, and such degrees provided much higher returns in terms of pay and potential promotions.

5. By the 1990s there is a convergence similar to those of labor force participation rates: Austrian women were catching up with men at the universities. The other side of the analogy does not work, however: Hungarian women's access to universities did not decline after the collapse of communism.

6. I also compared a more formal model of the *transition* to postsecondary education, given a completed secondary education in the two countries (S. Szelenyi 1998). Although I do not present the output here, my findings are consistent with the discussion above: there is practically no statistically significant difference in the class-based intergenerational inheritance of educational attainment in the two countries. However, in the early 1980s women faced vastly smaller degrees of discrimination in Hungary than in Austria.

7. In Hungary, on the other hand, strict entrance exams were instituted. These did not lower the admission chances of young women, however, who in many critical subjects performed better than men in a classroom context. Let me add a personal story here to illustrate this point. In the mid-1980s as a student representative I sat in on a series of oral entrance examinations at the University of Arts and Sciences in Budapest. For the particular major for which we were admitting students (Russian language and literature) female applicants outnumbered men by a factor of approximately ten. By the middle of the 1980s gender-based positive discrimination policies in university admissions had been completely phased out: men and women were supposed to be treated equally. Therefore, I was somewhat surprised to find that the committee lowered the standards for male applicants practically to zero in an effort to balance out the ratio of male and female students at the college. Any man who could put together two coherent Russian sentences got in, while women had to converse about sixteenth-century Russian poetry for a good half hour. Yet, the committee admitted overall fourteen students, only three of whom were men. The point of this story is, of course, that entrance examinations in and of themselves do not necessarily block women's access to university education, even when there is an obvious bias against them in the admission process.

Larger factors influencing students before they even make it to the exam do a more efficient job of affecting admission.

8. Characteristics also include: coming from a blue-collar, propertyless family; no children; and not in a supervisory position.

9. I interviewed a number of older female cadres and found that several of them participated in these unimaginably heroic activities. For example, Judit, the wife of a famous communist leader killed by the right-wing Hungarian police in an anticommunist raid, operated a printing press in a Budapest apartment and produced fliers and posters protesting the Nazi rule. Before the war Helga organized labor protests and strikes among textile workers, and before her own arrest during the war she spent time producing fake documents for underground comrades.

10. This should come as no surprise. Like other ideologies stemming from the same roots, Marxism-Leninism had great faith in science, which was found relevant for the household as well. Numerous articles in women's magazines described the scientifically correct way of feeding a family, and courses were organized to teach women how to keep house in the most efficient possible manner. Party leaders believed that scientific innovations, rather than the contributions of individual men, would free women from household duties.

11. Note the use of the possessive ("our") here, which indicates a move away from male domination over women as husbands to the power of the state over women as a subject group. I discuss this more fully in the next chapter.

12. Gender is coded as 0 = male, 1 = female; and the postsecondary degree is coded as 1 = has it, 0 = doesn't have it. Thus the product of the two variables, their interaction term, describes the additional effect for women graduates.

13. This relationship between the gendering of a capital and its usefulness for women also holds in terms of the different types of degrees in Hungary. Women's returns for *university* degrees were not significantly lower than those of men, but they were much lower for *college* degrees. Although the college degree was easily obtainable by women, university education was still dominated by men. As the proportion of men decreased, so did the degree's usefulness for women in both countries. (It should be noted again that in terms of usefulness for gaining managerial positions I found no difference between college and university degrees, which is what justifies treating these two types of degrees as one.)

14. Let's ignore for the moment the question of why Bourdieu conceptualized gender this way (for an interesting discussion of this question, see McCall 1992).

6. Conditions of Inclusion: Examining State Policies in Austria and Hungary, 1945–1995

1. Recently, feminist scholars have suggested transcending Mary Wollstone-craft's classic "equality" versus "difference" dilemma (Fraser 1994; Scott

1988). I believe their recommendations are valid for policymaking or feminist strategizing, but, as I demonstrate in this chapter, I find the distinction a useful tool in comparing and contrasting policymaking in Austria and Hungary.

2. More recent regulations on pregnancy in the Family and Medical Leave Act of 1993 mandates that employers grant parental leave to both male or female employees. This effort points toward a somewhat different principle of policymaking, although it formally assumes, as in previous legislation, the similarly situated status of men and women. In reality, however, because women are most likely to take the leave, its effect is different. Earlier, in 1978, states such as California began to experiment with "affirmative action"-based pregnancy regulations. Kelly and Dobbin (1999) argue that this approach, in contrast to what they call "equal opportunity" laws represented by the 1978 legislation, was more effective in forcing employers to grant leaves to pregnant women.

3. This is sometimes referred to as the "equality principle." I am using the term "similarity" because I want to emphasize that it is in contrast to the difference principle.

4. Interestingly, segregation is an outcome that also characterizes latent exclusion, the cell at the opposite end of my table. More and more often, women's inability fully to adopt the male norm forces them to take jobs specifically created for "inferior" workers (e.g., less than full-time jobs, jobs without benefits, lower-paid jobs in certain sectors of the economy deemed fit for women, etc.). In principle, the difference between the two cells lies in the degree of women's participation. In the case of limited exclusion (in state socialist Hungary, for example), women participate full time for their entire careers in the labor market, but this is not the case with latent exclusion (in capitalist Austria, for example). The fact that we see increasingly more women participating in the labor market in the United States and other Western capitalist societies (and doing so in a segregated fashion) is an indication that the principles of integration are shifting—for at least a segment of the female population—toward limited inclusion in these parts of the world as well.

5. The discussions in this chapter, therefore, characterize the social construction of gender carried out in decisionmaking bodies in Austria and Hungary. These constructions are obviously different from the variety of popular constructions of gender that people created, reproduced, or revolutionized in their everyday lives. An exploration of these latter ideas, while admittedly significant, is beyond the scope of this work.

6. The Austrian women's situation was even more difficult than that of Rosie the Riveter. In Austria, unlike in the United States, the proportion of women in the paid labor force actually declined after the war (Renzetti and Curran, 1992, 179, table 8.1).

7. The number of men in the labor force also declined, and thus the proportion of the female labor force remained around 39 percent between 1951 and 1971.

8. In contrast, by 1991 age at first marriage increased sharply to 25.6 years for

women, and the birthrate fell to 11.9 babies per 1,000 population. In the early 1990s women on average had 1.4 children in Austria (Frauenbericht 1995).

9. Party and state decrees do not need to be differentiated in Hungary. The party had the ultimate power over decisionmaking, and all important national-level regulations were first discussed in the Politburo. Whether the actual regulation was published in the form of a law and passed by Parliament or in the shape of a party decree and voted on by the Central Committee (or by both, as was the case most often) meant only a formal difference.

10. The occupation "tractor driver" was singled out as a particularly good example of how women could enter male occupations. Pictures of tractor-driver women appeared at the time in the newspapers and newscasts, and on political posters and other party propaganda materials. Many of the party documents I reviewed discussed the specific case of women tractor drivers and recruitment into this occupation. Although tractor driving was perhaps the job most often mentioned, women were mobilized just as intensively for many other types of agricultural and industrial jobs.

11. At least this was what Politburo documents claimed would happen. In reality very few men returned to blue-collar positions from office jobs.

12. Andrea Pető discusses a similar process at recruitment for police work in her book *Nőhistóriák* (Women's histories) (1998).

13. With one caveat: although the party leadership took pleasure in images of true communist women in a few previously male-typed professions, most women were still doing traditionally female-typed jobs and even the ones laboriously recruited often abandoned their new profession (PIA 276/88/656 in 1952; see also Goven 1993b). This is an early indication that the similarity principle was not completely genuine or successful even at its inception.

14. Interestingly though, just as the ideal woman was "masculinized" this way, the ideal man was also "feminized" to a degree. In an effort to assess the most important personal qualities necessary for advancement to leadership positions, I counted the descriptive terms used to characterize cadres in their personnel files in the first half of 1960. Cadre departments in the party secretariat collected personnel files, and when a person was nominated for a position (always a high-level leadership position in the party or in the state or economic apparatus) a brief nomination was written that described in a few sentences the cadre's past and present activities as well as his personality. In 1960, the terms most often used other than "politically reliable" and "educated" included the following: modest, reliable, disciplined, honest, or "has good people skills." Except for the last term, these are hardly the words that would be used to favorably characterize a CEO in a capitalist corporation. Those traits, usually associated with Western masculinity—e.g., creativity, risk-taking, competitiveness, ambition, or aggressive drive—did not once appear in the nominations.

15. The weekly women's journal (*Asszonyok*, and later *Nők Lapja*) is filled with examples of Stahanovite women, and the magazine's style and content in the

early 1950s is practically no different from the daily papers, except for the fact that the protagonists in the stories are mainly women.

16. These efforts at transforming the domestic division of labor were much less concentrated and effective than those directed at recruiting women for the labor force.

17. The Austrian Social Democratic Party was in some periods also called Austrian Socialist Party. I will refer to both as Social Democratic Party (SPÖ) and to their members as social democrats or socialists.

18. Austria was not, of course, the only country whose performance was occasionally critiqued by the EC. In fact, Austria was one of the first to ratify the New York Convention in 1979, as EC documents noted approvingly.

19. The prohibition against night work was still upheld, although some occupations were excused (such as nurses, waitresses, and actresses, for example).

20. Among many other examples, a report to the Department of Party and Mass Organizations complains that in Debrecen, a major Hungarian city, 607 girls and 102 boys who just graduated from high school could not find any work (PIA 288/21/1962/13).

21. "Elég a fejkendős Mariskák ispánságából!" in Hungarian (author's interview with Ibolya Ujlaki of the National Council of Hungarian Women, 1990).

22. I'd like to thank Julie Press for clarifying this distinction for me in one of our many conversations about this work.

23. The example of the United States that I give at the beginning of this chapter is the exception rather than the rule. Most countries provide targeted maternity benefits of some sort to new mothers. Historically, maternity policies were first introduced by Bismarck in Central Europe, and thus the commonality of the Austrian and Hungarian cases is no surprise (Kamerman, Kahn, and Kingston 1983). Indeed, pregnancy and maternity provisions, meager as they were, already existed in Hungary before World War II (Grád 1988). All European countries provided some sort of maternity benefits to women by this time.

24. A report to the Politburo says: "The women's organization for many years has been organized like the party. We must avoid these mistakes in the future. The women's organization should in the future place more emphasis on child-care issues, defending people's interests" (PIA 288/5/24).

25. The name Johanna Dohnal, the first State Secretary (later Minister) of Women's Affairs, is often mentioned as the key force behind these new labor market policies in Austria.

26. A year later this law was modified, and mothers were allowed to get a discount of two years on their retirement age for each child they raised.

27. By 1998, the Austrian Parliament did indeed legislate men's responsibilities in household chores.

28. In fact, some representatives suggested differentiation among women with children and those without (although not between men with children and those without), suggesting that only women with children should retain their

right to an earlier retirement age. This position, although not successful, would have produced an interesting, new variation on the difference principle, where gender would have been explicitly tied to reproductive responsibilities, and women without children would have been treated as men.

29. When talking about positive role models, the same Austrian legislators cited the example of their Western neighbors (e.g., Germany).

30. A better-known, albeit sometimes pejorative term for Roma is "Gypsy."

31. Or at least politicians could and did argue that their gender policies (especially maternity leave policies) were carried out at the urging of these financial institutions.

32. Goven (2000) argues that Hungarian legislators went further in these cuts than even demanded by IMF experts. Others such as Duina (1994) claim that the implementation of EU policies varied according to the institutional and historical differences in the receiving countries. Nevertheless, it can still be argued that the social policy recommendations and requirements of the EU exerted significant influence on the *principles* of policymaking in both countries.

33. Less than a decade later Hungarian policymakers also started to take EU regulations seriously in preparation for membership. In the first part of the 1990s, however, the influence of structural adjustment policies initiated by the IMF were stronger than the more woman-friendly social legislation proposed by the EU.

34. Austria repealed its protective legislations in 1995 as a direct response to an EU requirement.

7. Difference at Work: A Case Study of Hungary

1. Thanks to Gil Eyal for calling my attention to this term.

2. There are exceptions to this formulation, however. In some instances the documents singled out "housewives" or "urban housewives" as potential sources of labor supply, but in most instances they referred to the group simply as "women."

   The Women's Council is, to some extent, also an exception to this rule, and even top-level party organs changed their position somewhat after the 1970s. In several of the Women's Council documents, the need for separate programs and propaganda for women of different strata is mentioned. Still, the Women's Council prided themselves on their "unified gender politics" (*egységes nőpolitika*), which expressed their desire to "help the friendly communication and understanding between all women: peasant women in the co-ops, factory workers, white-collar women, as well as housewives" (PIA 288/5/36).

3. There was only one official women's organization at any one point in time, but the name and program changed a few times throughout the period. The first organization, established in the late 1940s, was called the Democratic Alliance of Hungarian Women (Magyar Nők Demokratikus Szövetsége, or

MNDSZ), which in 1956 was somewhat reorganized and then renamed the National Council of Hungarian Women (Magyar Nők Országos Tanácsa, or MNOT).

4. In fact, to represent the political leadership of the country the Politburo made a point of sending a male member (even though there was always at least one woman who also could have participated) to these celebrations or to the opening ceremonies of the congresses of the Women's Council. They considered such representation to be "polite," as evidenced by a discussion in the 1960s that included the phrase "for a man to greet the Women's Congress"; another subtle reinforcement of the "us, men"/"they, women" separation.

5. However, it should be noted that at a meeting in November 1950, party leader Mátyás Rákosi described women as "naturally" better communists than men: "The long serfdom has oppressed the proletariat, his lungs cannot expand, his muscles cannot contract. This is not true for young people and, to some extent, for women. . . . Women were doubly oppressed before the revolution, and like the youth can really see the advantages of the people's democracy [socialism]" (PIA 276/53/64). Either way, of course, the point here is that women as a group are constructed in opposition to the "proletariat" and seem to have certain characteristics in common—be it a lesser or stronger propensity toward being devoted communists.

6. To be precise, the document says "married women" (asszonyok), which was the way the Women's Council usually referred to its members, even though Politburo documents usually used the term "women" (nők). Asszonyok was perhaps seen as more friendly, less official sounding, and certainly less "feminist," which was the last thing the Women's Council would have wanted to subscribe to. The emphasis on married women rather than all women reflects the failure of Kollontai's position to take hold, even among those officially representing women in Eastern Europe.

8. Capitalist and State Socialist Gender Regimes

1. After 1998, when a more conservative, right-wing government took control of Parliament, the restrictions in maternity leave regulations were revoked. Parental leave policies after 1998 can be claimed as a universal right and they guarantee a very modest income to mothers (or fathers after the child's first birthday) for three years after the birth of each baby.

2. Hidden unemployment within companies and factories was an open secret toward the end of the state socialist era. No information exists on the gender breakdown of those who had jobs and salaries but no actual work in the 1980s in Hungary.

References

Acker, Joan. 1991. "Hierarchies, Jobs, Bodies: A Theory of Gendered Organizations." In *The Social Construction of Gender*, ed. Judith Lorber and Susan A. Farrell. Newbury Park, Calif.: Sage Publications.

Albelda, Randy, and Christopher Tilly. 1999. *Glass Ceilings and Bottomless Pits.* Boston: South End Press.

Allison, Anne. 1994. *Nightwork: Sexuality, Pleasure, and Corporate Masculinity in a Tokyo Hostess Club.* Chicago: University of Chicago Press.

Baker, Paula. 1990. "The Domestication of Politics: Women and American Political Society, 1780–1920." In *Women, the State, and Welfare*, ed. Linda Gordon. Madison: University of Wisconsin Press.

Benkő, Pálné, ed. 1982. *A nők helyzetének alakulása a KSH adatainak tükrében, 1970–1981 között* (Trends in the social situation of women in light of data from the Central Statistical Office). Budapest: Szakszervezetek Elméleti Kutató Intézete.

Böröcz, József. 1989. "Mapping the Class Structure of State Socialism in East-Central Europe." *Research in Social Stratification and Mobility* 6: 279–309.

Böröcz, József, and Ákos Róna-Tas. 1995. "The Formation of New Economic Elites in Hungary, Poland, and Russia." *Theory and Society* 24 (5): 751–81.

Bourdieu, Pierre. 1984. *Distinction: A Social Critique of the Judgement of Taste.* Cambridge: Harvard University Press.

———. 1986. "The Forms of Capital." In *Handbook of Theory and Research for the Sociology of Education*, ed. John G. Richardson. New York: Greenwood Press.

Bruszt, László. 1988. " 'Without Us but For Us': Political Orientation in Hungary in the Period of Late Paternalism." *Social Research* 55 (1–2) (spring/summer): 43–76.

Buchmayr, Renate, Branka Ivancevic, and Ingrid Wagner. 1992. *Vergleichsweise Ungleich: Zur Situation der Frau in Wirtschaft, Wissenschaft und Forschung* (Contrasting inequalities: on the situation of women in the economy, in the sciences and research.) Vienna: Service Fachverlag.

Census: Summary Data (*Népszámlálás: Összefoglaló adatok*). 1990. Budapest: Központi Statisztikai Hivatal.

Comparison of Social Indicators in Austria and Hungary. 1982. Budapest: Központi Statisztikai Hivatal.

Connell, R. W. 1987. *Gender and Power: Society, the Person, and Sexual Politics.* Stanford: Stanford University Press.

Corrin, Chris. 1992. *Magyar Women: Hungarian Women's Lives, 1960s–1990s.* London: St. Martin's Press.

Cyba, Eva. 1991. "Frauen—Akteure im Sozialstaat?" (Women—welfare state actors). *Österreichische Zeitschrift für Soziologie* 1: 25–42.

———. 1996. "Modernisierung im Patriarchat? Zur Situation der Frauen in Arbeit, Bildung, und privater Sphäre, 1945 bis 1995 (Modernizing patriarchy: On the situation of women in work, education, and the private sphere, 1945–95). In *Österreich 1945–1995: Gesellschaft, Politik, Kultur,* ed. Reinhard Sieder, Heinz Steinert, and Emmerich Tálos. Vienna: Verlag für Gesellschaftkritik.

Dahrendorf, Ralf. 1959. *Class Conflict in Industrial Societies.* London: Routledge.

Demographic Yearbook of Austria. 1981. Vienna: Österreichischen Statistischen Zentralamt.

Djilas, Milovan. 1957. *The New Class: An Analysis of the Communist System.* New York: Praeger.

Duina, Francesco. 1994. *Harmonizing Europe: Nation-States within the Common Market.* Albany: State University of New York Press.

Duncan, Simon. 1996. "Obstacles to a Successful Equal Opportunity Policy in the European Union." *European Journal of Women's Studies* 3: 399–422.

Egan, Michelle. 1998. "Gendered Integration: Social Policy and the European Market." *Women and Politics* 19 (4): 23–52.

Einhorn, Barbara. 1993. *Cinderella Goes to Market: Citizenship, Gender, and Women's Movements in East Central Europe.* London: Verso.

Eisenstein, Zillah. 1988. *The Female Body and the Law.* Berkeley: University of California Press.

Engels, Frederick. 1985. *The Origins of the Family, Private Property, and the State.* 1884. New York: International Publishers.

Esping-Andersen, Gosta. 1990. *The Three Worlds of Welfare Capitalism.* Cambridge, Mass.: Polity Press.

Eyal, Gil, Ivan Szelenyi, and Eleanor Townsley. 1998. *Making Capitalism without Capitalists: Class Formation and Elite Struggles in Post-Communist Central Europe.* London: Verso.

Feigl, Susanne. 1986. *Frauen in Österreich, 1975–1985* (Women in Austria 1975–1985). Vienna: Staatsecreteriat für Allgemeine Frauenfrage in Bundeskanzelleramt.

Firestone, Shulamith. 1970. *The Dialectic of Sex: The Case for Feminist Revolution.* New York: William Morrow.

Fodor, Éva. 1997. "Gender in Transition: Unemployment in Hungary, Poland, and Slovakia." *East European Politics and Societies* 11 (3) (fall): 470–500.

Fraser, Nancy. 1994. "After the Family Wage: Gender Equity and the Welfare State." *Political Theory* 22: 591–617.

Fraser, Nancy, and Linda Gordon. 1994. "A Genealogy of Dependency: Tracing a Keyword of the U.S. Welfare State." *Signs: Journal of Women in Culture and Society* 19 (21): 309–35.

Frauenbericht: Bericht über die Situation der Frauen in Österreich (Women's report: Report on the situation of women in Austria). 1995. Vienna: Bundesministerin für Frauenangelegenheiten / Bundeskanzleramt.

Freeman, Carla. 1999. *High Tech and High Heels in the Global Economy: Women, Work, and Pink-Collar Identities in the Caribbean.* Durham: Duke University Press.

Frey, Mária. 1996. "A nők munkaerőpiaci helyzete Magyarországon: Nemzetközi összehasonlításban" (Women's position in the labor market: An international comparison). In *A nők munkaerőpiaci helyzete Magyarországon: A vállalkozás alternativa* (Women's labor market position in Hungary: Entrepreneurship as an alternative), ed. Zsuzsa Laczkó and Anikó Soltész. Budapest: Aula.

Funk, Nanette, and Magda Mueller, eds. 1993. *Gender Politics in Communism: Reflections from Eastern Europe and the Former Soviet Union.* New York: Routledge.

Gal, Susan, and Gail Kligman, eds. 2000a. *The Politics of Gender after Socialism.* Princeton: Princeton University Press.

——. 2000b. *Reproducing Gender: Politics, Publics, and Everyday Life After Socialism.* Princeton: Princeton University Press.

Gehler, Michael, and Hubert Sickinger. 1995. "Politische Skandale in der Zweite Republic" (Political scandals in the Second Republic). In *Österreich 1945– 1995: Gesellschaft, Politik, Kultur.* Vienna: Verlag für Gesellschaftkritik.

Giddens, Anthony. 1971. *Capitalism and Modern Social Theory: An Analysis of the Writings of Marx, Durkheim, and Max Weber.* Cambridge: Cambridge University Press.

Gordon, Linda, and Nancy Fraser. 1994. " 'Dependency' Demystified: Inscriptions of Power in a Keyword of the Welfare State." *Social Politics* 1: 14–31.

Goven, Joanna. 1993a. "Gender Politics in Hungary: Autonomy and Antifeminism." In *Gender Politics in Communism: Reflections from Eastern Europe and the Former Soviet Union,* ed. Nanette Funk and Magda Mueller. New York: Routledge.

——. 1993b. "The Gendered Foundations of Hungarian Socialism: State, Society, and the Anti-Politics of Anti-Feminism, 1948–1990. Ph.D. diss., University of California, Berkeley.

Goven, Joanna. 2000. "New Parliament, Old Discourse? The Parental Leave Debate in Hungary." In *Reproducing Gender: Politics, Publics, and Everyday Life After Socialism,* ed. Susan Gal and Gail Kligman. Princeton: Princeton University Press.

Grád, András. 1988. "A jogi szabályozás kapcsolata a gyermekszületéssel és a gyermekvállalással" (The relationship between legal regulations concerning childbirth and actual birth). In *Terhesség-Szülés-Születés I,* ed. Ágnes Losonczi. Budapest: MTA Szociológiai Kutató Intézete.

Graham, Ann, and Joanna Regulska. 1997. "Expanding Political Space for Women in Poland: An Analysis of Three Communities." *Communist and Post-Communist Studies* 30 (1): 65–82.

Grisold, Andrea, and Ruth Simsa. 1992. "Die Situation von Frauen am Österreichischen Arbeitsmarkt. Ein Überblick" (The situation of women in the Austrian labor market: An overview). *Vergleichsweise Ungleich: Zur Situation der Frau in Wirtschaft, Wissenschaft and Forschung,* ed. Renate Buchmayr, Branka Ivancevic, and Ingrid Wagner. Vienna: Service Fachverlag.

Gross, Inge, Beatrix Wiedenhofer, and Werner Vötsch. 1994. *The Economic and Social Role of Women in Austria: Statistical Analysis.* 1994. Vienna: Austrian Federal Ministry of Labour and Social Affairs.

Gutknecht, Brigitte. 1993. "Gleichbehandlung von Mann und Frau und Allgemeine Gleichheitsgrundsatz" (The equal treatment laws and the equal treatment of men and women). In *Die "andere" Hälfte der Wirtschaft: Von den Chancen der Frauen im Wirtschaftsleben,* ed. Regina Bendl. Vienna: Schriftenreihe Frauen, Forschung und Wirtschaft 3.

Haller, Max, Tamás Kolosi, and Péter Róbert. 1990. "Social Mobility in Austria, Czechoslovakia, and Hungary: An Investigation of the Effect of Industrialization, Social Revolution, and National Uniqueness." In *Class Structure in Europe: New Findings from East-West Comparisons of Social Structure and Mobility,* ed. Max Haller. Armonk, N.Y.: M. E. Sharpe.

Haney, Lynn. 1997. "But We Are Still Mothers": Gender and the Construction of Need in Post-Socialist Hungary." *Social Politics.* 4 (2) (summer): 208–45.

Hartmann, Heidi. 1981. "The Unhappy Marriage of Marxism and Feminism: Toward a More Progressive Union." In *Women and Revolution: A Discussion of the Unhappy Marriage of Marxism and Feminism,* ed. Lydia Sargent. Boston: South End Press.

Heineman, Elizabeth D. 1999. *What Difference Does a Husband Make? Women and Marital Status in Nazi and Postwar Germany.* Berkeley: University of California Press.

Heitlinger, Alena. 1979. *Women and State Socialism: Sex Inequality in the Soviet Union and Czechoslovakia.* London: St. Martin's Press.

Hochschild, Arlie. 1975. "Inside the Clockwork of Male Careers." In *Women and the Power to Change,* ed. Florence Howe. New York: McGraw-Hill.

Hornung, Ela, and Margit Sturm. 1996. "Stadtleben: Alltag in Wien 1945 bis 1955" (Everyday life in Vienna: 1945–1955). In *Österreich 1945–1995: Gesellschaft, Politik, Kultur,* ed. Reinhard Sieder, Heinz Steinert, and Emmerich Tálos. Vienna: Verlag für Gesellschaftkritik.

Horváth, Ágnes, and Árpád Szakolczai. 1992. *The Dissolution of Communist Power: The Case of Hungary.* New York: Routledge.

Hoskyns, Catherine. 1996. *Integrating Gender: Women, Law, and Politics in the European Union.* New York: Verso Press.

Hungarian Mobility Survey (Társadalmi Mobilitás Kérdőív). 1992. Budapest: Központi Statisztikai Hivatal.

Jones, Kathleen B. 1993. *Compassionate Authority: Democracy and the Representation of Women.* London: Routledge.

Jowitt, Kenneth. 1987. *New World Disorder: The Leninist Extinction.* Berkeley: University of California Press.

Kamermann, Sheila, Alfred Kahn, and Paul Kingston. 1983. *Maternity Policies and Working Women.* New York: Columbia University Press.

Kanter, Moss Rosabeth. 1977. *Men and Women of the Corporation.* New York: Basic Books.

Kelly, Erin, and Frank Dobbin. 1999. "Civil Rights Law at Work: Sex Discrimination and the Rise of Maternity Leave Policies." *American Journal of Sociology* 94: 455–92.

Kligman, Gail. 1992. "The Politics of Reproduction in Ceausescu's Romania: A Case Study of Political Culture." *East European Politics and Societies* 6 (3) (fall): 364–418.

——. 1994. "The Social Legacy of Communism: Women, Children, and Feminization of Poverty." In *The Social Legacy of Communism*, ed. James R. Miller and Sharon L. Wolchik. Washington, D.C.: Woodrow Wilson Center Press; Cambridge University Press.

——. 1998. *The Politics of Duplicity: Controlling Fertility in Ceausescu's Romania.* Berkeley: University of California Press.

Kollontai, Alexandra. 1971. *The Autobiography of a Sexually Emancipated Communist Woman.* New York: Herder and Herder.

——. 1981. *A Great Love.* New York: Norton.

Koncz, Katalin. 1985a. "Eredmények és feszültségek a női foglalkoztatásban" (Positive effects and tensions in women's employment). *Egyetemi Szemle* 4: 33–47.

——. 1985b. "A nemek szerinti bér és keresetkülönbségekről valamint ennek okairól" (On the gender gap in wages and its causes). *Munkaügyi Szemle* 39 (2): 1–7.

Konrád, György, and Szelenyi Iván. 1989. *Az értelmiség útja az osztályhatalomhoz* (Intellectuals' road to class power). Budapest: Gondolat Kiadó.

Kreisky, Eva, and Birgit Sauer. 1997. "Women in Decision Making in Politics, Economy, and Society: Access and Barriers for Women in Austria. Final Report." Vienna. Manuscript.

Krymkowski, Daniel H. 1991. "The Process of Status Attainment among Men in Poland, the U.S., and West Germany." *American Sociological Review* 56 (February): 46–59.

Lee, Ching Kwan. 1998. *Gender and the South China Miracle: The Two Worlds of Factory Women.* Berkeley: University of California Press.

Lengyel, György. 1996. *Cadres and Managers: Changing Patterns of Recruitment of Economic Leaders in the Planned Economy.* Budapest: Aula Kiadó.

Lewis, Jane. 1993. *Women and Social Policies in Europe: Work, Family, and the State.* Hants, U.K.: Edward Elgar.

Lewis, Jane, and Ilona Ostner. 1994. "Gender and the Evolution of European Social Policy." In *European Social Policy: Between Fragmentation and Integration*, ed. Stephans Leibfried and Paul Pierson. Washington, D.C.: Brookings Institution.

Littleton, Christine A. 1991. "Reconstructing Sexual Equality." In *Feminist Legal Theory: Readings in Law and Gender*, 2d ed., ed. Katharine T. Bartlett and Rosanne Kennedy. Boulder: Westview Press.

Luijx, Ruud, Peter Robert, Paul M. de Graaf, and Harry B. G. Ganzeboom. 1995. "From Ascription to Achievement: The Status Attainment Process in Hungary from 1919 to 1993." Paper presented at the second conference of the European Sociological Association, Budapest, August 30 to September 2, 1995.

Mach, Bogdan W., and Jules L. Peschar. 1990. "Family Background and Educational Attainment in Czechoslovakia and the Netherlands: The Analysis of Cultural and Economic Sources of Inequality in Comparative Perspective." In *Class Structure in Europe: New Findings from East-West Comparisons of Social Structure and Mobility*, ed. Max Haller. Armonk, N.Y.: M. E. Sharpe.

MacKinnon, Catharine. 1991. "Difference and Dominance: On Sex Discrimination." In *Feminist Legal Theory: Readings in Law and Gender*, 2d ed., ed. Katharine T. Bartlett and Rosanne Kennedy. Boulder: Westview Press.

Magyarország Statisztikai Évkönyve (Statistical yearbook of Hungary). 1990. 1993, 1996. Budapest: Közgazdasági és Jogi Könyvkiadó.

Markens, Susan, Carol Browner, and Nancy A. Press. 1997. "Feeding the Fetus: On Interrogating the Notion of Maternal-Fetal Conflict." *Feminist Studies* 23: 351–72.

Matkovits, Susanne. 1995. "Staatliche Gleichstellungspolitik zum Abbau geschlechtsspezifischer Segmentation auf dem Arbeitsmarkt: Österreichische und Internationale Bildungs- und Arbeitsmarktpolitik im Vergleich (State policies to reduce gender-specific labor market segregation: Austria and international labor market and education policies compared). Ph.D diss., University of Vienna.

Mazey, Sonja. 1998. "The European Union and Women's Rights: From the Europeanization of National Agendas or the Nationalization of the European Agenda." *Journal of European Public Policy* 5 (1) (March): 131–52.

McCall, Leslie. 1992. "Does Gender Fit? Bourdieu, Feminism, and Conceptions of Social Order." *Theory and Society* 21 (6): 837–69.

McGuire, Gail M., and Barbara F. Reskin. 1993. "Authority Hierarchies at Work: The Impact of Race and Sex." *Gender and Society* 7 (4): 487–507.

Microcensus of Austria. 1982. Vienna: Österreichischen Statistischen Zentralamt.

Microcensus of Austria. 1988. Vienna: Österreichischen Statistischen Zentralamt.

Microcensus of Austria. 1996. Vienna: Österreichischen Statistischen Zentralamt.

Mikrozensus Jahresergennisse. 1997. Wien: Österreichischen Statistischen Zentralamt.

Milkman, Ruth. 1987. *Gender at Work: The Dynamics of Job Segregation by Sex during World War II*. Urbana: University of Illinois Press.

Molyneux, Maxine. 1981. "Women in Socialist Societies: Problems of Theory and Practice." In *Of Marriage and Market: Women's Subordination Internationally and Its Lessons*, ed. Kate Young, Carol Wolkowitz, and Roslyn Mc-Cullagh. New York: Routledge.

Mueller, Walter, Paul Luttinger, Wolfgang Konig, and Wolfgang Karle. 1990. "Class and Education in Industrial Nations." In *Class Structure in Europe: New Findings from East-West Comparisons of Social Structure and Mobility*, ed. Max Haller. Armonk, N.Y.: M. E. Sharpe.

Nationalrat XIV. Gesetzgebungsperiod, 120. Sitzung, Feb. 23, 1979. (Stenographische Protokolle)

Nationalrat XIV. Gesetzgebungsperiod, 136. Sitzung. March 20, 1986. (Stenographische Protokolle)

Nationalrat XVIII. Gesetzgebungsperiod, 90. Sitzung, Dec. 1, 1992 (Stenographische Protokolle)

Nationalrat XVIII. Gesetzgebungsperiod, 90. Sitzung, Nov. 30, 1992. (Stenographische Protokolle)

Nee, Victor. 1991. "Social Inequalities in Reforming State Socialism: Between Redistribution and Markets in China." *American Sociological Review* 56 (June): 267–82.

Nelson, Barbara. 1990. "The Origins of the Two-Channel Welfare State: Workman's Compensation and Mother's Aid." In *Women, the State, and Welfare*, ed. Linda Gordon. Madison: University of Wisconsin Press.

Neyer, Gerda. 1997. "Frauen in Österreichischen politischen System" (Women in the Austrian political system). In *Handbuch des Politischen Systems Österreichs: Die Zweite Republik*, ed. Herbert Dachs et al. Vienna: Manzsche Verlags- und Universitatbuchhandlung.

Nőszövetségi Dokumentumok (Documents from the women's organization). 1988. Budapest: Magyar Nők Országos Tanácsa.

Oktatás, Művelődés 1950–1990 (Education, culture). 1991. Budapest: KSH, 1991.

Omnibusz. 1997. Budapest: TÁRKI.

Ong, Aihwa. 1987. *Spirits of Resistance and Capitalist Discipline*. Albany: State University of New York Press.

Orloff, Ann Shola. 1993. "Gender and the Social Rights of Citizenship: The Comparative Analysis of Gender Relations and Welfare States." *American Sociological Review* 58: 303–28.

———. 1996. "Gender in the Welfare State." *Annual Review of Sociology* 22: 51–78.

Österreichische Hochschulstatistic, Studienjahr 1997/98 (Austrian educational statistics). 1999.

Ostner, Ilona, and Jane Lewis. 1995 "Gender and the Evolution of European Social Policies." In *European Social Policy: Between Fragmentation and Integration*, ed. Stephan Liebfried and Paul Pierson. Washington, D.C.: Brookings Institute.

Párttörténeti Intézet Archívuma (PIA). Magyar Országos Levéltár, Budapest. File 288/5/406, Politburo meeting, 1966.

Párttörténeti Intézet Archívuma (PIA). Magyar Országos Levéltár, Budapest. File 288/5/962, Report to the Politburo, 1986.

Párttörténeti Intézet Archívuma (PIA). Magyar Országos Levéltár, Budapest. File 288/5/783, Report to the Politburo, 1979.

Párttörténeti Intézet Archívuma (PIA). Magyar Országos Levéltár, Budapest. File 288/5/247, Politburo meeting, 1961.

Párttörténeti Intézet Archívuma (PIA). Magyar Országos Levéltár, Budapest. File 288/5/140, Politburo meeting, 1959.

Párttörténeti Intézet Archívuma (PIA). Magyar Országos Levéltár, Budapest. File 288/21/1972/28, Department of the Party and Mass Organizations, 1972.

Párttörténeti Intézet Archívuma (PIA). Magyar Országos Levéltár, Budapest. File 288/5/234, Politburo meeting, 1961.

Párttörténeti Intézet Archívuma (PIA). Magyar Országos Levéltár, Budapest. File 288/21/1958/12, Report by the National League of Trade Unions to the Department of the Party and Mass Organizations, 1958.

Párttörténeti Intézet Archívuma (PIA). Magyar Országos Levéltár, Budapest. File 288/5/639, Report to the Politburo, 1974.

Párttörténeti Intézet Archívuma (PIA). Magyar Országos Levéltár, Budapest. File 288/5/24, Politburo meeting, 1957.

Párttörténeti Intézet Archívuma (PIA). Magyar Országos Levéltár, Budapest. File 288/5/227, Politburo meeting, 1961.

Párttörténeti Intézet Archívuma (PIA). Magyar Országos Levéltár, Budapest. File 276/94/886, Report to the Politburo, 1956.

Párttörténeti Intézet Archívuma (PIA). Magyar Országos Levéltár, Budapest. File 276/94/444, Report to the Politburo, 1951.

Párttörténeti Intézet Archívuma (PIA). Magyar Országos Levéltár, Budapest. File 288/5/401, Politburo meeting, 1966.

Párttörténeti Intézet Archívuma (PIA). Magyar Országos Levéltár, Budapest. File 288/21/1970/51, Department of the Party and Mass Organizations, 1970.

Párttörténeti Intézet Archívuma (PIA). Magyar Országos Levéltár, Budapest. File 288/21/1962/13, Report to the Politburo, 1962.

Párttörténeti Intézet Archívuma (PIA). Magyar Országos Levéltár, Budapest. File 288/5/511, Report to the Politburo, 1970.

Párttörténeti Intézet Archívuma (PIA). Magyar Országos Levéltár, Budapest. File 288/5/24, Politburo meeting and report, 1957.

Párttörténeti Intézet Archívuma (PIA). Magyar Országos Levéltár, Budapest. File 288/21/1959/7, Department of the Party and Mass Organizations, 1959.

Párttörténeti Intézet Archívuma (PIA). Magyar Országos Levéltár, Budapest. File 288/21/1973/24, Report to the Department of the Party and Mass Organizations, 1973.

Párttörténeti Intézet Archívuma (PIA). Magyar Országos Levéltár, Budapest. File 288/21/1958/24, Report to the Department of the Party and Mass Organizations, 1958.

Párttörténeti Intézet Archívuma (PIA). Magyar Országos Levéltár, Budapest. File 288/5/36, Politburo meeting, 1957.

Párttörténeti Intézet Archívuma (PIA). Magyar Országos Levéltár, Budapest. File 288/21/1957/12, Department of the Party and Mass Organizations, 1957.

Párttörténeti Intézet Archívuma (PIA). Magyar Országos Levéltár, Budapest. File 288/21/1958/15, Department of the Party and Mass Organizations, 1958.

Párttörténeti Intézet Archívuma (PIA). Magyar Országos Levéltár, Budapest. File 288/21/1961/18, Department of the Party and Mass Organizations, 1961.

Párttörténeti Intézet Archívuma (PIA). Magyar Országos Levéltár, Budapest. File 276/89/273, Department of Propaganda, 1951.

Párttörténeti Intézet Archívuma (PIA). Magyar Országos Levéltár, Budapest. File 288/21/1959/3, Department of the Party and Mass Organizations, 1959.

Párttörténeti Intézet Archívuma (PIA). Magyar Országos Levéltár, Budapest. File 288/5/509, Politburo meeting, 1970.

Párttörténeti Intézet Archívuma (PIA). Magyar Országos, Levéltár, Budapest. File 276/53/116, Politburo meeting, 1953.

Párttörténeti Intézet Archívuma (PIA). Magyar Országos Levéltár, Budapest. File 288/5/182, Politburo meeting, 1960.

Párttörténeti Intézet Archívuma (PIA). Magyar Országos Levéltár, Budapest. File 288/5/394, Politburo meeting, 1966.

Párttörténeti Intézet Archívuma (PIA). Magyar Országos Levéltár, Budapest. File 288/5/267, Politburo meeting, 1962.

Párttörténeti Intézet Archívuma (PIA). Magyar Országos Levéltár, Budapest, File 276/53/108, Report to the Politburo, 1953.

Párttörténeti Intézet Archívuma (PIA). Magyar Országos Levéltár, Budapest. File 288/5/255, Politburo meeting, 1962.

Párttörténeti Intézet Archívuma (PIA). Magyar Országos Levéltár, Budapest. File 288/5/592, Politburo meeting, 1972.

Párttörténeti Intézet Archívuma (PIA). Magyar Országos Levéltár, Budapest. File 288/5/293, Report to the Politburo, 1963.

Párttörténeti Intézet Archívuma (PIA). Magyar Országos Levéltár, Budapest. File 276/88/656, Department of the Party and Mass Organizations, 1952.

Párttörténeti Intézet Archívuma (PIA). Magyar Országos Levéltár, Budapest. File 276/53/64, Politburo meeting, 1950.

Párttörténeti Intézet Archívuma (PIA). Magyar Országos Levéltár, Budapest. File 288/4/243, Report to the Central Committee, 1988.

Pateman, Carole. 1988a. "The Patriarchal Welfare State." In *Democracy and the Welfare State*, ed. Amy Gutman. Princeton: Princeton University Press.

———. 1988b. *The Sexual Contract*. Stanford: Stanford University Press.

Pateman, Carole. 1989. *The Disorder of Women: Democracy, Feminism, and Political Theory*. Stanford: Stanford University Press.

Pető, Andrea. 1998. *Nőhistóriák* (Women's histories). Budapest: Seneca.

Petrova, Dimitrina. 1993. "The Winding Road to Emancipation in Bulgaria." In *Gender Politics in Communism: Reflections from Eastern Europe and the Former Soviet Union*, ed. Nanette Funk and Magda Mueller. New York: Routledge.

Phillips, Ann. 1991. *Engendering Democracy*. University Park: Pennsylvania State University Press.

Pierce, Jennifer. 1995. *Gender Trials: Emotional Lives in Contemporary Law Firms*. Berkeley: University of California Press.

Renzetti, Claire M., and Daniel J. Curran. 1992. *Women, Men, and Society*. 2nd ed. Needham Heights, Mass.: Allyn and Bacon.

Reskin, Barbara. 1991. "Bringing Men Back In: Sex Differentiation and the Devaluation of Women's Work." In *The Social Construction of Gender*, ed. Judith Lorber and Susan A. Farrell. New York: Farrell and Sage Publications.

Reskin, Barbara F., and Catherine E. Ross. 1992. "Jobs, Authority, and Earnings among Managers: The Continuing Significance of Sex." *Work and Occupations* 19 (4): 342–65.

Reskin, Barbara F., and Patricia Roos, eds. 1990. *Job Queues, Gender Queues: Explaining Women's Inroads into Male Occupations*. Philadelphia: Temple University Press.

Rich, Adrienne. 1986. *Of Woman Born: Motherhood as Experience and Institution*. New York: Norton.

Ridgeway, Cecilia L. 1997. "Interaction and the Conservation of Gender Inequality: Considering Employment." *American Sociological Review* 62 (2): 218–36.

Róna-Tas, Ákos. 1998. *The Great Surprise of the Small Transformations: The Demise of Communism and the Rise of the Private Sector in Hungary*. Ann Arbor: University of Michigan Press.

Rosenberger, Sieglinde. 1995. "Frauenpolitik: Moderne zwischen Megatrends und Backlashes" (Gender politics: Between megatrends and backlashes). *Österreichische Zeitschrift für Politikwissenschaft* 24 (1): 35–51.

—. 1996. "Lieber gleich-berechtig als später" (Equal rights now). In *Österreich 1945–1995: Gesellschaft, Politik, Kultur*, ed. Reinhard Sieder, Heinz Steinert, and Emmerich Tálos. Vienna: Verlag für Gesellschaftkritik.

—. 1997. "Frauen- und Gleichstellungspolitik." (Women and equal treatment policies). In *Handbuch des Politischen Systems Österreichs: Die Zweite Republik*, ed. Herbert Dachs et al. Vienna: Manzsche Verlag- und Universitätsbuchhandlung.

Rowhani, Inge. 1989. "Frauenarbeit in Verwaltungsinstitutionen" (Women's work in state administration). *Österreichische Zeitschrift für Soziologie* 2: 40–49.

Rueschemeyer, Marylin, ed. 1998. *Women in Politics of Post-Communist Eastern Europe*. 2d ed. Armonk, N.Y.: M. E. Sharpe.

Sainsbury, Diane. 1996. *Gender, Equality, and Welfare States*. Cambridge: Cambridge University Press.

Salzinger, Leslie. 1997. "From High Heels to Swathed Bodies: Gendered Meanings under Production in Mexico's Export-Processing Industry." *Feminist Studies* 23 (3): 549–75.

Scagnetti, Claudia. 1987. "Die Stellung der Frau in der Österreichischen Arbeitnehmervertretung" (The status of women in the Austrian labor force). Ph.D. Diss., Wirtschaftsuniversität, Vienna.

Scott, Joan W. 1988. *Gender and the Politics of History*. New York: Columbia University Press.

Siklova, Jirina. 1993. "Are Women in Central and Eastern Europe Conservative?" In *Gender Politics and Post-Communism: Reflections from Eastern Europe and the Former Soviet Union*, ed. Nanette Funk and Magda Mueller. New York: Routledge.

Slomczynski, Kazimierz, and Tadeusz Krauze. 1987. "Cross-National Similarity in Social Mobility Patterns: A Direct Test of the Featherman-Jones-Hauser Hypothesis." *American Sociological Review* 52: 598–611.

Stark, David. 1986. "Rethinking Internal Labor Markets: New Insights from a Comparative Perspective." *American Sociological Review* 51: 492–504.

Statistisches Handbuch für die Republic Österreich (Statistical Yearbook of Austria). 1951. Vienna: Österreichischen Statistischen Zentralamt.

Status of Women in Austria. 1976. Vienna: Federal Ministry of Social Affairs.

Steininger, Barbara. 1991. "Frauen in der Österreichischen Politik: Eine Empirische Analyse 1945 bis 1991" (Women in Austria: An empirical analysis, 1945–1991). *Österreichisches Jahrbuch für Politik* 643–666.

Szalai, Erzsébet. 1990. "Az Uj Elit" (The new elite). In *Gazdaság és Hatalom*. Budapest: Aula Kiadó.

Szalai, Julia. 2000. From Informal Labor to Paid Occupations: Marketization from Below in Hungarian Women's Work." In *The Politics of Gender After Socialism*, ed. Susan Gal and Gail Kligman. Princeton: Princeton University Press.

Szelenyi, Iván. 1978. "Social Inequalities in State Socialist Redistributive Economies." *International Journal of Comparative Sociology* 19: 63–87.

———. 1982. "The Intelligentsia in the Class Structure of State Socialist Societies." *American Journal of Sociology* 88: 287–326.

Szelenyi, Iván, and Eric Kostello. 1996. "The Market Transition Debate: Toward a Synthesis?" *American Journal of Sociology* 101 (4): 1082–96.

Szelenyi, Iván, and Szelenyi, Balázs. 1994. "Why Socialism Failed: Toward a Theory of System Breakdown—Causes of Disintegration of East European State Socialism." *Theory and Society* 23: 211–31.

Szelenyi, Szonja. 1987. "Social Inequality and Party Membership: Patterns of Recruitment into the Hungarian Socialist Workers' Party." *American Sociological Review* 52 (3): 559–73.

———. 1998. *Equality by Design: The Grand Experiment in Destratification in Socialist Hungary*. Stanford: Stanford University Press.

Sztalin, J. V. 1950. *Válogatott beszédek* (Selected speeches). Budapest: Kossuth Kiadd.

Tálos, Emmerich, and Bernhard Kittel. 1996. "Sozialpartnerschaft—Zur Konstituierung einer Grundsäule der Zweiten Republik" (Social partnership—on the basic principles of the Second Republic). In *Österreich 1945–1995: Gesell-*

schaft, Politik, Kultur, ed. Reinhard Sieder, Heinz Steinert, and Emmerich Tálos. Vienna: Verlag für Gesellschaftkritik.

Tóth, Olga. 1990. "Conservative Gender Roles and Women's Work." Manuscript.

Útmutató. 1987. Budapest: Párttörténeti Intézet.

Van derLippe, Tanja, and Éva Fodor. 1998. "Changes in Gender Relations in Eastern Europe." *Acta Sociologica* 41 (2): 131–49.

Verdery, Katherine. 1996. *What Was Socialism, And What Comes Next?* Princeton: Princeton University Press.

Walder, Andrew G. 1986. *Communist Neotraditionalism.* Berkeley: University of California Press.

—. 1995. "Career Mobility and the Communist Political Order." *American Sociological Review* 60 (3): 309–28.

Walder, Andrew G., Bobai Li, and Donald J. Treiman. 2000. "Politics and Life Chances in a State Socialist Regime: Dual Career Paths into the Urban Chinese Elite, 1949–1996." *American Sociological Review* 65 (April): 191–209.

Weber, Max. 1978. *Economy and Society.* Berkeley: University of California Press.

Williams, Wendy. 1993. "Equality's Riddle: Pregnancy and the Equal Treatment–Special Treatment Debate." In *Feminist Legal Theory: Foundations*, ed. D. Kelly Weisberg. Philadelphia: Temple University Press.

Wolf, Wendy, and Neil Fligstein. 1979. "Sexual Stratification: Differences in Power in the Work Setting." *Social Forces* 58: 94–107.

Wong, Raymond Sin-Kwok. 1996. "The Social Composition of the Czechoslovak and Hungarian Communist Parties in the 1980s." *Social Forces* 75 (September): 61–89.

Wright, Eric O. 1985. *Classes.* New York: Verso.

—. 1997. *Class Counts: Comparative Studies in Class Analysis.* Cambridge: Cambridge University Press.

Wright, Eric O., Janeen Baxter, and Elisabeth Gunn Birkelund. 1995. "The Gender Gap in Workplace Authority: A Cross-National Study." *American Sociological Review* 60 (June): 407–35.

Zeitlin, Maurice. 1987. "Corporate Ownership and Control: The Large Corporation and the Capitalist Class." In *Class, Power, and Conflict: Classical and Contemporary Debates*, ed. Anthony Giddens and David Held. Berkeley: University of California Press.

Zetkin, Clara. 1934. *Reminiscences of Lenin.* New York: International.

Index

Éva Fodor is Assistant Professor of Sociology at Dartmouth College.

Library of Congress Cataloging-in-Publication Data
Fodor, Éva.
Working difference : women's working lives in
Hungary and Austria, 1945–1995 / Éva Fodor.
p. cm.
Includes bibliographical references and index.
ISBN 0-8223-3077-6 (cloth : alk. paper)
ISBN 0-8223-3090-3 (pbk. : alk. paper)
1. Women—Employment—Hungary. 2. Women—Employment—Austria.
3. Hungary—Economic conditions. 4. Austria—Economic conditions. I. Title.
HD6142.5 .F63 2003   305.48'9623'09436–dc21   2002011679